MW00980339

THE CALGARY PROJECT
urban form / urban life

THE CALGARY PROJECT
urban form / urban life

Beverly A. Sandalack and Andrei Nicolai

Published by the
University of Calgary Press
2500 University Drive NW
Calgary, Alberta, Canada T2N 1N4
www.uofcpress.com

We acknowledge the financial support of the Government of
Canada through the Book Publishing Industry Development
Program (BPIDP) and the Alberta Foundation for the Arts
for our publishing activities. We acknowledge the support of
the Canada Council for the Arts for our publishing program.

This book has been published with the help of a grant from
ENMAX Power.

Library and Archives Canada Cataloguing in Publication

Sandalack, Beverly A. (Beverly Ann), 1953-
The Calgary Project : urban form/urban life
Beverly A. Sandalack and Andrei Nicolai.

Includes bibliographical references.
ISBN 1-55238-217-6

1. Urbanization--Alberta--Calgary--History. 2. Calgary (Alta.)--History.
I. Nicolai, Andrei, 1950- II. Title.

HN49.C6S35 2006   307.1'409712338   C2006-903894-5

Design: Andrei Nicolai, Francisco Alaniz Uribe, Beverly A. Sandalack
Cover photo: Braden Abrams Reid, downtown Calgary looking east
            from Crowchild Trail SW
Printed by Houghton Boston, Saskatoon, Canada

UNIVERSITY OF
CALGARY
PRESS

The Canada Council for the Arts
Le Conseil des Arts du Canada

Financial support provided by the Alberta Foundation for the Arts,
a beneficiary of Alberta Lotteries.

COMMITTED TO THE DEVELOPMENT OF CULTURE AND THE ARTS

CONTENTS

ACKNOWLEDGMENTS

This book had its origins in a series of discussions over several years of research and projects that dealt with urban design at various scales. We had completed a study of the city of Halifax in 1998, and there seemed to be a need for a similar project dealing with Calgary that looked at the evolution of the city form, its public realm, and the influences on this development. It was impossible to know at the outset that *The Calgary Project* would be infinitely more complex and take much longer than we expected; and the rapid growth of the city further complicated the work. But we did not anticipate how much there was to learn about city form and process by looking at Calgary. This book has also helped to inform and inspire the developing Urban Design Program at the University of Calgary.

Many graduate research assistants participated in various aspects of *The Calgary Project* through The Urban Lab at the Faculty of Environmental Design. Jinwei Zhang and Julio Marce Santa completed several of the studies and assisted in the development of many of the analytical methods, and were long-term participants and contributors to the work. Francisco Alaniz Uribe completed several studies and drawings and provided assistance in graphic design and final layout of the publication, as well as much logistical support over the last two years of the project. Other assistants included Chen Chen, Ryan Perry, Kate Lambert, Fraser Shaw, Kristina Meehan-Prins, Patric Langevin, Gian Carlo Carra, Andrew Mackie, Mackenzie Stonehocker, Liisa Tipman, Steve Denyer, Chris Gill, Darren Lee, and Braden Abrams Reid.

Discussions with Don Smith, Max Foran, Hugh Dempsey, Jennifer Bobrovitz, and Michael McMordie (Calgary history), Fred Sandalack (parks and open space), and Bill Sandalack (electrical infrastructure), provided insight and information. We appreciate very much the helpful staff and the resources of the University of Calgary Library, the Glenbow Archives, the City of Calgary Archives, and the Calgary Public Library, and thank the City of Calgary and the Glenbow Museum for mapping and photographs.

ENMAX Power provided major funding over several years to permit the extensive research and investigations of various aspects of the city form. We are most grateful for this important support and for their commitment to the city. Judy Duncan provided much support over the long process of the development of the book, and we are very grateful for her enthusiasm for the project and for her ongoing assistance. Thank you as well to Cathy Pitts, B. J. Arnold, and Leanne Pottinger for their involvement with the project as it developed.

Initial funding was provided through a Professional Faculties Research Cluster Grant at the University of Calgary. The University of Calgary provided two additional grants for parts of the research. This support is greatly appreciated. Some of the research was conducted during the course of several smaller projects, and the funding and support from the Calgary Cultural District Partnership, the Cliff Bungalow-Mission Community Association, the Calgary Foundation, the Inner City Forest Committee, the Beltline Community Association, and the Faculty of Environmental Design is appreciated and acknowledged. A grant from the Community Initiatives Program, administered by Alberta Gaming and funded through the Alberta Lottery Fund, for a series of publications related to the 2005 project "Sense of Place" provided additional assistance with publication.

Thanks also to Blane Hogue for his support and creative energy during the early stages of the project, to Marino Vardabasso and Anne Johnston, Faculty of Environmental Design, who provided much valuable support and assistance, to EVDS Deans Mary-Ellen Tyler and Brian Sinclair for their support, to Mike Quinn and Maureen Wilson for their participation in the early days of the project, and to Ann Davis, Len Novak, and Bob Sandford who, through the series of activities called "Sense of Place" that commemorated Alberta's centennial, helped to situate this project within a broader regional context of place. Thanks also to John King and Peter Enman of the University of Calgary Press for editorial advice and for guiding this project through to completion.

We are grateful for the support and contributions from students, colleagues, and other friends, however any errors or omissions are the responsibility of the authors.

This book is dedicated to all students of the city.

FOREWORD

Aristotle said, "If you would understand anything, observe its beginning and its development."

The Calgary Project: urban form / urban life offers us insight into Calgary's development and as a result, helps us gain a clearer understanding of our city. It explores the history of our urban structure, how Calgary has grown, and why it has developed the way it has. When we understand this history, we are better prepared to make decisions to strengthen infrastructure such as land development, roads, power, and water systems.

The publication of this book brings particular joy to ENMAX as we recently celebrated our 100th anniversary of providing safe, reliable, cost-effective electricity to Calgarians. We have grown right along with Calgary, since our predecessor, The City of Calgary Electric System, first assumed responsibility for street lighting in 1905. Today we continue to work with the Urban Development Institute, builders, developers, and city planners to meet the needs of our community as it continues to expand and change.

New challenges require innovative and responsible thinking from all parties to ensure we develop the infrastructure, maximize technology and harness resources in a way that will ensure the city remains vibrant for our children and our children's children.

At ENMAX, we are proud to be part of *The Calgary Project*. This book helps us reflect on how the great city of Calgary has evolved and challenges us to explore new solutions for the future.

Allan R. Buchignani, P.Eng.
President and COO
ENMAX Power Corporation

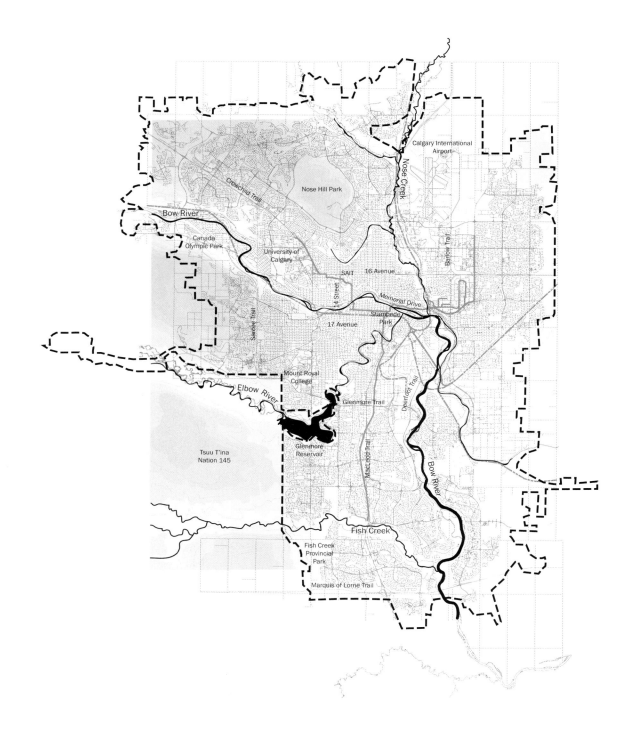

Crowchild Trail

Nose Hill Park

Calgary International Airport

Nose Creek

Bow River

Canada Olympic Park

University of Calgary

Barlow Trail

SAIT

16 Avenue

14 Street

Memorial Drive

Sarcee Trail

17 Avenue

Stampede Park

Mount Royal College

Elbow River

Glenmore Trail

Deerfoot Trail

Glenmore Reservoir

Tsuu T'ina Nation 145

MacLeod Trail

Bow River

Fish Creek

Fish Creek Provincial Park

Marquis of Lorne Trail

INTRODUCTION

Calgary is a young city – it has gone from pioneer beginnings to modernity in little over a century. Although it still has a relatively compact downtown, most of Calgary's post-war growth has taken the form of single-use and low-density neighbourhoods, and it is now almost overwhelmed by its suburbs. Getting around the city is far more complex now than ever, and discussions of Calgary's development and growth usually centre on transportation issues and ideas of orderly expansion rather than on sustainable development and urban design.

How did we get here? The evolution of the city reflects the evolution of ideas and ideologies, and of changing theories and practices of urban design and planning. The values cultures place on the built landscape are reflected in changing patterns of land ownership and land development, and consequently in the spatial qualities of the public realm. The city form is therefore a manifestation of societal values.

The first phase of urban development in Calgary, as in most other western cities, lasted up to approximately World War II and was marked by incremental change (see Relph [1987] for a discussion of the phases of urban development). New development usually extended and grafted onto the existing grid framework, and the street was considered a public space. Efforts to make the prairie city more livable included significant street tree plantings. Most neighbourhoods exhibited a mix of uses, with retail areas within easy walking distance or accessible by streetcar. Neighbourhoods developed during this phase are still the most walkable, with the permeable grid providing a high degree of choice of routes.

The second phase of urban development corresponds to the period of post-war economic growth. Land use zoning was developed to remedy some Victorian urban conditions by separating incompatible uses, but soon gave way to oversimplification and an almost obsessive desire to regulate land uses. A result of functional land use zoning was a greater separation of places of living, from places of work, from places to shop. One of Calgary's most explosive periods of growth coincided with this phase, and much of the city form exemplifies the processes and practices that dominated urban planning, design, and architecture for several decades.

The third, current phase of urban development is no longer so much the result of functional requirements or of cultural constraints but is more often determined by the marketplace. New suburban neighbourhoods in Calgary are carefully promoted on some aspect of uniqueness; this distinction is emphasized by the edges of most new communities, which are defined by high-volume collector roads, with huge land buffers on either side. Sometimes just crossing one of these roads requires getting in the car.

1
Calgary main features.
drawing F. Alaniz Uribe, A. Nicolai

1

The Calgary Project is a result of over five years of research, observation, and discussion. It seeks to add to the debate about what kind of city Calgary should strive to become and to help frame the discussion. This book therefore has several objectives, with the general goal of providing a better understanding of Calgary's urban form and process while contributing to the account of Canadian settlement evolution and development.

Firstly, it attempts to document the urban structure of Calgary at various scales, from the city as a whole, to the neighbourhood, to the street, in order to provide a record and a resource. The form of an object or organism (including the form of a city or a neighbourhood) is a "diagram of the forces" that have acted upon it (Thompson 1961, 11), and in the case of urban form, these forces are physical as well as cultural.

In order to understand the processes of urban change, an evolutionary approach to urban analysis and design is taken. This approach to urban design emphasizes a methodology for understanding, in detail, the make-up and functioning of a place. It assumes that each place is the product of the inter-relationship of natural form and process with built form and community, over time. The history of the city is reviewed, with a particular focus on events and processes that relate to urban form and structure, as a way of gaining a better understanding of how the city has been shaped. As the analysis evolves, so does a developing sense of place.

The evolution of the city is considered during several periods, determined by selecting key moments in the city's history when transformation was most evident. The fire of 1896; the outbreak of World War I in 1914 and the beginning of economic depression; the end of World War II and the beginning of a new age of prosperity and modernist ideals in 1945; the beginning of the period of urban renewal in the mid-1960s; the 1988 Winter Olympics and the emergence of Calgary into the international scene – these were selected as defining moments in the city's history, and as slices through time that capture the story of the city.

For each time slice, the overall physical form of the city is considered, and the relationships of the constituent parts are discussed. Each era of city-building is characterized by certain downtown, commercial, and neighbourhood types that reflect changing values and conceptions of the urban landscape. The built forms vary widely in character and quality, and Calgary's urban landscape today is an amalgam of many development types.

Typical neighbourhoods are studied in more detail, including consideration of overall layout, street patterns, and street design. These neighbourhoods are illustrated in several ways to represent spatial characteristics and indicate how each provides the basic functions of housing, services, a sense of community, and both natural features and urban amenities, but with significant difference in arrangement and land use patterns. These neighbourhood studies are intended to provide a record as well as a resource for future planning and urban design.

A representative section of the downtown is analyzed as well and followed through the city's evolution. The development of city infrastructure and services such as water, sewer, and power and their relationship to urban form and quality are also outlined.

Secondly, the city's evolution is discussed with an emphasis on certain qualities that are believed to be important. Urban analysis must be grounded in a vision of what the city should be; otherwise, it remains only descriptive. In this research, each period of time, and each street, neighbourhood or place, was analyzed in terms of the degree of environmental responsiveness, permeability, legibility, variety, civility, and expression of place. The relationships between landscape, settlement form, infrastructure, land development, sustainability, human comfort, and cultural identity are all important aspects of an integrated approach to looking at the city.

The Calgary Project particularly emphasizes the quality of the public realm as the receptacle for urban life. The urban form is, and should be, more than a collection of streets and buildings – it is also an arrangement of places to which people may develop significant ties. The public realm is important as the deepest and longest-lasting element of urban infrastructure. This is an underlying principle that provides a lens through which to analyze city form and its evolution.

As well, this research approach advocates continuity between a city vision and development strategies, emphasizing the public nature of all development and the importance and potential permanence of the public realm. Issues related to urban structure and urban design are identified, and some recommendations for future planning, development and urban design are proposed.

The Calgary Project is not intended as a detailed history of the city. There are much better sources for that, and the reader is advised to consult the list of references and further reading. Rather, this document is intended to be a story about the evolution of the city form and its relationship to urban life and urban quality, with the intention of helping to provide better understanding of the city of Calgary and to contribute to better decision-making in guiding the processes of urban development.

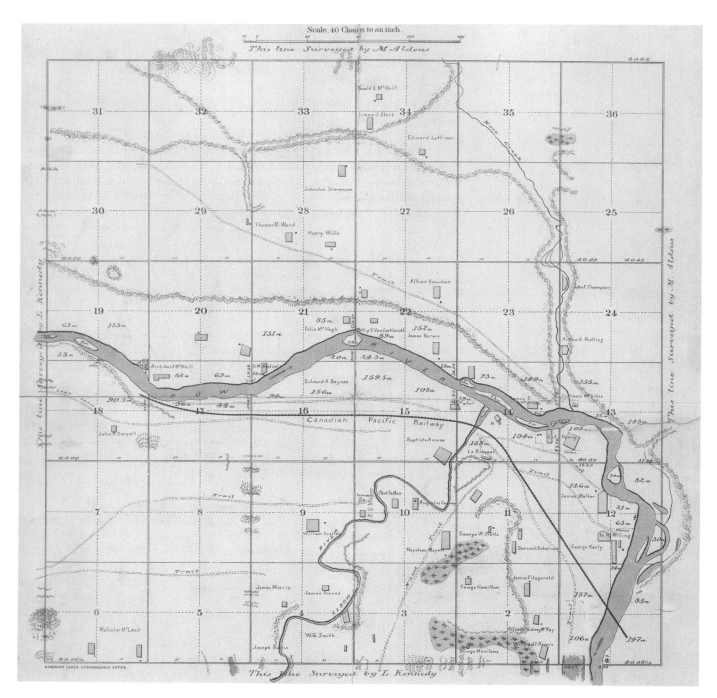

Scale, 40 Chains to an inch.

This line Surveyed by M. Aldous

This line Surveyed by L. Kennedy

This line Surveyed by L. Kennedy

This line Surveyed by M. Aldous

DOMINION LANDS LITHOGRAPHIC OFFICE.

4

2 THE EARLY DAYS: EXPEDIENCY, OPPORTUNISM, AND SPECULATION

2.1 NATURAL PROCESS AND FORM

The prairie landscape is vast and largely uniform, and only occasionally do features of strong relief such as the river valleys and plateaus occur. Much of the landscape around Calgary is the result of glaciation and the action of spillways carrying away meltwater and carving out steep-sided, flat-floored river valleys. Urban evolution is influenced by natural form and process, especially in the early years of the city when the first locational decisions are made. The situation of Fort Calgary at the confluence of the Bow and Elbow rivers acknowledged the importance of the water supply, and also started the city's relationship with these rivers. Calgary's physical site, set against the backdrop of the Rocky Mountains, is the most dramatic and commanding of all the prairie cities. The broad Bow valley, with its steep walls and dynamic river, and its tributaries, the Elbow River and Nose Creek, subdivide the city into a series of plateaus.

The Bow River, renowned in recent decades for trout fishing, canoeing, and kayaking, originates in the Bow Glacier in the Rocky Mountains and occupies an old valley several kilometres wide. The source of the clear waters of the Elbow River is further west in the Elbow valley, and the river reaches Calgary as a sparkling foothills stream. The delta of the Elbow, created in the 1930s by the construction of Glenmore Reservoir, is known as the Weaselhead and is very rich in wildlife habitat. The north-facing escarpments of both rivers are vegetated by white spruce, aspen, and stands of Douglas fir. South-facing slopes are dominated by grassland and shrubland. Riverine forest and several islands are found in the lowlands. Calgary is a city of considerable landscape diversity.

Alberta's river valleys became corridors for migratory populations, eventually developing into aboriginal routes. When Europeans began to settle the prairies, these paths were adopted for trade and transportation, as it was economical to use the routes that native peoples had already developed. Once Fort Calgary was established, these trade routes were protected and formalized, and many of the early trails eventually became major thoroughfares.

River and stream valleys were used for shelter, campsites, navigation, and other strategic purposes. Above Calgary, the plateaus are windswept and less hospitable, and settlement was concentrated in the side valleys such as Big Hill Springs and Coal Creek to the north and Jumping Pound Creek to the south. Settlements were also common along Fish Creek. The Nose and Beddington Creek valleys are broader and hence more exposed, and were used less for settlements. The Elbow River above the Glenmore Dam area was comprised of low, wet, forested areas, and there were fewer settlements here as

2
The township map of 1884 shows the rivers and railway as well as some early trails and buildings in what would develop as Calgary's downtown.
courtesy Glenbow Library

well. Below the Glenmore Dam area, the deep and narrow valleys were more sheltered and better suited for settlement (see Rasporich and Klassen [1975] for a more complete discussion).

Calgary's early form was directly influenced by its varied terrain. Local relief, degree and direction of slope, and natural drainage patterns influenced the location of residential areas. These factors also directly influenced the provision of city utilities. In Calgary's earliest decades, development occurred only where services could be easily extended. The city therefore expanded on the relatively flat river valley bottoms, and the escarpments and ravines presented barriers to growth.

Topography is a determinant of urban form and land use locations, and the west-to-eastward slope of the land has been important in Calgary's urban form evolution. This simple and obvious fact has influenced some urban development – water and sewage run downhill, and Calgary's development to the east has so far been less extensive than that to the west. East Calgary has also had a stigma attached to it because of actual and perceived lower environmental quality, and reflected in lower property values. Calgary's industrial land was located south of the downtown and east along the CPR. The CPR shops, stockyards and oil-related industries were all located there, and Calgary's sewage treatment plants are situated at the eastern edge of the city, where they collect wastewater and discharge it into the river downstream of the city. As the populations of Canmore and Cochrane increase, both to the west and upstream from Calgary, the issue of disposing of wastewater and sewage in the Bow River becomes a more critical issue for Calgary.

2.2   EARLY URBAN FORM

Calgary was established as a small North West Mounted Police Fort in 1875 and its future as a settlement was assured with the completion of the Canadian Pacific Railway through the area in 1883. Perched between the prairies and the foothills landscapes to the west, Calgary's fortuitous setting at the intersection of the early north-south and east-west routes gave it a strategic nodal location and great growth potential.

The CPR's decision to take a southerly route through the western prairies determined Calgary's future and was followed by rapid expansion of the cattle industry. Dozens of eastern capitalists followed the lead of Senator M.H. Cochrane and amassed vast land holdings where they ran thousands of cattle. These early years laid the foundations of a major beef industry in the foothills of the Rocky Mountains and on the open ranges. These successful ranchers, who owned the stockyards, slaughterhouses, tanneries, and brewery, became the most important source of local investment capital and financed

3
View of Calgary looking southwest showing the junction of the Bow and Elbow rivers, ca. 1886. Considerable diversity is found within the Calgary region, ranging from the prairie landscape of south-facing escarpments to the spruce and Douglas fir found in the moister north-facing slopes.
Glenbow Archives NA-431-2

4
Western imagery is still part of Calgary's identity, for example, this restaurant door, 11th Avenue SW.
photo B. Sandalack 2000

much of the significant early building in the city. Calgary's image and character still owe much to its ranching roots. Calgary and other towns, such as Fort Macleod, Lethbridge, Medicine Hat, and Maple Creek, eventually developed into supply and shipping points for the ranching areas. Ranching created a different culture than farming, and those towns developed a character distinct from that of the farming communities (Thomas 1986).

Despite these early influences, it wasn't until the CPR selected Calgary as its principal maintenance centre for the western prairie provinces that the future of the city was truly solidified. The coming of the railway led to the opening up of the western prairies for agriculture, and Calgary became the focal point of several branch railway lines. The city served for several decades primarily as a service and supply centre for the agricultural industries that surrounded it.

Many histories of Calgary (see, for example, Dempsey [1994], Foran [1978], or Foran and MacEwan Foran [1982]) discuss the hectic and colourful period in which the town location was consolidated and the early patterns established. One of the earliest maps is the Plan of Township 24 prepared by the Dominion Lands Office as part of its survey of the West in advance of settlement (figure 2). The geometry of the National Land Survey grid was superimposed on the irregularity of the landscape. The river patterns and escarpments gave a sense of the shape of the land, and the early fort and later the town was centred in the more sheltered river valley and near the water sources. The small cluster of buildings around the confluence of the Bow and Elbow rivers, evident in early maps and drawings, gave little indication of the speed with which the city would develop and with which it would evolve from these primitive marks on the land, to modernity.

The railway strongly influenced Calgary's urban structure, growth and character. There is a logic in the way a city develops and, in Calgary's case, the relationship between the rivers, the railway, and the topography set the stage for its urban form patterns. The railway companies took advantage of the generally broad and flat Bow River valley in laying the east-west line, and the line north to Edmonton roughly paralleled Nose Creek.

The Sarcee Reserve (now the Tsuu T'ina Nation) was established with the signing of a treaty in 1881. The reserve has been one of the only physical barriers to Calgary's expansion, and it was likely difficult in the early years to imagine that the city would eventually spread to its edge.

By the late 1800s most of the Canadian prairies had been surveyed into townships six miles square. Each township was made up of thirty-six sections of one mile square, or

640 acres (259 hectares). (This grid pattern is clearly discernible from the air.) It is on top of this larger grid that Calgary's layout was imposed by the CPR. The typical procedure for townsite development involved the selection of a promising site by the railway company, platting as a series of streets/blocks, and then division into lots. Calgary's street grid was misaligned three degrees from the Dominion Land Survey grid. The correction between the two grids ultimately created several interesting spaces, including Tomkins Park on 17th Avenue SW.

Following the decision of the CPR to locate its major maintenance centre for the western prairie region, Calgary became the supply and service centre for the farm and ranch land that the railway opened up, and it also became the focal point for a number of branch rail lines. When the CPR arrived in 1883, it found a town that already had eight hotels, three billiard halls, six laundries, ten stores, and one photographer, although all these were housed in tents. In 1882, when the CPR confirmed its plans to extend the main line through Calgary, the present-day downtown (Sections 15 and 16) was reserved for grazing North West Mounted Police horses. Most of the businesses in the old townsite moved across the Elbow River following the CPR's subdivision of Section 15 and the establishment of a rival townsite west of the fort.

Calgary incorporated as a town in 1884 with a population of 428. The CPR was again the major factor in defining the extent of the early business district. By placing the railway station north of the tracks and by withholding lands immediately to the south from sale at the first auction of townsite lots, the CPR provided for a business district between the rails and the river, concentrated around the railway station and a few blocks towards the fort. The railway company reinforced this by donating land in that area for civic purposes. Access to the south was across bumpy level crossings that were also chosen arbitrarily by the railway company. The differentiation of commercial activity north and south of the tracks was further consolidated by the emergence of wholesale facilities south of the line, directly opposite the business centre.

The CPR owned and controlled the wide rights-of-way on either side of the tracks. The most prominent building was the railway station, whose attractiveness as a social centre grew with the planting of the railway garden, a nation-wide practice that began voluntarily but eventually became company policy. Station gardens were valued as a means of convincing settlers of the land's fertility, of appealing to their cultural values (which were often conditioned by experiences in England and Europe), and as a way to make new arrivals feel more at home (see Rees [1988] and Von Baeyer [1984]).

5
Gardens, Canadian Pacific Railway station ca. 1900–1903.
Glenbow Archives NA-1126-3

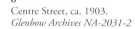
6
Centre Street, ca. 1903.
Glenbow Archives NA-2031-2

7
Power plant at Eau Claire Lumber Mill, 1901.
Glenbow Archives NC-32-4

The new town included the railway station and post office constructed in 1884 and a commercial district along Stephen Avenue. Housing was built in a concentric pattern around the downtown, a pattern that established early on the urban structure. Lots were put on the market and a house was constructed as each lot was sold. This created a stable residential neighbourhood characterized by low turnover and well-maintained houses, and although there was some uniformity of house size, style and value, there was also considerable opportunity for individuality. Churches and schools were located within the residential areas and provided social gathering places in addition to their institutional functions. A public market and stockyards were also established at this time.

An industrial area began to form as a strip along the CPR line to the east. Calgary's early industries were related to city building, including lumber mills and quarries, and to agriculture. These industries included grain storage and processing, and livestock handling and meatpacking, together with various related services and businesses. The construction industry established itself from the beginning. The Calgary area is under-lain with soft sedimentary bedrock, mainly sandstone and shale. Excavation is therefore relatively easy, and several quarries were established. Local building materials included this sandstone, as well as clay brick from nearby Brickburn and other sites, and lumber from several mills.

Peter Prince established the Eau Claire Lumber Company in 1886 across from what is now Prince's Island. Prince blasted through the neck of connecting land to make the peninsula into an island and to create a separate, controllable stream with which to run his mill. The presence of the Eau Claire Lumber Mill on the south bank of the Bow River, almost adjacent to the business area, had a marked impact on subsequent land development patterns in the area. Other small manufacturing enterprises located nearby, with the result that the area between the river and the business centre became associated with manufacturing. By granting the Eau Claire Company substantial rights in 1886, town council temporarily relinquished its control of development along the south bank of the Bow River. By the end of the century, this attitude of civic indifference to the river was reinforced by periodic floods, log jams, and the tendency of nearby residents to use the south bank of the Bow River as a dumping ground for refuse.

A sawmill in Inglewood operated by Colonel James Walker was responsible for supplying much of the lumber that built the city's sidewalks, buildings, and bridges. Timber and some brick were seen as the best available and cheapest building materials, but this era ended in 1886 with a catastrophic fire that wiped out over a dozen of Calgary's best buildings.

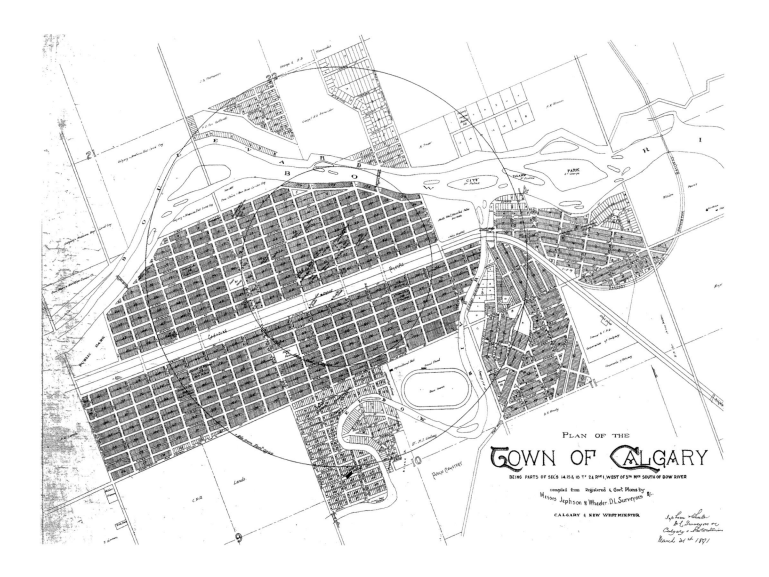

PLAN OF THE

TOWN OF CALGARY

BEING PARTS OF SECS 14,15 & 16 T⁹ 24 R⁹⁴ I, WEST OF 5ᵗʰ Mᵉʳ SOUTH OF BOW RIVER

compiled from Registered & Gov.ᵗ Plans by

Messrs Jephson & Wheeler D.L. Surveyors &c.

CALGARY & NEW WESTMINSTER

3 CITY DEVELOPMENT TO 1914

3.1 INTRODUCTION

Calgary's urban development, and much of its city image, has been characterized by vigourous but intermittent growth. The period between the devastating 1886 fire and the outbreak of World War I in 1914 saw the transformation of Calgary from a frontier town into an affluent urban centre. This dramatic growth was enabled by the construction of the Canadian Pacific Railway, which opened the west to agriculture and settlement, and by a general improvement in the world economy that was reflected in high wheat prices, strong demand for cattle, and favourable freight rates. Calgary's population increased more than tenfold during this period, from 4,000 residents at the turn of the century to over 50,000 at the beginning of World War I.

The task of rebuilding much of the downtown after the 1886 fire produced many substantial sandstone and brick commercial buildings concentrated along Stephen Avenue and, to a lesser degree, 1st Street SW, that would define a new image of prosperity and permanence for the city. The downtown was therefore established as the commercial and symbolic centre, and many of Calgary's important parks and streets such as Central Park and Memorial Drive were established at this time and reflected a strong commitment to civic values. City evolution was driven by visionaries and entrepreneurs, including William Pearce and Fred Lowes, and during this time the Mawson Plan, Calgary's first major urban design blueprint, was completed, although it was not adopted due to an economic recession and the persistence of a pioneer-town mentality in the city.

The direction of residential development was largely a response to the location of the railway and to the expansion of municipal transportation infrastructure such as streetcar lines. Industrial activities, related primarily to construction, agriculture and the railway, were clustered in an emerging industrial precinct in the eastern part of the city.

The outbreak of World War I marked the end of Calgary's first major growth period, one in which the early street patterns and functional relationships were established. The war had a huge impact on the settlement of the west and on the economy, and European immigration and investment declined dramatically. Property values fell, speculators lost fortunes, and the suburban developments planned in the early years would not be realized until the 1950s. However, in 1914, oil was struck at Turner Valley thirty miles south of the city, marking the birth of the industry that was to generate much of Calgary's wealth and development over the next century. Deep roots in the oil industry and a gradually diversifying economic base gave Calgary competitive advantages when further oil discoveries were made in Alberta in later decades.

8
Early land subdivision took the form of a grid laid out parallel and perpendicular to the railway. The post office was at the centre, and most development was within a half-mile (.8 km) or one-mile (1.6 km) radius as shown on the map. Inglewood and Ramsay to the east of the city centre were laid out according to a modified grid. Mission (then Rouleauville) was located south of 17th Avenue SW.
courtesy Glenbow Library

3.2 IDEAS, PLANS, AND PLANNING

Many North American cities and towns are barely a century old and developed rapidly from relatively primitive circumstances to modernity. The first phase of urban development, which would last until approximately 1940, was characterized by its foundation in relation to natural features, and by the establishment of the patterns of land survey and subdivision, and then by incremental changes to older forms with the introduction of new building and transportation technologies and planning concepts. Architects and urbanists considered the problems of town planning and design in terms of historical precedent, context, and propriety, and street forms and patterns were grafted onto existing urban frameworks.

In Calgary, the intersection of the rivers, the Canada Land Survey grid, the railway line, and the railway company grid determined early town form. The Canadian Pacific Railway Company effectively acted as the first town planner, establishing a grid of streets aligned parallel and perpendicular to the rail line. The railway station and post office marked the town centre, and the downtown commercial district and warehouses developed around this centre. The street grid was then easily subdivided into twenty-five-foot lot frontages and adapted readily to the city's rapid growth.

Significant ideas regarding land use and development emerged in pre-World War I Calgary. William Pearce was one of the early city's most influential figures and strongest advocates and was responsible for establishing many of the important concepts that would govern this era. Pearce was a surveyor for the Dominion Land Survey and settled in Calgary when the Dominion Land Office was established in what was then a town

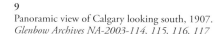

9
Panoramic view of Calgary looking south, 1907.
Glenbow Archives NA-2003-114, 115, 116, 117

10
William Pearce's estate "Bow Bend Shack" and extensive tree plantings, 1902, demolished in the 1950s to make way for construction of a warehouse.
Glenbow Archives NA-2289-6

11
William Pearce's gravestone in Union Cemetery, with a portion of his signature.
photo B. Sandalack 2005

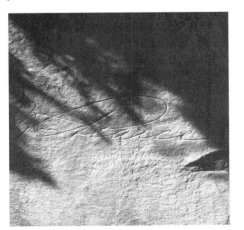

of 500. Pearce was also superintendent of mines and had jurisdiction over land claims and surface rights between Winnipeg and the Rocky Mountains and the 49th and 56th parallels.

Pearce saw natural features as prime determinants of urban development, and his views on the potential for agriculture on the prairies and the role of irrigation in establishing an urban forest were to have a profound and lasting effect on the city. He envisioned Calgary as a city of trees, dotted with parks, and his own land on the southwest quarter of Section 13 became a model of landscaping and horticulture. Pearce's home, which he named Bow Bend Shack, was considered by some to be the grandest house west of Winnipeg. (The house and grounds were destroyed in the 1950s to make way for a warehouse.)

Several key ideas advocated by Pearce were passed in a town council motion in 1887:

- Land along the Bow and Elbow rivers was to be set aside and provided with road access and pleasant vistas. Pearce saw to it that the City also acquired the Bow River islands.
- Many of today's well-known parks were to be established, including Central Memorial Park, the General Hospital land, the Bonnybrook park reserve, and several areas owned by the CPR that were subject to flooding and unsuited for development.
- The proposed city parks were to be connected like links in a chain. This was a powerful idea but would take nearly a century to come to fruition.

Calgary's population reached 45,000 in 1911, a startling tenfold increase that occurred within just a decade. The young city's subdivided land mass was equal to that of Toronto, which had ten times Calgary's population. The early influence of the railway and of land speculators led to rather disorderly residential development in Calgary, with servicing often lagging behind housing construction. Before 1911, City Council had limited authority to regulate residential subdivision, and zoning had yet to be introduced. A building bylaw was the sole mechanism by which Council regulated development, and there were no means to control lot frontages, street width, and the provision of public areas and green space. Moreover, the city's administration lacked permanent staff with the skills to manage urban growth.

At the peak of this early boom, Calgary's first Town Planning Committee (which became the City Planning Commission, or CPC, in 1912) was formed and began to grapple with what were to become the familiar challenges of growth. The CPC's aims were to provide "better traffic facilities; better housing conditions; equipped playgrounds for children; a system of parks connected by drives; [and] an economical and convenient grouping of our public buildings" (Foran 1980, 33). The most urgent tasks then facing City Council were the provision of infrastructure and other services, and Council's solutions tended to be reactive rather than directive with respect to the form and quality of urban growth.

In 1912, William Pearce and influential entrepreneur Fred C. Lowes, both members of the Planning Commission, retained British landscape architect Thomas Mawson to prepare the city's first physical plan. Pearce was instrumental in hiring Mawson and "imparted to him his views on the need for an extensive network of scenic drives, a green belt, a park system connected with boulevards, an improved tree-planting program, and an experimental nursery" (Donaldson 1983, 240). Indeed, Mawson observed that:

> … all the many beauty spots and lovely views which exist in your locality, and which, when they were shown to me by the President of your City Planning Commission, William Pearce, Esq., D.L.S., came as a perfect revelation to me, accustomed as I was to imagine your City to be set down on a featureless prairie. No greater mistake could possibly have been made (Mawson 1912, 71).

Mawson, with significant advice from Pearce, prepared a visionary plan that proposed the following:

> The parks, public gardens, and playgrounds of any city must necessarily play a very large part in its civic life…. Included in the areas which I propose to acquire, will be found many spots of natural beauty…. They follow to a large extent the banks of your two rivers, the Bow and Elbow, which should be rigidly preserved for the use of the public.
> As regards the centre of your city, all that it has been possible to do in the way of adding to your open spaces is to suggest the acquisition of Prince's Island and the formation of riverside promenades on both your rivers, and that St. Patrick's Island should be laid out as an addition to the St. George's Island Park with connecting bridges.
> A little further out to the east we have proposed the purchase of a considerable tract of country, which is at present finely timbered in the north east portion of Bow Bend, and also the rifle range on the opposite bank of the river.
> We strongly recommend the purchase of a large area of flat country too low lying for successful building operations between the existing Shaganappi Park and the Bow River, which … is most exceptionally beautiful, and would need very little alteration to make it into one of the most sought after resorts in the whole district.

12
Mawson's town planning scheme, 1912.
Glenbow Archives NA-2018-1

13
Sketch of Mawson's proposed Civic Centre, ca. 1910s.
Glenbow Archives NA-1469-55

There is an island in the river close to it, and this should form part of the park and would allow of very effective treatment for the bridge, which will be necessary to connect with the other bank and the Bowness car route by which it will be very easily reached from the city.

Taken as a whole, what we propose to do is to expropriate all ground which is too low and marshy … and all ground which is too steep for building upon.… It is fortunate that these are the very pieces of ground which will make the finest and most picturesque parks.… With regard to the smaller recreation grounds, which it will be necessary to provide … the great thing is to make sure that there will be at least one small open space within easy reach of every dwelling in the city.

Along your two rivers also, the Bow and Elbow, there are numberless beauty spots, and even where these do not exist, or have been somewhat destroyed by the type of development allowed along their banks, there is no doubt that they can be restored to a type of beauty more suited to their urban surroundings, and that at comparatively little expense, another advantage which seems never to have been realized by the people living in Calgary (ibid., 8).

Although Mawson's words alone convey the passion and intelligence of his plan, they are almost secondary to the gorgeous set of drawings that illustrate the plan (the originals are housed in the Canadian Architectural Archives at the University of Calgary). Mawson envisioned a system of streets, civic spaces and squares, focused on the rivers and modelled after the City Beautiful movement, an urban planning model that had risen to prominence with the 1893 Chicago World's Fair.

The plan was clearly based on a strong vision of the public realm and its importance. It proposed locating Calgary's civic centre near what is now Eau Claire Market and orienting the buildings in relation to the Bow River. Splendid civic boulevards would connect other major public spaces, which included the railway station, the fairgrounds, and several parks. The downtown core was seen as the heart of the city, and various neighbourhoods were laid out around it. Formal techniques of the City Beautiful movement employed by Mawson included the connection of landmarks, placement of important buildings or public spaces at the termination of significant axes, and emphasis of the visual and aesthetic aspects of city form.

His plan was also very sensitive to Calgary's environmental features, emphasizing relationships to the landscape with public spaces and paths orienting to the rivers and escarpments. Mawson also proposed more detailed plans for new housing areas. Although his urban design ideas were visionary, his design of a series of neo-Classical civic buildings was not appropriate to the early Calgary context and would be a factor in the ultimate rejection of the plan.

After the Calgary Planning Commission passed along Mawson's plans to City Council, it declared its work completed and dissolved itself. The plans were then passed over to the Parks and Playgrounds Committee to consider what actions should be taken, but little would be done. William Reader was appointed Parks Superintendent in 1913, and he attempted, within the constraints of the war and the economic depression, to continue the vision of Pearce and to add his own ideas to the beautification effort.

But by the time World War I and the economic depression had run their course and Calgary began to recover from its financial troubles, the age of idealism had passed. Civic spirit turned to solving "problems" and most visions faded (Perks 1985, 11).

3.3   SPATIAL STRUCTURE

The CPR and real estate speculation spurred and directed the city's early growth. A land subdivision map of the time illustrates the speculative fever that gripped the city. Prior to the war, the city subdivided sufficient land to house over half a million people, a population Calgary would not reach until the middle of the twentieth century. By 1914, the City had provided graded streets, sewer and water services, and streetcar service to 26,000 undeveloped lots, or more than twice the number of properties that were built on at that time (P.J. Smith 1971, 10).

Speculative activity resulted in the transfer of most land holdings from private to corporate interests such that by 1911 virtually all land within three to five miles of the post office was concentrated in the hands of local real estate agents. A series of land annexations between 1882 and 1911 increased the city's tax base, extended services into outlying areas, and increased land values. Thus, while Calgary comprised fewer than three sections of land in 1900, the city had expanded to cover more than forty sections by 1911.

The railway was both directly and indirectly responsible for most city developments. Rail access was a key determinant in the location of many industries and wholesaling activities. A strip of warehouses served by spur lines developed north and south of the railway, and a tentacle of industrial development extended for more than five miles east and south of the city centre along the Bow River valley. Stockyards, food and beverage industries such as the Calgary Brewery, agricultural service industries and, later, oil

14
Bird's-eye sketch of Calgary looking north, 1911.
Glenbow Archives NA-1209-2

refineries and construction materials manufacturers developed to the south and east of the confluence of the Bow and Elbow rivers. Railway shops were established in Alyth and later in Ogden, leading to the development of small working-class neighbourhoods.

The main roads into and out of town followed old trails. What were to become Edmonton Trail, Crowchild Trail, Macleod Trail, and Richmond Road, for example, originated as trading routes or paths established by First Nations people. The grid pattern of streets laid out by the CPR formed a concentrated business core, and residential development expanded around this core. During these early decades, residential areas were confined mainly to the broad river valleys below the escarpments.

Eventual construction of bridges at Centre Street N, 10th Street N, and 4th Street S allowed development to extend north of the Bow and south and east of the Elbow and, for the most part, Calgary spread to the west and south. Natural drainage patterns and the slope of the land controlled where water and sewer services could be reasonably provided.

Rebuilding following the fire / downtown development

After the 1886 fire, Calgary began rebuilding the town core in more permanent materials of sandstone and brick, establishing a more substantial physical presence and creating a distinctive identity. The rebuilt downtown focused on Stephen Avenue and, with the construction of many landmark buildings and of the Palliser Hotel nearby, this street was secured as Calgary's commercial centre.

At the heart of the downtown was the CPR railway station. The station's early simple frame building was soon replaced by two masonry structures whose standardized design reflected the railway's importance as a symbolic and vital functional link across the vast nation. A railway garden was a part of this assemblage and was important as a means of encouraging civic pride and in the CPR's promotion of the West as a place to settle and farm. The two station buildings were later taken to High River and Claresholm, where they both now serve as museums.

15
Calgary's railway station was at the terminus of Centre Street and included a plaza in front.
Glenbow Archives NA-1436-2

A much larger sandstone station was built in 1908 on 9th Avenue at the base of Centre Street. The building's axial relationship with Centre Street situated the railway station at the centre of Calgary's urban structure in a deliberate, legible way. A modest plaza at the station's entrance underscored the importance of the arrival and departure experience in the early city. Although never developed into a space of much elegance, the plaza was maintained for a brief period in conjunction with the railway garden.

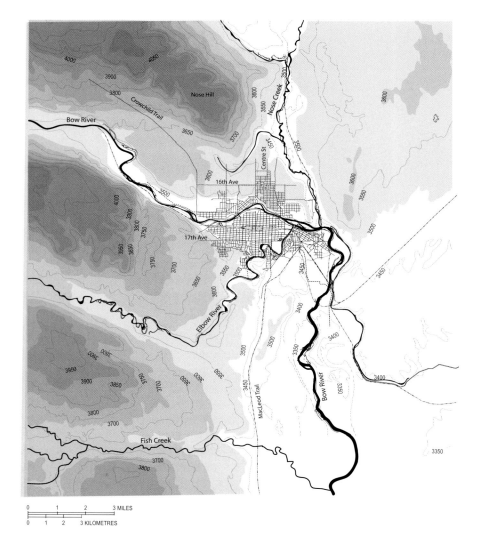

Labels on map:
4000
4050
3900
3800
Crowchild Trail
Nose Hill
Bow River
3600
3550
Nose Creek
3600
3650
3700
3650
Centre St
3800
16th Ave
3500
3800
4000
3800
3750
17th Ave
3950
3850
3750
3700
3650
3600
3500
3550
Elbow River
3600
3450
3400
3500
3600
3550
3500
3450
3500
3500
3350
3400
3600
3400
3450
3500
MacLeod Trail
3400
Bow River
3350
3800
3900
3950
3900
3850
3750
3700
3650
3600
3800
3700
Fish Creek
3700
3800
3400
3350
3350

0   1   2   3 MILES
0   1   2   3 KILOMETRES

16
Calgary's early street pattern, ca.1914, shows a city core concentrated around the rail lines that paralleled the Bow River.
drawing A. Nicolai

17

The city was experienced inside-out, with people and goods arriving at the railway station. The downtown commercial district extended north from the station, and a band of warehouses and related industrial uses grew to the south. Most industrial land was concentrated around the railway lines to the east and along the Bow River, and working-class neighbourhoods grew up near them. Streetcar lines permitted additional development of residential neighbourhoods and some small-scale commercial streets.
drawing F. Alaniz Uribe and B. Sandalack

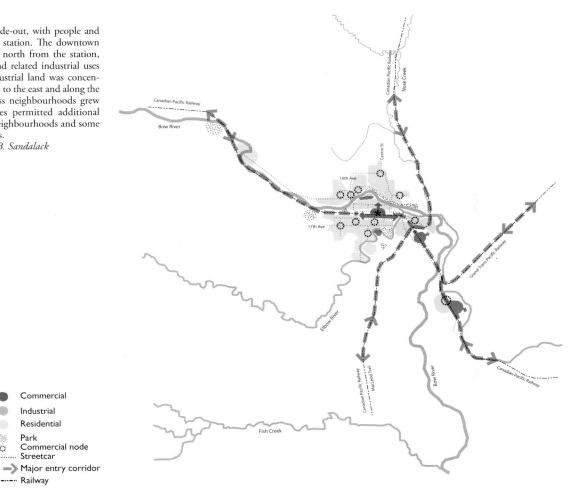

● Commercial
● Industrial
● Residential
⋯ Park
○ Commercial node
⋯⋯ Streetcar
←-→ Major entry corridor
—·—· Railway

With the exceptions of the Grain Exchange Building at seven storeys, and the Palliser Hotel at its original eight, building heights were restricted by city bylaw to six storeys, the maximum extent of water pressure for effective fire fighting at the time. Western development of the downtown core was focused along 8th Avenue and to a lesser extent 9th Avenue, and consisted of retail and wholesale businesses. This pattern was associated with the emergence of a warehouse district south and west of the railway tracks.

The CPR constructed freight sheds between 1st Streets SE and SW in 1903 and additional sheds east of 2nd Street E in 1905. Trains coming from the east or west were uncoupled in the adjoining rail yards and switched to a series of spur lines that served the so-called "wholesale street" along 10th Avenue west of the yards. Heavy rail traffic and shunting necessitated the construction of underground railway crossings. By 1912, spur lines served a well-defined district of warehouses on both sides of the tracks and as far west as 8th Street SW.

1st Street SW was the first north-south street to achieve commercial prominence. 2nd Street had originally been expected to fulfill this role, and the CPR chose it as the site of the first crossing under the tracks, but it was ignored in favour of the level crossings on 1st Streets E and W. 1st Street W had some significant buildings and better connections to Macleod Trail, and it took priority over 1st Street E for an underpass (it was also more directly connected to the CN station).

Commercial development in areas outside the downtown followed the street railway routes established after 1909. Commercial main streets developed across the 10th Street Bridge in Hillhurst, in east Calgary (today's Inglewood) and along 17th Avenue SW. By 1910 17th Avenue was known as "the coming business street." Commercial street success was in some cases a function of whether or not the CPR decided to open or maintain a railway crossing. For example, commercial areas on 8th and 11th Streets SW emerged as the CPR opened them as crossings while others were closed at 7th and 10th.

Chinatown was a part of the early city and was first situated around 8th and 9th Avenues between Centre and 4th Streets SE, in what is now East Village. A second community developed around 10th Avenue between Centre and 3rd Street SW. In 1910, the CNR announced a proposed route into the city south of the main CPR line that would terminate near St. Mary's Church, causing land prices to soar and displacing the Chinese community. Several Chinese merchants purchased land at the intersection of 2nd Avenue and Centre Street and established a new Chinatown in that neighbourhood.

18
Warehouse located at 437-10th Avenue SE.
Glenbow Archives NA-3514-8

19
Calgary stockyards, ca 1907.
Glenbow Archives NA-468-14

Railways were also influential in the development of the Mission district. A parish hall built by the Oblate Fathers in 1905 east of St. Mary's Church was sold to the CNR as a terminus building and at the time it was thought that all of the St. Mary's property might be bought for expansion. There were also plans for the Calgary-based Inter-Urban Railway which would deliver produce daily via electric trains from a terminus proposed in the Calgary Market to points south.

It was around this time that the first efforts were made to develop a university in Calgary. Seven hundred and fifty acres of land west of the city were donated for a university, money was raised for an endowment, and classes were held in the public library. However, the provincial government refused to grant degree-giving status and recommended instead the establishment of a Provincial Institute of Technology and Art in Calgary.

Industrial development

In 1887 the city acquired part of the northeast quarter of Section 11 for stockyard purposes. In 1890, the development of Patrick Burns' meat packing plant gave the industrial strip southeast of the downtown additional impetus and lent the area a character that would distinguish it for decades. The stockyard's location on Section 11 ensured that meat packing and processing plants would develop in east Calgary and not west of the city limits as originally preferred by the CPR and City Council.

This placed industries both downwind and downstream of the city's commercial and residential development, while giving the east part of the city a more industrial and working-class character. A brewery, tannery, and soap works located on Section 11, just outside city limits. In 1890, a donation of thirty-five acres of land to the Calgary and Edmonton Railway Company for freight yards helped to consolidate manufacturing in east Calgary. A city policy further influenced the location of manufacturing and industrial uses to City-owned land clustered along the railways headed north and south, although industries already located on low-rent land along the south bank of the Bow River remained in place.

The CPR's decision to build its shops at Ogden provided an impetus to the local economy and influenced neighbourhood development, while the anticipated arrival of the Grand Trunk Pacific and Canadian Northern Railways sparked an unprecedented series of land transactions. The railway shops were to employ more than 5,000 men, and the locomotive sheds alone were to cover six acres. The new subdivision, named Ceepeear, was sold to Fred Lowes in what was considered to be the most important real estate deal ever put through in Calgary. Within a year, several subdivisions surrounded the shops and the projected route of the street railway that would connect the district to the city.

Street railway system

In the early 1900s, the possession of a street railway system was considered to be the hallmark of a mature municipality. Before the development of the streetcar system, Calgarians' mobility was limited and development generally clustered around the business district. The streetcar system, however, extended into outlying areas and promoted tentacles of growth from the city core. Paved roads, together with the CPR's agreement to construct subways under its tracks, contributed to the feasibility of a street railway system.

Transit projects in Calgary had a profound influence on the city's growth and prosperity. The first local attempt at public transportation took place in 1905 with the inception of the Calgary Car Company Limited. The bus service operated by this private company turned out, however, to be unsuccessful as a result of unreliable roads and buses. In March 1907, Council ratified a bylaw providing funds for the building and equipping of a street railway system, and the City decided to construct and operate a street railway under municipal patronage. The new railway's first run took place in 1909 from downtown (8th Avenue and 1st Street SW) to the Fair (Stampede) Grounds (2nd Street SE via 8th Avenue), with early expansion of the system driven by real estate development.

Residential growth favoured areas near streetcar lines, and schools, apartment buildings, and boarding houses were also located close by. Developers entered into agreements with the city for streetcar extensions. Tuxedo Park (with a park around which the line looped), Pleasant Heights, Killarney, and Elbow Park were among the neighbourhoods that also gained early prominence from streetcar line connections. Forest Lawn was intended as an intensive industrial area along the Grand Trunk Pacific line, but the area attracted the interest of developers who sold lots on the guarantee of street railway service.

Elsewhere, the City agreed to provide service from the Bowness area to the downtown in exchange for eighty-six acres for park purposes and construction of a steel bridge across the Bow River. Similarly, Calgary secured the location of the CPR shops at Ogden with the promise to provide water, sewer, and electrical service as well as a street railway extension. The Kensington Road and Capitol Hill lines were added during 1913, and the South Calgary loop and the 17th Avenue SW extension followed.

20
1st Street SW looking north, Grain Exchange Building on the left, 1919.
Glenbow Archives NA-2399-180

Construction costs of the street railway lines were relatively low. Land speculators often built their own lines linking subdivisions to the city's system and later donated the track to the city. The result of this was an unplanned expansion of the street railway network that led to the development of far-flung residential districts in the city's outlying areas. The provision of utilities, however, was more costly and lagged behind residential construction.

Neighbourhoods that had streetcars, utilities, and building restrictions were generally considered to be more valuable. Nonetheless, a line proposed to serve the emerging Mount Royal neighbourhood, which lay within reach of existing lines and had a sufficient population base to justify a new line, never materialized because of opposition by the influential Mount Royal Improvement Association.

In addition to political and economic factors, the street railway network responded to technical constraints and local topography. The locations of railway crossings and underpasses determined the routes between the city centre and the area to the south, while bridge locations determined access to the north. The topography also prohibited certain street railway alignments. Rails were laid up 10th Street NW rather than along Centre Street where the slope was steeper. The Shaganappi coulee effectively blocked extensions to the area west of Bankview and Sunalta, and Killarney and Altadore were accessible only when rail lines were laid to the south up 14th Street SW to circumvent the meandering Elbow River.

The street railway system also made commercial enterprises feasible beyond the city centre along such streets as 17th Avenue South, Kensington Road NW, 10th and 14th Streets NW, and 11th Street SW. Rents in these areas were lower than in downtown, and clusters of small single-owner and family establishments began to appear around major intersections.

The outbreak of war in 1914 temporarily halted the development of the Calgary Municipal Railway.

21
Panoramic view looking south, 1911.
Glenbow Archives NB-41-15, 16, 17, 18

Residential development and expansion

Residential development in Calgary was generally compact and linked to the city's transportation infrastructure. The City encouraged the development of workers' housing near industrial areas in keeping with the urban planning approach of the time that endeavoured to form whole districts composed of inter-related industrial and residential uses. Ogden, Manchester, and Bonnybrook were examples of this practice, with other clusters of workers' housing developing in Mills Estate and Albert Park. East Calgary, near the brewery, became the fastest growing area in the city. In Bowness, a private developer reached an agreement with the City by creating a garden suburb and riverside park, in return for which the City built a streetcar line parallel to the river that connected Bowness and the city centre. East of the downtown, Forest Lawn was promoted as a suburban community on the strength of a promise of a streetcar connection.

22
Mount Royal residential street, 1911.
Glenbow Archives NA-2022-2

The CPR played an influential role in residential growth and developed several neighbourhoods outside the downtown. It reserved and subdivided the southeast quarter of Section 15 in anticipation of an eastward expansion of the city and in 1892 offered these lots to working families at affordable prices. Victoria Park was annexed in 1901 and, by the following year, most of the neighbourhood's homes had been built and were occupied in many cases by employees of the CPR. However, the CPR's decision to locate its shops in Ogden drew many railway workers from Victoria Park. In their absence, Victoria Park evolved into a middle-class neighbourhood.

The CPR developed its residential subdivisions strategically. Mount Royal, for example, was designed on a steep bluff by the railway as an exclusive residential area with a view over the city. The area's picturesque, curvilinear streets distinguished it from other city neighbourhoods, which were laid out in a more or less uniform grid. A strong lobby on Council further promoted Mount Royal as the city's only true luxury suburb by placing building restrictions (and thereby a premium) on lots in that neighbourhood. The CPR also laid out Scarboro using a curvilinear street pattern that responded to the area's sloping terrain, an approach which at the time was unique to it and Mount Royal.

In the Mission district in 1899, a group of 500 predominantly Roman Catholics bought land south of the town's corporate limits and established the village of Rouleauville. This village was annexed by the city in 1907. Farther south along the Elbow River were numerous subdivisions, some of which weren't built up until the 1960s. In these areas, a skeletal urban structure persisted for many decades.

23
View north from Mission Hill to 4th Street SW, ca 1890.
Glenbow Archives NA-431-4

North of the Bow lay a sparse residential district on the lands along the Bow River flats comprised of Hillhurst–Sunnyside (subdivided in 1904) near the Bow Marsh Bridge and an area near the brewery appropriately named Breweryville. The city expanded northwards after the construction of a privately owned bridge across the Bow River at the approximate location of today's Centre Street Bridge. The new bridge, and the greater mobility allowed by the street railway, prompted development and subdivision farther than ever from the downtown core. Over a dozen subdivisions were laid out more than ten miles from the city centre, although there was little real building activity in these areas at the time.

Further north, the village of Crescent Heights incorporated in 1908 as a quiet, middle-class suburb and was annexed by the City in 1910. By 1912, lots in Mount Pleasant and Rosedale had been sold and the CPR had developed Bridgeland and Balmoral. A group of German-speaking immigrants settled in Riverside (subsequently called Germantown) near the Langevin Bridge. Lutheran and Moravian churches were built on the north side of the river, and this area has continued to be one of Calgary's most ethnically diverse neighbourhoods.

Parks, public spaces, and streets

One of town council's first undertakings after incorporation of the town of Calgary in 1884 was to set aside land for a cemetery, as requested by the federal government. Council's first choice was land that is now the site of Shaganappi Golf Course. This was rejected due to the rocky nature of the site, and an alternative site of about sixty acres at Macleod Trail (now Spiller Road) was made available for purchase. In 1891, a survey and plan for Union Cemetery was laid out by the town engineers, and in 1899, eighty-eight trees were planted. A bridge was constructed across the Elbow River at 2nd Street East to afford better access to the cemetery. In 1909, additional land was reserved for a tree nursery.

Through the authority of William Pearce, parkland was reserved for Central Park as part of the survey plan of the town site. Other early park areas obtained by the town were a thirty-acre property adjacent to the Bow River and the land reserve provided by the federal government at the Shaganappi site.

On Pearce's advice, the Bow River Islands opposite and east of the North West Mounted Police (NWMP) barracks were secured in 1890 and public parks named after Saints George, Andrew, and Patrick were established. As well, land adjacent to the Bow River was also set aside for park purposes and in 1906 the area was ploughed, fenced, and named Mewata Park. In 1912, an armoury building was approved, and it was completed in 1917. The land west of the armoury was eventually developed for what would become a series of recreational facilities, from polo fields, to a football stadium, to skateboarding today.

In 1889, the Calgary Agricultural Society purchased ninety-four acres of land from the Dominion Government for fairgrounds, with the restriction that none of the land was to be subdivided and sold. This set in place one of Calgary's defining elements and established a physical presence that would greatly influence the city's urban development.

The Society's first large fair, known as the Dominion Exhibition, took place in 1908 and the exhibition grounds were named Victoria Park in honour of the reigning Queen. Over time, the adjacent residential community took this name as well. In 1911, the city assumed the property debt and with it, ownership of the grounds. The following year, four wealthy ranchers who came to be known as the Big Four – Patrick Burns, A.E. Cross, George Lane, and A.J. McLean – financed Guy Weadick's vision of what was initially intended to be a one-time rodeo and agricultural fair. This event eventually became the Calgary Stampede.

In 1890, City Council's public works committee was instructed to work towards construction of a public park near the railway station. Although the railway garden had been established earlier in a pattern typical of many western communities, Central Memorial Park on 4th Street between 12th and 13th Avenues SW would be Calgary's first formal park. A South African Soldiers' Memorial at the park's centre and a bandstand at the west end were added later, and a public library, constructed with grants from philanthropist and industrialist Andrew Carnegie and the City of Calgary, was opened in 1912.

A committee formed in 1892 took an active role in the development of parks and cemeteries. William Pearce encouraged the committee to plant trees and establish an urban forest in Calgary. This undertaking took place over many years, despite the hindrances of the harsh climate, a general shortage of water, desiccating Chinook winds in the winter, alkaline soils, and lack of experience in the cultivation of trees in western Canada's environment. Tree-planting efforts were also hampered by insufficient funding, the absence of a comprehensive plan, and conflicts with city utility companies that frequently dug up boulevards and ruined tree plantings when installing water, gas, or electrical services.

24
Central Park (Memorial Park) looking west, ca 1900-1915.
Glenbow Archives NA-920-20

25
6th Avenue SW, with treed boulevards and sidewalks, ca 1900-1903.
Glenbow Archives NA-468-7

Boulevard tree planting began in 1895, and approximately eighty trees were planted on Atlantic (9th) Avenue E. Trees were brought from the mountains by railroad, and spruce and poplar, along with Manitoba maple from Brandon were planted on boulevards. Saplings could also be obtained by residents, who were encouraged to plant trees on their own lots. The gradual replacement of wooden walks with concrete sidewalks also contributed significantly to city development. By 1911, the city had nearly fourteen miles of improved boulevards, and thousands of trees had also been planted by private citizens. Many of these early plantings can still be found in Calgary's older neighbourhoods, and the remaining leafy inner city streets are a legacy of Pearce's vision and the early commitment of the City to a strong ideal.

Pearce and the Reverend Dean Paget, another advocate of neighbourhood improvements, urged the City to acquire more children's playgrounds and recommended that a playground be provided at each school. They also proposed numerous locations as park reserves, the additional development of islands, and the establishment of an experimental tree plantation at Victoria Park to be managed by the Dominion Tree Planting Division of Indian Head, Saskatchewan.

During this time, riverside land in the downtown was perceived to have low value, and Calgary's river banks were the site of lumber yards, garbage dumps, and industrial uses that would remain, with little comment, until the 1960s. An exception was Bowness Park, a sizeable riverside property acquired by the City in 1911 from landowner John Hextall in exchange for an extension of the city streetcar line to the area.

The philanthropy of notable Calgarians also played a vital role in park development. Ezra H. Riley, a local rancher, donated approximately twenty acres of land (now Riley Park) to the City, and Frank Shouldice, also a rancher, provided one hundred acres on the condition that the city's street railway extend to the Shouldice Bridge. Both areas were dedicated to public use along with more than ninety acres of land at Shaganappi Point.

As the city expanded westward and north of the Bow and embraced settlements in need of services, Council ruled in 1911 that no further subdivision plans would be approved unless a minimum of five percent of proposed subdivisions was deeded to the City for parks purposes. As a result of City initiatives, co-operation with the CPR, and the campaigns of private citizens and visionaries like William Pearce, Calgary's Parks Department managed approximately 300 acres of parks and cemetery grounds by 1911 (see Barraclough [1975] and the Calgary Field Naturalists' Society [1975] for a discussion of the history of Calgary's parks up to 1975).

Infrastructure and urban form

City physical infrastructure is interrelated with and interdependent on urban form and, accordingly, Calgary's evolution is closely tied to the physical necessities of water, sewer, and power. Provision of basic services and infrastructure were the main preoccupation of the first era of city building, and much was accomplished.

By the early 1900s, Calgary's built-up areas were serviced with water and power. Road paving and laying of sidewalks were also carried out in the areas adjacent to the downtown section.

Water

The Bow and Elbow rivers supplied water to the city's drinking and municipal services. During Calgary's early years, water was sold door-to-door by the barrel, but the destruction of eighteen buildings by the 1886 fire pointed out the need for a more efficient, pressurized water system. The first freshwater main was laid in 1889 from the Eau Claire Lumber Mill to the NWMP fort, with water pressure provided by a steam-driven pump at the mill. Residents could pump their own water from public wells located throughout town, and these wells were also used to aid in dousing fires.

In 1899, Calgarians approved a publicly owned water utility. A gravity-fed pipeline was constructed from an intake on the Elbow River west of Twin Bridges and an elevation drop of ninety metres provided the necessary pressure. While sufficient as a drinking water supply, this system was inadequate to fight fire in tall buildings, a limitation that obliged Council to pass a bylaw restricting building heights to six stories.

In 1900, the City assumed the responsibility of supplying water when it purchased the operations of the Gas and Waterworks Company. Over the next decade, the city was to experience explosive growth accompanied by an exponential increase in the demand for water. In 1910, the Currie reservoir was constructed in a natural depression at the southwestern edge of Calgary. Located sixty-one metres in elevation above the city centre, the new reservoir helped meet the demand with the addition of new pumphouses, the second of which is the present-day Pumphouse Theatre near the Bow River.

Sewer

The removal of human waste from city dwellings was originally the responsibility of the Town Scavenger. Householders also disposed of sewage from their windows or doors, and the practice of depositing waste from indoor plumbing into cesspools became increasingly common during Calgary's economic boom. The provision of piped water further increased wastewater and sewage volumes.

In the early days, sanitary and storm sewers shared the same lines. By 1906, the city's sewer system extended for nearly twenty-six linear kilometres, with outfalls into the Bow River located at 1st Street SE and at the NWMP fort. Storm sewers also needed to be sufficiently large and numerous to handle the sudden surges of snowmelt that resulted from Chinook conditions. It was soon learned, however, that the sewer lines were too short to permit sufficient bacterial breakdown of effluent before it was discharged into the river, but plans to implement sewage treatment were not to be realized until 1932.

Sewer lines in the downtown were typically laid beneath the streets. In residential areas, however, back lanes were preferred for sewer lines. It was less disruptive to lay pipes beneath an unpaved surface, where they could be more easily dug up for repairs and upgrades.

As Calgary grew, so did the City's Engineering Department, and the development of the sewer system included more deeply buried pipes and other innovations. A notable expansion of the system occurred when the construction of the CPR's Ogden shops necessitated water and sewer services almost five miles from the downtown.

Power

Electrical structures are perhaps the most visible element of the service infrastructure, and many of Calgary's facilities can be traced back to the city's founding decades. Street lighting was first provided by a system of oil lamps overseen by Calgary's Fire, Water and Light Committee. While gaslights persisted into the twentieth century, electricity proved to be greatly superior in light output, efficiency, and cost.

Calgary's first electric utility, the Calgary Electric Lighting Company, provided some street lighting as early as 1887 with electricity supplied by the city's first power station on McIntyre Avenue. This company was soon overtaken by Peter Prince's Calgary Water and Power Company. In 1905, the City of Calgary assumed the responsibility of lighting streets and inaugurated a municipally owned electric light plant. Some street lighting would also be provided by gaslights between 1907 and 1918 through the Calgary Natural Gas Company, but the service's high costs led to its replacement by electric lighting. Natural gas was also piped from Bow Island to Calgary homes as early as 1912 by the Canadian Western Natural Gas, Light, Heat and Power Company.

In 1905, the City of Calgary Electric System opened its first coal-fired steam plant on Atlantic Avenue at the corner of 9th Avenue and 5th Street SW. It was replaced shortly thereafter by a brick veneer powerhouse, a building that subsequently served as a municipal garage, an outlet for the Alberta Liquor Control Board, and a nightclub. A steam power plant built in 1910 in Victoria Park supported the Calgary's ongoing industrial expansion with inexpensive electricity and supplied direct current, rather than alternating current, to the city's new streetcar system as well as other users. This new facility was conveniently located beside the Elbow River as a water supply and received coal by way of a railway spur from the main CPR line. An underground conduit system was constructed in the downtown and, by the mid-1920s, most of the city's distribution system within the commercial areas of Sections 15 and 16 had been placed underground.

26
Number One Substation, 9th Avenue SW.
photo D. Lee 2005

Additional needs for electricity led to a contract with the Calgary Power Company to supply hydroelectric power generated on the Bow River. (See Hawkins [1987] for a detailed account of the politics and practicalities of this venture, as well as for a more comprehensive history of the power industry in Calgary.) The dam constructed at Horseshoe Falls ninety kilometres west of the city is still in operation, and the legacy of Peter Prince's company lives on in the TransAlta Corporation. The combination of coal and hydro power was vital to meeting the city's year-round demands for electricity. The hydroelectric plant alone was not a continuous, reliable source, since the rivers' lowest water levels coincided with the times of peak demand in winter. In 1913 a second hydro plant was completed by the Calgary Power Company at Kananaskis Falls, upstream of Horseshoe Falls. Although the City continued to generate some of its own electricity, it purchased much of its power from the Calgary Power Company. This eventually led to the practice of purchasing its entire power supply from a wholesaler, with the City utility focusing its resources on the transmission and distribution of electricity.

By 1911, the city limits encompassed one township, or an area of thirty-six square miles, excluding Ogden, the CPR Shops, and the Manchester extension. A 12,000-volt power line ring main was erected around the perimeter of the city, feeding in two directions from the Victoria Park power station. Number One Substation was built at the corner of 9th Avenue and 7th Street SW, and a second substation was built opposite the Ogden Shops, where transformers reduced the voltage to 2,200 volts for local distribution. Both of these structures still stand. Number One Substation, a compact structure with an attractive tile veneer, still plays a pivotal role in providing power to Calgary's downtown core. It delivers almost half of the downtown load and contains space-saving switchgear within the building, as opposed to the usual "lattice-type" equipment seen in substation yards.

27
Telephone exchange building on 14th Avenue SW.
photo B. Abrams Reid 2006

Telephone

In 1887, the Bell Telephone Company provided Calgarians a new means of communication and held a monopoly on telephone service until 1908, when the Alberta Government bought out Bell's holdings. The physical infrastructure for telephone service included lines and exchange buildings. Cedar telephone poles first carried the telephone lines down Stephen Avenue and other downtown streets; the practice of burying cable was first introduced in Calgary in 1907.

One of the earliest telephone exchanges was the Liston Block on 8th Avenue and 1st Street SE, but this service soon moved to a new building on 7th Avenue where the company made a strong physical statement. Several smaller exchange buildings were constructed during this period using a so-called "thermos jug" principle: a space created between the concrete outer walls and an inner shell of terra cotta blocks allowed air to circulate within the buildings and maintained a constant operating temperature for the telephone equipment. Several of these small buildings still exist and are a part of their neighbourhood's fabric.

3.4   URBAN FORM AND URBAN TYPES

Much of what makes a city distinctive is a result of the particular patterns, types, and relationships of the building blocks of urban form. Combinations of buildings, lots, streets, and city blocks make up the physical form of the city, and the layout and visual relationships between these elements are an important aspect of how people experience a place.

Different eras produce distinct urban forms, all of which contribute to the physical record of the community and influence the quality and nature of the public realm. In a young city like Calgary, this physical legacy is less established and more vulnerable to change than that of more mature cities. Documenting the urban forms and building types of each era helps in understanding both the physical attributes and experiential qualities of places that make the city unique and provide ingredients and tools for the construction of future urban forms.

While any city consists of various land uses, including commercial, residential, industrial, and institutional, it is the commercial and residential streets, blocks, and buildings that are the most prevalent, distinctive, and useful as a basis for reviewing Calgary's physical evolution.

Calgary's urban form in the early twentieth century characterized a city in rapid transformation. Shack towns beyond the city limits were common in western Canada during this time. Early bridge development made possible some development north of the river, such as a German settlement that emerged in Bridgeland near the Langevin Bridge, and a string of brothels that sprung up in the Nose Creek area. By the time North Hill was incorporated within the city limits in 1907 and 1910, its reputation was already established as a less desirable place to live than the south and southwest neighbourhoods.

The primitive early tents and shacks transformed into one of the country's finest collections of sandstone commercial buildings in just a few decades. Several notable institutional buildings also started to provide a structure and visual character to the new city.

Downtown

Commercial streets differed from residential development in that buildings in these areas were normally built flush with the property line. This provided a continuous frontage for passers-by, and commercial buildings took further advantage by incorporating large display windows. Commercial lots normally had a twenty-five-foot frontage, resulting in a block with considerable variety and visual interest. This "main street" commercial type was constructed in several locations in early Calgary, including Stephen Avenue, 17th Avenue SW, 1st, 4th, 11th, and 14th Streets SW, 10th and 19th Streets NW, and 2nd Avenue NE.

The buildings on commercial streets were typically of timber or frame construction faced either in brick veneer or wood siding. A notable exception was Stephen Avenue, where handsome sandstone buildings helped to define Calgary building in the early twentieth century and earned Calgary the name "Sandstone City." Sandstone is one of the materials that is particularly expressive of downtown Calgary's sense of place: it glows in the bright sun of the prairies and has a distinctive warmth in the oblique light of sunrise and sunset. A direct link between materials and form, and between place and time, was created by the use of sandstone from local quarries (although imported sandstone also had a similar quality).

In the evolution of the downtown core can be read much of the story of the city. 8th Avenue has maintained its position as Calgary's premiere retail street. 1st Street SW was once one of Calgary's earliest commercial main streets, and its position now is one more of promise than of fact. The intersection of these two streets is arguably the most

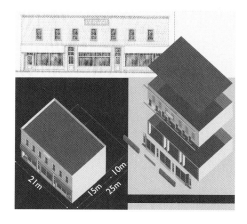

28
Main Street buildings were typically two storeys and included commercial space at the ground floor with residential units above. Subdivision within the building allowed multiple small businesses, and large windows permitted display of goods.
drawings J. Marce Santa

29
Stephen Avenue (8th Avenue), 1892.
Glenbow Archives NA-1702-7

30
A series of drawings of a transect of the city, ca. 1914, centred on 8th Avenue and 1st Street SW, shows the commercial core concentrated north of the railway tracks, a warehouse district to the south, and residential areas to the north and south. A three-dimensional computer model illustrates the fabric and texture of the city that resulted from a combination of street and block pattern, land subdivision, and building type. A land use diagram shows the general distribution of the commercial, warehouse, residential and industrial uses.
drawings J. Zhang, F. Alaniz Uribe, K. Meehan-Prins, A. Nicolai, B. Sandalack

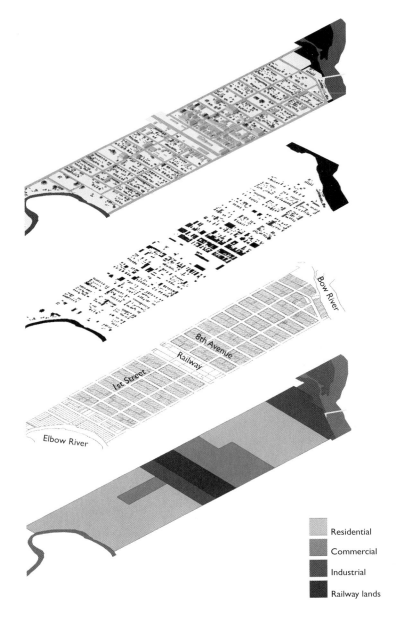

	Residential
	Commercial
	Industrial
	Railway lands

potent place in the city in the sense of its history, energy, and entrepreneurial activity. Various planning ideas have played out over the decades, and the urban form has gone through several stages, from its early establishment and traditional form, through urban renewal and the consequent decimation of the urban fabric, through to a rebirth and rejuvenation.

A transect through the city between the Bow and Elbow rivers, centred on the intersection of 8th Avenue and 1st Street is documented and followed through several development eras in this and subsequent chapters.

In 1914, the pattern of streets and blocks north and south of the railway tracks represents a permeable grid, separated by the expanse of rail lands, and connected by only a few crossings. Calgary's early commercial blocks were laid out in a grid pattern aligned with the rail line.

Building footprints show the concentration of larger commercial structures on 8th and 9th Avenues with the development of a warehouse district south of the tracks. A few institutional buildings are identifiable by their larger footprint.

Neighbourhood types

With the exception of some apartment buildings such as the Devenish Block, Calgary's residential areas were, as now, made up primarily of low-density, single-family housing.

During this time, home ownership was valued and encouraged among all economic classes. Calgary's home buyers preferred single-family detached housing, which was the mainstay of the city's residential construction industry. Workers from the United Kingdom, Europe, eastern Canada, and the eastern United States, who had grown up in crowded and often less desirable industrial communities, aspired to the independence and social respectability represented by home ownership.

Apartments were intended mostly for the well-to-do and were usually located near the downtown. They included such notable buildings as the Devenish Block, Houlton House near the Lougheed Mansion, the Lorraine Apartments opposite the Burns and Hull estates, and the Hermitage. Other apartments were intended for single people and were located in East Calgary near the industrial districts and streetcar lines. Most of these buildings were constructed of brick veneer over a timber or steel frame, and many offered retail space at the ground level to increase revenue for the building owners.

31
Devenish Apartments and streetcar on 17th Avenue and 8th Street SW, ca 1912.
Glenbow Archives NA-4385-2

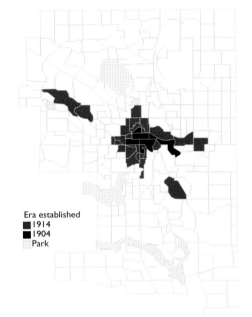

Era established
■ 1914
■ 1904
Park

32
Calgary's earliest neighbourhoods (superimposed on a current outline map) show a concentrated city core and the outlying suburbs of Bowness, Ogden, and Forest Lawn.
drawing J. Zhang, J. Marce Santa, F. Alaniz Uribe

The occupancy of apartments changed with the flood of immigration into the city during the peak years of 1912 and 1913 when the demand for housing outstripped the supply and rental property construction took off as investors seized opportunities for high returns.

Calgary's early housing varied enormously and reflected the social and economic divisions of the day. Despite the affluence of Calgary's elite neighbourhoods, the homes of workers and their families predominated in the urban landscape. Workers' housing was generally humble, utilitarian, and mass-produced from standardized plans. Pre-fabricated house packages included a variety of bungalow designs popular in city neighbourhoods.

Residences of the entrepreneurial elite were rugged and massive, with sandstone, brick, and half-timbered motifs lending an air of solidity to the urban residential environment. Many of Calgary's most luxurious residences were built in the Beltline, while Mount Royal, Scarboro, Sunalta, Elbow Park, Elboya, Glencoe, and parts of Bowness became the enclaves of capitalists, entrepreneurs, and professionals. Owners frequently erected houses near their places of business. Some of the finest houses were concentrated to the south along 12th and 13th Avenues SW behind the developing wholesale district, providing a measure of privacy and exclusiveness while still being within walking distance of the centre. Many mansions, such as James A. Lougheed's Beaulieu and Patrick Burns' sandstone mansion, were constructed here.

Hillhurst

Hillhurst lies just across the river from the downtown and was first populated in 1907 by a wave of mostly English and Scottish settlers. Kensington Road is one of the few city streets to retain its British name after the city's adoption of a numbered street scheme in 1904. A wooden bridge at 10th Street NW connected the neighbourhood with the rest of the city. Only a few houses lay along 10th Street, a dirt road known as Morleyville Road since it followed the trail to the Methodist mission at Morley.

Originally part of the extensive land holdings of the Riley family, Hillhurst was purchased by the City in 1904 and was soon being surveyed and sold. The neighbourhood was laid out in a grid pattern, with the exception of Gladstone Road, an old trail that once skirted the edge of a slough and that was formalized into a street. (The low-lying area would experience frequent floods until the construction of dikes and deepening of the river channel helped control water levels.) The area now known as Riley Park was a farm that the Riley family donated to the City for use as a recreation park, with the unusual stipulation that cricket was to be the only sport permitted in the park.

The survey grid, streetcar lines, and a growing population supported the development of commercial areas on 10th Street, Kensington Road, and 14th Street as well as more limited commercial development on 5th Avenue. The Red Line ran across the Louise Bridge to 10th Street, followed Kensington Road to 14th Street, up 14th Street to 5th Avenue, and then returned along 10th Street. At this time, a special CPR streetcar also served Sunnyside, a more working-class neighbourhood east of Hillhurst, to take railroad employees to their jobs at the Ogden Shops. Hillhurst's early commercial areas persist today and define the edges of the neighbourhood. Its mix of residential and commercial areas, parks, and schools contributes to its sustained popularity.

Garages and outbuildings are placed at the rears of the lots. Lanes, found in most blocks, allow access for municipal and household services and result in a much more hospitable pedestrian environment along the street fronts. This lot arrangement, an abundance of sidewalks, and treed boulevards create a highly permeable grid. The heavy canopy of trees created through the City's early street tree planting program contributes to the exceptionally walkable, high-quality pedestrian environment of Hillhurst's streets.

33
Hillhurst's street pattern is a grid, with the exception of the diagonal Gladstone Road. Residential blocks include back lanes, and schools are set on larger institutional blocks. Commercial strips developed along 10th Street, 14th Street, and Kensington Road and were supported by streetcar lines and a concentrated residential population.
drawings J. Marce Santa

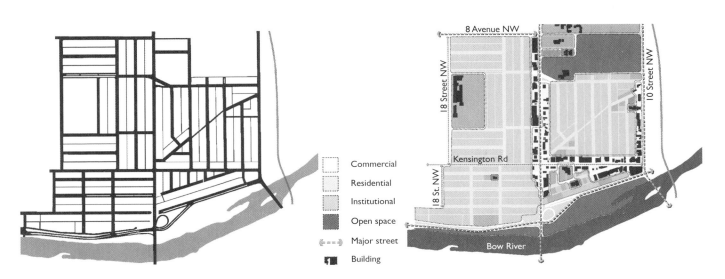

Commercial

Residential

Institutional

Open space

Major street

Building

8 Avenue NW

18 Street NW

10 Street NW

Kensington Rd

18 St. NW

Bow River

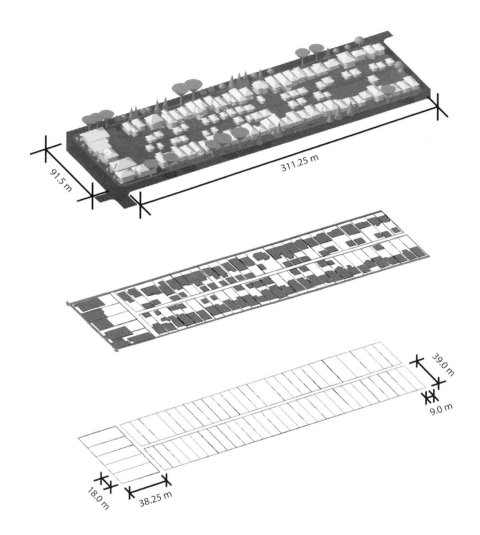

311.25 m

91.5 m

39.0 m

9.0 m

18.0 m

38.25 m

34
Typical blocks and streets in Hillhurst show a pattern in which houses are sited fairly close to the sidewalk, but with sufficient setback to allow for the development of a semi-private area and for private landscaping. Most of the houses have two storeys, and this creates a comfortable sense of enclosure on the streets.
drawings J Marce Santa, streetscape drawing C. Chen

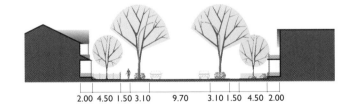

2.00 4.50 1.50 3.10   9.70   3.10 1.50 4.50 2.00

Rosedale

Following the opening up of the north hill after 1910, Rosedale was subdivided and developed as a middle-class neighbourhood. While most of the area conformed to the grid pattern, the streets along the escarpment followed the topography and created some spectacular viewpoints. The grid here produced shorter blocks than in Hillhurst and most of the blocks also included back lanes.

The primary land use in Rosedale was, and still is, single-family residential. An elementary school and community centre are located within the community and have park space associated with them. Other large green spaces are created by the undevelopable sloped land. 16th Avenue NW at the north edge is the most accessible commercial street (a project to widen and the street, which also serves as the Trans Canada Highway, commenced in 2005) and streetcar lines once connected the neighbourhood to Kensington and to the downtown.

Rosedale's block and street structure have resulted in a walkable and comfortable neighbourhood. As in Hillhurst, back lanes allow garages and services to be located at the rear of the lots, giving the streets a strong pedestrian quality. Street tree plantings are extensive, and most streets have treed boulevards that act as a buffer between the sidewalk and the street.

35
Rosedale's street pattern is a grid modifed to the topography. Strong edges are provided by the escarpment to the south and west and 16th Avenue to the north. A school and community centre are important central features within the residential blocks.
drawings J. Marce Santa

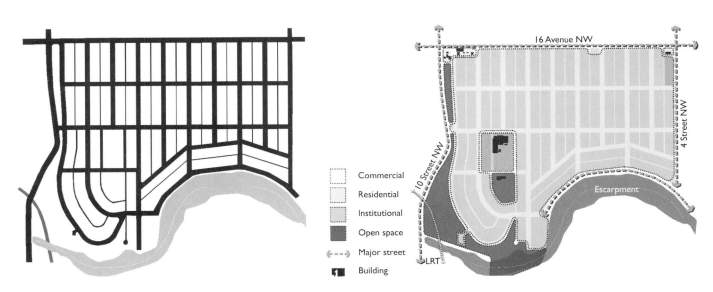

Commercial

Residential

Institutional

Open space

Major street

Building

16 Avenue NW

10 Street NW

4 Street NW

Escarpment

LRT

41

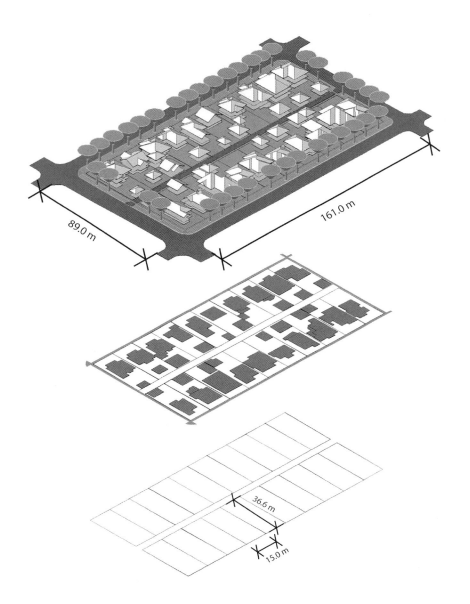

89.0 m

161.0 m

36.6 m

15.0 m

36
Most blocks have back lanes, allowing treed boulevards at the front. Front porches are common, giving a strong public presence on the streets. Houses are one or two storeys, with a variety of styles.
drawings J. Marce Santa, streetscape drawing C. Chen

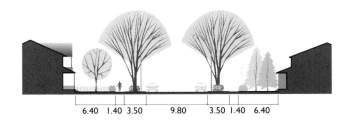

6.40 1.40 3.50 9.80 3.50 1.40 6.40

Mount Royal

In 1905, the CPR registered the first plans for Mount Royal, which was subsequently developed in stages as a unique and prestigious neighbourhood. The first houses were unserviced, since they lay outside city limits. However, with the expansion of the city boundaries, the CPR neighbourhood was incorporated into the city, and water, sewer, and electrical services entered the area along with roads and sidewalks.

Although the railway company typically imposed a rigid grid on its townsites, it often retained outside design advice in the development of its own subdivisions. In the case of Mount Royal, it consulted the Olmsted Brothers, a firm that had evolved directly out of the partnership of Fredrick Law Olmsted and Calvert Vaux, the designers of Central Park in New York City and Mount Royal in Montreal. In Calgary's Mount Royal, the grid was modified so that streets followed the contours of the hilly topography. Lots were large and irregularly shaped, featured deep setbacks and sideyards, and were arranged to make the most of the views. Several small parks were incorporated into the layout of the neighbourhood, and the CPR also planted roadside trees resulting in today's park-like environment.

The numerous building restrictions imposed in Mount Royal, which included caveats dealing with land uses, number of outbuildings, and a minimum house cost, contributed to the area's cachet and exclusiveness. The neighbourhood is varied and includes both laned and laneless blocks. Lot and house size both vary greatly. Some blocks consist of lots that extend from street to street, providing a double frontage. Street quality throughout the neighbourhood is high, and treed boulevards provide shade, shelter, and spatial definition.

The primary land use is single-family residential. Two schools are located within the neighbourhood, and Western Canadian College (now High School) lies just to the north. At one time Mount Royal also included a golf course, built in 1919 by residents on remaining undeveloped land. The Earl Grey Golf Course later relocated as housing spread south.

The edges of Mount Royal are defined by the river escarpment to the south and east, and by 14th Street SW to the west. A streetcar line once extended up 14th Street, and some residents sought the construction of a line through the neighbourhood, a controversial proposal that was defeated.

37
Mount Royal street pattern follows the contours of the hilly topography. Edges are formed by the escarpment to the south and 14th Street at the west.
drawings J. Marce Santa

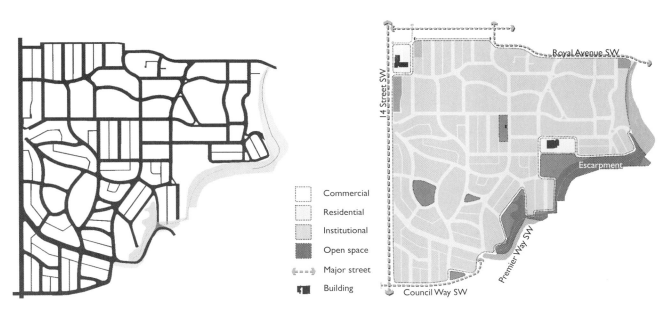

Commercial

Residential

Institutional

Open space

Major street

Building

14 Street SW

Royal Avenue SW

Escarpment

Premier Way SW

Council Way SW

45

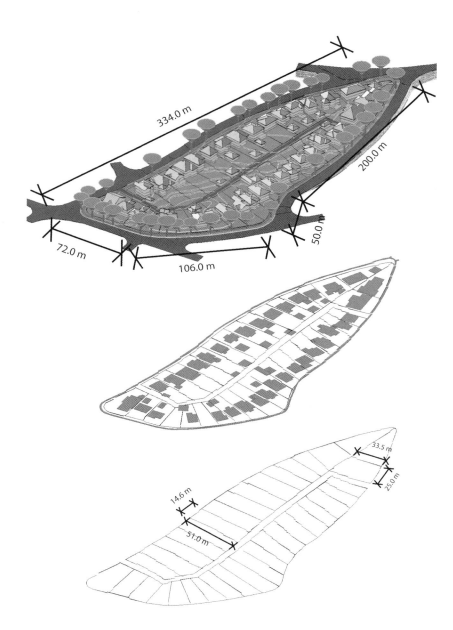

334.0 m

200.0 m

72.0 m

106.0 m

50.0 m

33.5 m

25.0 m

14.6 m

51.0 m

38
Large houses on large lots with abundant landscaping
give Mount Royal a distinctive character.
*drawings J. Marce Santa, streetscape drawing C. Chen,
photo B. Sandalack*

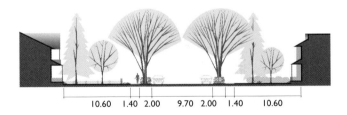

10.60   1.40   2.00   9.70   2.00   1.40   10.60

Roxboro / Rideau

Roxboro typifies both the spirit of development and entrepreneurship that character-ized the early city as well as the strong civic nature of much of its early urban form. Its interesting story begins prior to World War I, when Roxboro was located at the southern edge of Calgary approximately 1.6 kilometres from the city centre. The city was growing rapidly and the most exciting residential developments by far were those of Fred Lowes & Company.

A colourful character and tireless booster of Calgary and the West, Freddy Lowes was one of Calgary's biggest developers and is credited with initiating Calgary's growth to the south. His company owned, developed, and sold enormous amounts of land and at one time listed five million acres of farmland for sale. The company's Calgary properties included the neighbourhoods of Glencoe, Elbow Park, Britannia, Windsor Park, Stanley Park, and Rideau Park.

Lowes purchased the Roxboro lands from the Oblate Fathers for $100,000 with the vision of developing a high quality suburb that would compete with the CPR's prestigious Mount Royal. "Along the river and between the trees" was the slogan that he used to promote Roxboro, a neighbourhood now recognized for its high environmental and urban quality, but that was somewhat ironically created by what would seem now to be environmentally extreme interventions.

Lowes provided graded boulevards, curbs, sidewalks, street lighting, and trees for Roxboro before putting the property on the market and, ultimately, selling 525 large lots. An analysis of Roxboro today shows how landscape features of the Elbow River and its escarpment define three edges of the neighbourhood, with a major street forming the western edge. The street layout is a permeable grid, within the limits of the river and escarpment. All of Roxboro's housing consists of single-detached dwellings, with public green space and a community hall making up the other land uses. However, just to the north of the neighbourhood, and easily accessible by foot, lies a commercial street containing most services and amenities. Schools are located within easy walking distance.

The block structure consists of houses placed towards the front of the lots and rear garages accessed by a lane. Houses face the street, and most include a front porch or stoop. A combination of house type, building placement, private landscaping, street design, and trees in Roxboro lends the street a pedestrian scale, clearly demarcates public and private spaces, and establishes the high visual quality and character of this neighbourhood.

39
Hydraulic pumps and high-pressure streams of water were operated for three months to carve 100,000 cubic yards of earth from Mission Hill and fill a wetland, raising the land above reach of the Elbow River floods and preparing for construction.
Glenbow Archives NA-2957-3

40
The street pattern of Roxboro and Rideau is permeable, with good connection. It is a constructed landscape, but with a high quality public realm, and reflecting the strong edges of the river and escarpment. The block pattern is a grid and includes back lanes. The dominant land use is single-family housing, with a school at the west, and park space along the escarpment. The 4th Street commercial area is easily accessed to the north.
drawings J. Marce Santa

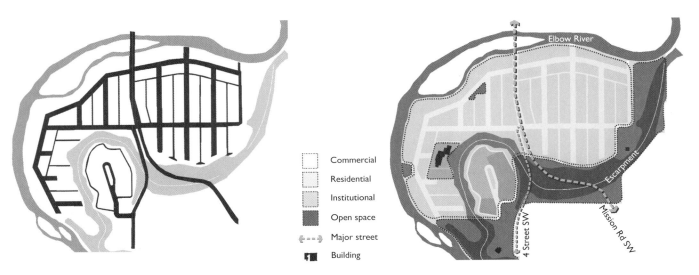

Commercial
Residential
Institutional
Open space
Major street
Building

Elbow River

Escarpment

4 Street SW

Mission Rd SW

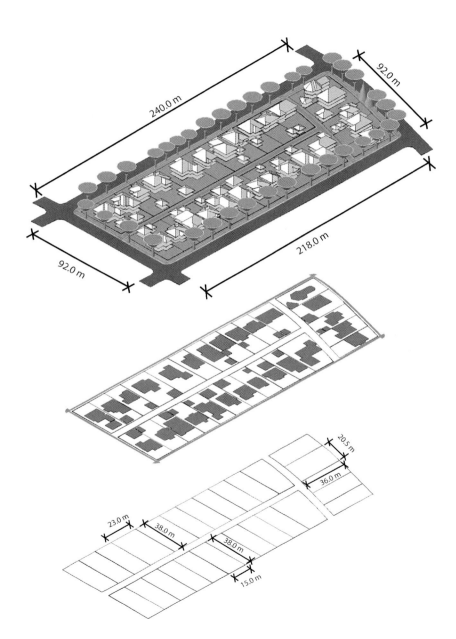

41

Lot subdivision, building massing, and a three-dimensional model show houses oriented to a public street and garages and services accessed via back lanes. The typical lot size is 50 by 120 feet (15 by 36 metres), including the lanes that provide service access at the rear of the lots. Street trees on boulevards separate the pedestrian sidewalk from the street and help distinguish public and private space. The result is a human-scaled environment. There is a variety of one- and two-storey house form and design with doors and windows addressing the street and unified by the landscape.

drawings J. Marce Santa, streetscape drawing C. Chen

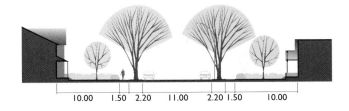

10.00   1.50 2.20   11.00   2.20 1.50   10.00

3.5 SUMMARY

Early town form was expressive of an "inside-out" development, a form that also reflected how the town was experienced. Goods and people typically arrived at the railway station and worked their way outward through successive layers of public function. The railway station was not only the first thing that people saw; it was the social and cultural heart of the town and was imbued with many layers of meaning and association. Calgary was a walking city during this period, and a resident could cross easily, reaching any part of the settlement on foot.

Physical expansion during Calgary's early formative period was constrained by major escarpments, ridges, and rivers, which made it difficult to establish roads and to lay utilities. Bridge construction was expensive. When the means of transportation was limited to horses and horse-drawn vehicles, the steep grades of the escarpments were an especially severe limitation to growth. The establishment of the town centre, the east-west railway corridor with its associated wholesaling and industry, the concentric layers of housing around the core, and the industrial strip to the east formed Calgary's early urban structure. Because of topographic and transportation-related constraints, Calgary was fairly compact for many years. A highly imageable town developed in the river valleys, and the shape of the land and the form of the town had an easy fit.

42
Warehouse on 11th Avenue SE.
photo B. Abrams Reid 2006

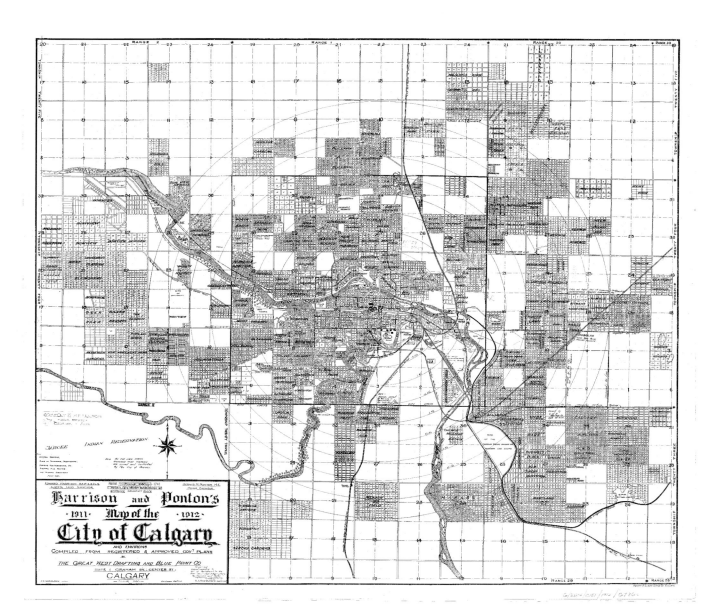

Harrison and Ponton's
· 1911 · Map of the · 1912 ·
City of Calgary
AND ENVIRONS
COMPILED FROM REGISTERED & APPROVED GOV'T PLANS
BY
THE GREAT WEST DRAFTING AND BLUE PRINT CO
SUITE 1, GRAHAM BK., CENTER ST.
CALGARY

4 WORLD WAR I, INTERWAR YEARS, WORLD WAR II

4.1 INTRODUCTION

Aside from a minor burst of building and population increase in the late 1920s, ending with the onset of the Depression, Calgary went through a period of several decades of slow growth and more austere economic conditions that would only be relieved by the post-World War II boom. Population growth reflected natural increase rather than immigration, and from 1916 to 1941 the city grew by 32,000 to 88,000. Calgary did not significantly expand its territory, and most development consisted of infilling of the land that had been subdivided during the previous period of speculation.

Calgary would develop an identity as a conservative society, with small economic disparities, relative ethnic homogeneity, and therefore a lack of radical influences. This conservatism was otherwise contrasted by the city's association with the individualistic and high-risk activities of ranching and oil, and Calgary developed a distinctive character that would continue to differentiate it from other western cities.

Calgary also gained prominence as a jumping off point to nearby scenic attractions such as Banff and to hunting areas in the mountains and wilderness. The city retained its frontier image, with the Calgary Stampede providing a focal point for the ranching and farming character and what would continue as a strong identification with the outdoors.

Calgary's futures were also secured by the beginnings of the oil industry, and its regional identity and commercial ambitions would be realized in full following World War II.

4.2 IDEAS, PLANS, AND PLANNING

The city underwent gradual expansion during this period, and most city planning was technical in nature and more concerned with the provision of essential services such as utilities and roads than with grand visions. Following the rejection of Mawson's plan for Calgary, no inspirational notions of city form came forward.

So decisive was the halt to Calgary's development post-1914 that residential zoning was introduced only in the 1930s (Perks 1985, 11), and the city planning department adopted a conservative stance. The Alberta Town Planning Act of 1929 empowered cities to appoint town planning commissions whose mandate included preparation of a zoning bylaw. Around this time, Calgary authorized the preparation of over thirty reports on recreational land use, transportation, civic art, and zoning, to be overseen by a town planner.

43
Harrison and Ponton's map of the City of Calgary 1911-1912.
courtesy Glenbow Library

The zoning bylaw was used primarily as a tool to accommodate the increasing need for multiple dwellings and to address a general housing shortage. The new zoning bylaw allowed for four districts (single-family, two-family, multiple-dwelling, and commercial) instead of the two it formerly described (residential and business), but this only applied to the inner city area. It was presumed that the existing commercial land use designation was sufficient to accommodate Calgary's growth indefinitely, and additional commercial land was not set aside.

The main urban development issues that were recognized at the time were a housing shortage and an emerging problem of traffic congestion in the core. A transportation plan was developed to try to address traffic problems, and a proposed system of arterial roads was based on the presumption that existing roads could be widened as required, but much of this plan was shelved during the Depression.

4.3   SPATIAL STRUCTURE

The pre-1914 boom had resulted in an over-extension of the city and produced a landscape of scattered houses, isolated from main roads and utilities, and most of these areas would not be in-filled until the next population boom following World War II. With the opening of Centre Street Bridge in 1916, it was now much easier to access land north of the Bow River, and development spread with the construction of the streetcar lines. In 1922, a report designated twenty-eight of Calgary's thirty-six sections as unimproved, and in 1930, over 80 per cent of the city's area was unoccupied.

Although the City did not undergo much net growth during this period, several developments occurred that would have significant impacts on the form, function, and character of the city.

In 1923, the Dominion Exhibition combined with the Calgary Stampede to form the Calgary Exhibition and Stampede, and it evolved as an annual agricultural fair and civic celebration of ranching culture.

Glenmore Reservoir was constructed, and it would have major impacts on the physical form of the city and become a recreational and ecological resource. Creation of Glenmore Reservoir involved flooding several farms, notably that of Sam Livingstone, an early settler. However, it also created one of Calgary's most important recreation amenities. The Weaselhead, a broad, ecologically rich delta, now one of Calgary's premiere natural recreation areas, was a result of the modifications upstream of the dam. Until Glenmore

44
View to the north with Calgary Exhibition and Stampede Grounds in foreground and downtown, 1941.
Glenbow Archives PA-3475-2

45
Glenmore Dam under construction, 1931.
Glenbow Archives ND-10-96

46
Sarcee Camp looking south, with future Glenmore Trail in middle ground, 1958.
Glenbow Archives NA-5093-476

Reservoir was constructed, the Elbow River was a minor and easily bridged edge. The reservoir and the enlarged Weaselhead ecological area would together present a barrier to transportation expansions as the city grew to the south.

Calgary also emerged as a military centre during this era. During World War I, Sarcee military camp was located in the southwest adjacent to the Sarcee Indian Reserve and was connected to the city by the Killarney section of the street railway line. During the 1930s, an area south of 33rd Avenue near 24th Street SW was acquired by the Department of National Defence for the development of Currie Barracks. Several years later, property for what became known as Lincoln Park was acquired including approach and takeoff zones for an airfield. With the war, additional developments took place, including in 1941 the conversion of the main locomotive shop at Ogden to a munitions factory by the Canadian government.

Calgary had at least six movie houses in the 1930s, but there was a relative lack of cultural facilities, reinforcing Calgary's identification with the outdoors and the frontier. The absence of a university, which would have fostered cultural institutions, was also a factor. It was up to the Art Department of the Provincial Institute of Technology (now the Southern Alberta Institute of Technology or SAIT), established on the North Hill, to provide cultural leadership, aided by organizations such as the Calgary Allied Arts Council who had facilities in a Mount Royal residence (Coste House). The Grand Theatre, located downtown in the Lougheed Building, was a notable and exceptional feature, bringing international-calibre acts to the city (D.B. Smith 2005).

The railway remained directly and indirectly responsible for most of Calgary's development; however, the street railway and an emerging highway system were also contributing to its form and function. The CPR and the CNR had main lines extending into the city. The CPR was the main east-west line and it owned and controlled significant amounts of land. The CNR had extensive holdings in what is now Lindsay Park and operated a station in Mission in what is now the Alberta Ballet building on 18th Avenue and 1st Street SW.

The Ogden shops continued to provide a source of employment and formed an industrial hub, and Ogden continued to develop as a working-class neighbour-hood, as did Inglewood and Ramsay, which served the Alyth railway yards and the stockyards. The warehouse district had consolidated to the south of the tracks, and several spur lines serviced it.

Bow River

Crowchild Trail

Nose Hill

Nose Creek

Centre St

16th Ave

17th Ave

17th Ave

Elbow River

MacLeod Trail

Bow River

Fish Creek

| 0 | 1 | 2 | 3 MILES |
| 0 | 1 | 2 | 3 KILOMETRES |

47
Calgary's expansion to 1945 was modest, taking the form of extensions to the grid. Residential neighbourhoods developed to the north, south and west, and industrial growth continued to the east, still within a general frame of the river valleys and escarpments.
drawing A. Nicolai

48

Up to 1945, Calgary was still centred on the railway, and the warehouse district and industrial areas expanded. The city's residential growth was related to the spread of streetcar lines, and served by local commercial streets and corner stores. The inter-city highway system was emerging, but had not yet had much influence on the urban structure.

drawing F. Alaniz Uribe and B. Sandalack

Commercial
Industrial
Residential
Park
Commercial node
Streetcar
Major entry corridor
Railway

Transportation and circulation

The Calgary Municipal Railway, the streetcar public transit network, was at its highest development stage during this period, providing an efficient public transit system and defining, in part, the settlement patterns of the city. The City exerted control over the extension of the utility lines as a way to limit growth; however, construction of houses still took place beyond the limits of the utilities in areas that were at the same time serviced by streetcar lines. Cheaper clusters of houses developed in these areas, and a differential of residential districts emerged.

Most streetcar routes connected to the downtown, and the corner of 8th Avenue and 1st Street SW was the epicentre of transit activity, with 75 per cent of the traffic coming from points west of 1st Street SW. The street railway system was the preferred mode of travel for several decades, and it also included a sightseeing car from 1912 to 1930.

As passenger use rose, the system continued to be upgraded. The final purchase of streetcars took place in 1929, with the delivery of cars 87 to 92. The delivery of the last cars coincided with the onset of the Depression, which brought a sharp decline in passenger traffic. In 1931, the first gas-powered buses were introduced, extending transportation beyond streetcar lines and heralding the arrival of what would develop as a very different age of transportation and urban form. After the start of World War II in 1939, increased industrial activity and rationed gasoline led to an increase in the demand for public transportation, and streetcars previously withdrawn from service were reintroduced.

Although the streetcar had a significant impact on the function and form of Calgary, road transportation of goods and people within the city, as well as nationally and regionally, started to have a major impact on the organization of the city and its function. As early as the 1920s, the automobile competed with the streetcar for space on roads and for passenger traffic. The increasing numbers of private automobiles meant a decline in use of public transportation, while increased automobile traffic on 8th Avenue started to interfere with the streetcar schedules. However, the comparatively high ridership of the streetcar system meant that the impact of the increasingly popular car was still minor.

Edmonton Trail connected to points north, the Banff Highway (now Highway 1A) led west, and Macleod Trail connected south. These roads were developed on what had become well-worn paths and ultimately became highways. 16th Avenue N and 17th

49
View of downtown from North Hill, ca. 1940-45.
Glenbow Archives PA-3538-35

50
Corner store on 17th Avenue and 7th Street SW.
photo B. Abrams Reid 2006

Avenue S ran the width of the city and extended into the hinterland beyond; however, the closest major settlements to the east were too great a distance to make regular travel feasible so these roads remained minor trails for some years.

Air travel emerged during this era, and Calgary's first Municipal Airport was developed in the Renfrew area. This would turn out to be a temporary location, but it functioned as a significant hub for a decade until it was located to McCall Field in 1939.

Downtown and other commercial

During this period, the downtown continued to dominate as the commercial and service centre, largely facilitated by the excellent streetcar service. The post-World War I period saw a stabilization of rents, meaning that small business owners could remain downtown. Civic policy of this time generally mitigated against commercial expansion outside the compact central business district, although clusters of businesses thrived along some of the streetcar routes. Numerous corner stores served more local needs for day-to-day groceries and sundry items.

Residential

The inter-war period saw the emergence of fringe settlements of variable quality ranging from shacks to more substantial brick and stone houses. Many were outside the city's legal limits and were therefore not subject to its building and subdivision controls, or to its tax rates; however, they were often constructed near one of the streetcar lines and had some locational advantages.

The 1920s saw a high rate of property tax delinquency, and the City of Calgary took possession of many thousands of acres of land through the enactment of tax recovery legislation. This land largely remained unused, and unproductive of tax revenue, as the city's demand for housing stalled for several decades. It was later to prove to be a valuable resource, as the post-war demand for housing was first accommodated by infilling within the earlier subdivided land.

However, with the removal of so much land from the assessment rolls, and to control the further spread of scattered populations, council initiated a policy of growth restriction. Streetcar services were curtailed, utilities were restricted beyond the inner-city area, high assessments were levied on outlying non-agricultural land, and incentive programs were initiated to encourage owners of outlying land to exchange for land closer to the core and move their existing houses to inner-city lots. A later bylaw even prevented the sale of property of outlying areas for residential construction unless the lot was adjacent to an existing building. As a result, land prices dropped in the outlying areas, with some of it reverting to agricultural use, and others being acquired by developers for very low prices. The settlements of Bowness and Forest Lawn were situated outside the city limits but were within commuting distance because of the streetcar lines, and they developed during this period as lower-priced areas.

In Calgary's inner area, the population increased by over 100 per cent between 1911 and 1946. This influenced the conversion of large single-family houses to multiple-dwelling units. Crowded and substandard conditions became more common, especially in the area that had come to be known as the Beltline. The City's policy of restricted growth promoted mixed land uses, and it was easy to convert existing buildings into suites. This was most prominent along the streetcar routes and near existing business areas, and clusters of higher density developed at several nodes.

With World War II came a housing shortage, the result of a lack of construction during the Depression, continuing migration to urban centres from the rural hinterland, and the attraction of labour to the new military bases. The Dominion government assumed responsibility for housing within the framework of the crown corporation Wartime Housing Ltd., tending to favour those cities that had contributed to the war effort, and Calgary's housing shortage was partially addressed through wartime housing developments, including areas in west Hillhurst and Altadore.

In addition to the federal housing program, City Council sold some of its land, first at 50 per cent of its assessed value, and later at 25 per cent, in order to generate some revenue and promote housing construction, and within a few years, the City disposed of much of the land that it had acquired. It wasn't until 1946 that a City lands committee recommended that the policy be discontinued, but not before much land had changed hands in a climate of speculation.

Industrial

Manufacturing land use in Calgary did not change significantly during this period as the City's industrial policy of 1911 allowed for expansion on the existing land. Most new industries were located in Manchester or along Macleod Trail, further establishing the character and function of these areas, and the city also set aside land in the Nose Creek area for future industrial parks.

51
Construction of Imperial Oil Company plant in Ogden, 1923.
Glenbow Archives NA-2849-136

Oil refining facilities were built in east Calgary, consolidating the industrial character between the stockyards and the Ogden repair shops. After the 1914 discovery of oil at Turner Valley, hundreds of exploratory wells were drilled in the area, and in 1921 the newly built Imperial Oil refinery (where today's Lynn Ridge is located) was connected by pipeline to the Turner Valley oil field. The Alberta government found it necessary to have a more direct regulatory role in this industry and located the Alberta Oil and Gas Conservation Board in Calgary, which gave the city a firm foundation as the management, financial, and regulatory centre of western Canada's petroleum industry. When the big post-war oil discoveries were made, Calgary's place in the petroleum industry was further secured.

The majority of the workforce still related largely to meatpacking, railway yards, and the Ogden shops. The residential areas near these industrial activities therefore became further consolidated as generally working-class housing, with a strong functional relationship to the industrial locations. Local service and commercial activities were located in local neighbourhood shops, but the downtown was the primary place for shopping for clothing and other consumer goods.

Parks, public spaces, and streets

Despite the austerity of this period, the early work inspired by the vision of William Pearce and Thomas Mawson provided a foundation for the continued evolution of the public realm of streets, parks, and squares, and Parks Superintendent William Reader laid the foundations of much of Calgary's infrastructure of public streets and spaces.

Perhaps most notable was the development of Memorial Drive as Calgary's premiere civic boulevard. Pearce had been instrumental in protecting the north bank of the Bow River from building encroachment, and the 1915 Parks Superintendent's Annual Report suggests Bow River Park development "before it's too late." In 1922 a committee composed of representatives of the Board of Trade, the Rotary Club and horticultural societies was formed to gather a fund for the purpose of providing trees to be planted along Memorial Drive between Hillhurst Bridge and St George's Island Bridge in memory of those who died in the war. Contributions to the fund came from forty businesses and 160 individuals, further establishing Memorial Drive in the minds of Calgary citizens.

That spring, a total of 900 trees were planted along the boulevard by parks employees, and a small tag bearing a soldier's name was fastened to each tree. A further 400 trees were planted over the next year, and in 1924 another 305 trees were planted and replacements made where necessary. In 1927, 450 trees were provided by the Kiwanis Club and planted east of Langevin Bridge, and each year the Kiwanis Club assisted further, so that an additional 992 trees were planted over the following four years. At the close of 1931, the plan prepared by William Reader of a double drive along Memorial was realized. The centre boulevard was seeded and lilac shrubs planted at intervals, and over time, the approaches at Hillhurst and Langevin bridges were improved. The construction and incremental planting of Memorial Drive resulted in a linear public park, commemorative landscape, and major element of the urban structure. This represents a staggering degree of dedication to a strong vision, as well as a commitment to establishing a high quality urban forest in this still-new city.

Reader contributed greatly to city beautification, and his horticultural background influenced his approach to design and conservationist attitude, which was no doubt partly due to the austere economic conditions under which he had to operate. However, Reader's concentration on boulevard planting made a huge impact on the city, creating many beautiful streets in the Beltline and elsewhere. Reader reported planting 1,500 Russian poplars and 1,500 spruce trees on boulevards in the area from 5th to 20th Avenues between 4th and 11th Streets SW, and other trees were planted in parks throughout the city.

Riley Park, Central Park, Mewata Park, and Prince's Island were improved, Tomkins Park was created from donated land, and Shaganappi Golf Course was developed under Reader's leadership. Three civic nurseries were in operation at Union Cemetery and Victoria Park and on St. Patrick's Island, where an ambitious program of propagation intended to provide trees and shrubs for the city.

Reader's crowning achievements were perhaps the rock gardens at Union Cemetery and at Riley Park. Reader had plans as well for a rock garden at Sunalta Ravine between 11th and 17th Avenues SW (now Crowchild Trail), but funds would not permit. The Reader Rock Garden at the northern edge of Union Cemetery transformed a bare sandy hillside to a horticultural showpiece and included rocks, exotic tree and shrub species, and alpine plants, connected by flagstone paths and steps. The garden thrived for many decades, although it fell into disrepair through the latter part of the twentieth century. The gardens have now been restored, and re-opened in 2006.

Bowness Park functioned as the major family park on land acquired by the City in 1911. Bowness Park was a place for family outings away from the city through the De-

52
William R. Reader in rock garden, n.d.
Glenbow Archives NA-1604-101

53
Bowness Park, ca 1920s.
Glenbow Archives NA-2365-35

54
Bandstand at St. George's Island Natural History Park, Calgary Zoo, ca 1940-1945.
Glenbow Archives PA-3538-12

pression years. Its amenities included a lagoon, facilities for boating and canoeing, picnic pavilion, playground, summer cottages, tenting, swimming pool, dance hall, trails, tea room and dining room, a fountain, music piped by orthophonic speakers throughout the park, a miniature golf course, a football field, and commercial amusements, including a shooting gallery, miniature railway, pony rides, and some mechanical rides.

Numerous playgrounds were constructed during this time, and by 1925 seventeen children's playgrounds were maintained. Baseball diamonds, cricket pitches, skating rinks, and tennis courts were also developed, and cemeteries were developed at Queen's Park and expanded at Union Cemetery. One hundred spruce trees were donated by William Pearce's widow to be planted on Rideau Island as a memorial to her husband, who died in 1930.

The Calgary Zoo was developed during this period on St. George's Island and eventually included development of the Natural History Park, featuring life size models of dinosaurs. The zoo soon became a popular place for family outings and concerts, assisted greatly by service clubs, businesses, and private individuals.

During this period an unusual amount of development and improvements were seen, largely as a result of individual vision and commitment. Calgary's streets, parks, and islands created an infrastructure of public space that expressed the civic values and ambitions of the period.

Infrastructure and urban form

Water

In 1929, the Glenmore Reservoir Project was initiated, which provided some, although not complete, control of the periodic Elbow River floods and provided a reliable drinking water resource for Calgary's growing population. The project also provided a much-needed source of employment during the Depression.

At the time, there was opposition to placing the buildings and filtration plant so close to the city (although Calgary's suburbs would not extend that far until the 1950s), and as a response, more attention was paid to the plant's site planning and architectural design. Along with the dam across the Elbow River and spillway, several buildings related to water treatment and control were constructed, and the strong civic nature of these buildings and the site is striking. The brick and Tyndall stone buildings have an elegance and beauty that belies their utilitarian function, and this area eventually evolved into a high quality part of the public realm. It is also one of the few places where it is possible to gain a direct appreciation for the complex processes involved in delivering a fundamental requirement of life to the city. The reservoir, the spillway, and the buildings are all accessible, and it is possible to understand the direct connection between the physical environment and what comes out when you turn on the tap.

Sewer

Calgary's sewer treatment system was somewhat slower to develop, and raw sewage continued to be disposed of in the rivers until the 1930s. The last raw sewage outfall wasn't eliminated until the construction of the Ogden Plant. In 1932 a Wastewater Treatment Plant was constructed at Bonnybrook.

Power

In 1927 Calgary Power became the sole supplier of electricity to the city, and during the same period, contracts were developed with Canadian Western Natural Gas, Heat, Light and Power Company Ltd. to provide other utilities. This represented a more mature era, where contracts with established companies replaced the free-wheeling earlier decades, in which unreliable and inefficient services were more the norm.

The presence of electrical infrastructure was an integrated part of the visible urban infrastructure. Street lighting, and a web of power lines and poles, defined the extent of the city that was serviced. Although the residential pattern was sparse in places, it was possible to get a sense of the limits of the urban landscape through the presence of the electrical infrastructure.

The first fully automated electrical substation was constructed in 1928 at 14th Street and 34th Avenue SW, where it still stands. Calgary continued to modernize and up-grade residential lighting from the corner intersection street lighting that dominated up to 1928. In 1948 the first mercury vapour light was installed.

Telephone

Telephone service lagged as well due to the wars and the Depression. Calgary's most notable physical structure related to telephone service was the exchange building design.

55
Glenmore water treatment plant.
Glenbow Archives NA-5093-390

56
South Calgary sub-station at 14th Street and 34th Avenue SW, constructed in 1928.
photo D. Lee 2003

4.4　URBAN FORM AND BUILDING TYPES

Downtown

The downtown developed a distinctive architectural character through construction of many significant buildings, many made of sandstone. The Hudson's Bay Building provided a commercial and visual anchor on 8th Avenue and 1st Street SW, incorporating a fine arcade, one of the few recommendations from Thomas Mawson's plan that was implemented. The downtown core further intensified, and 1st Street S also developed as a commercial centre, serving the residential district south of the railway tracks. The narrow lot subdivision still predominated north and south of the railway lands, and the grain and scale of the city was still fairly fine.

The corner store proliferated as a commercial type well adapted to serving the local needs of neighbourhoods.

57
Hudson's Bay building and streetcar, looking west down 8th Avenue at 1st Street SW, 1928.
Glenbow Archives ND-8-266

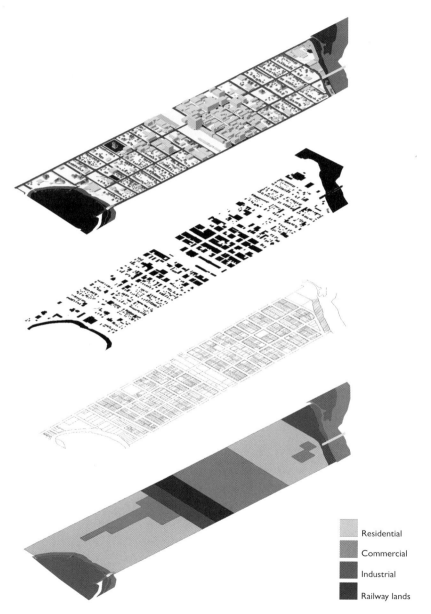

58
Drawings illustrate how the downtown, ca. 1945, consists of an expanded low-rise commercial area, with consolidation of 1st Street SW, Chinatown commercial on Centre Street N, further development of the warehouse district south of the tracks, and industrial development along the south bank of the Bow River.
drawings J. Zhang, F. Alaniz Uribe, K. Meehan-Prins, A. Nicolai, B. Sandalack

Residential
Commercial
Industrial
Railway lands

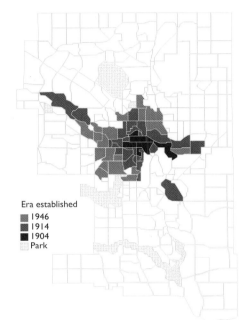

Era established
■ 1946
■ 1914
■ 1904
░ Park

Neighbourhood types

The contrast between the speculative view of Calgary shown in the 1912 map by surveyors and engineers Harrison, Ponton and Parker (figure 43), and the map indicating the neighbourhoods that were actually constructed during this period (figure 59) illustrates the difference between the ambitions of the early decade and the reality of the Depression. The 1912 map shows how much land was subdivided awaiting development that would not occur until after World War II. It also illustrates the dominance of the grid street plan as an approach to land subdivision and urban design. Few of the planned subdivisions deviated from the grid plan, lending continuity and coherence to the city. The grid was not a monotonous pattern as it was relieved by the rivers and escarpments and punctuated by parks and other open spaces.

59
Neighbourhood growth was modest up to 1945, and was clustered around the downtown, with the exception of the railway suburb of Ogden to the southeast.
drawing J. Zhang, J. Marce Santa, F. Alaniz Uribe

West Hillhurst

West Hillhurst was among several neighbourhoods across Canada that were constructed according to similar patterns. During the early 1940s, the federal government built some 26,000 single-family dwellings as rental housing to address the housing shortages that had emerged following the Depression. Only a few basic house plans were employed, leading to neighbourhoods that had a greater degree of conformity and uniformity than found elsewhere (see Evenden [1997] for a discussion of wartime housing in Canada).

While the neighbourhood generally conformed to the grid, creation of some cul de sacs distinguished West Hillhurst from other neighbourhoods and produced a somewhat distinct district. The wartime housing blocks were sandwiched between Queen Elizabeth School and a small commercial strip on 19th Street, and the neighbourhood was easily accessed by streetcar.

House types included the side-gabled or one-and-a-half-storey versions of a Cape Cod design, and a less common hip-roofed cottage. A few attached models were also built. The placement on the lot and the spacing between houses created a distinct and repetitive image that came to define a certain Canadian cultural landscape, and one that was found across the country in almost identical patterns.

60
The West Hillhurst area is outlined on a 1924 air photo. The survey grid defined the edges and set the frame for subsequent block subdivision. The neighbourhood is primarily single family housing, and includes Queen Elizabeth School at the centre, a community centre at the north, and the 19th Street commercial strip within easy walking distance.
drawings M. Stonehocker, J. Marce Santa

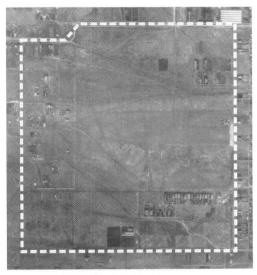

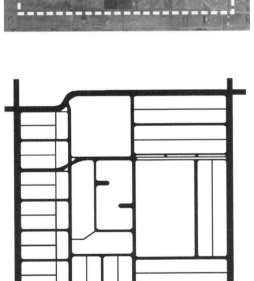

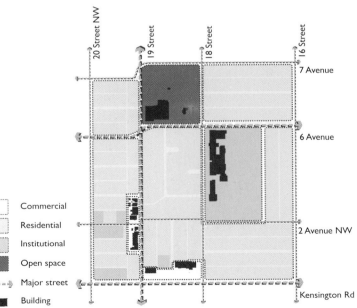

Commercial

Residential

Institutional

Open space

Major street

Building

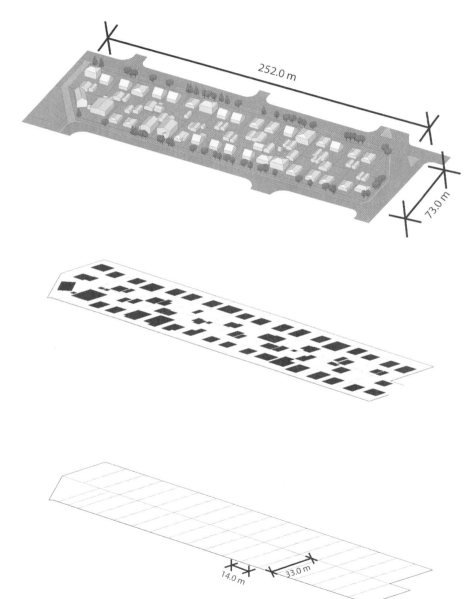

61
West Hillhurst representative block and street illustrate a modestly-scaled neighbourhood. Although the block shown here is laneless, the presence of garages and services is minor, due to the use of side driveways, some shared driveways, and placement of the garages at the rear of lots.
drawings M. Stonehocker, F. Alaniz Uribe,
photo M. Stonehocker

252.0 m

73.0 m

14.0 m   33.0 m

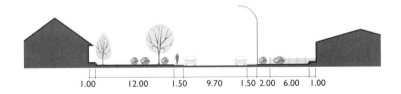

| 1.00 | 12.00 | 1.50 | 9.70 | 1.50 | 2.00 | 6.00 | 1.00 |

4.5   SUMMARY

Calgary's urban character was established during this period. Sandstone City defined the downtown, and a number of smaller commercial streets on the streetcar lines followed the mainstreet pattern. Residential development was concentrated around the core, with some development adjacent to industrial hubs at Ogden and Alyth. The city was a coherent whole, centred on the downtown core and railway, and with an emerging infrastructure of public parks, gardens, and streets.

Most of the urban development during this time consisted of extensions to the existing grid. History and tradition were the determinants of urban form, and it was expected that new developments would graft onto the existing. A few departures from the strict grid likely derived their inspiration from Thomas Mawson's City Beautiful notions; for example, Tuxedo and Renfrew included some street patterns and public spaces that have a much more formal expression than was the norm.

62
Side of warehouse on 11th Avenue SE.
photo B. Abrams Reid

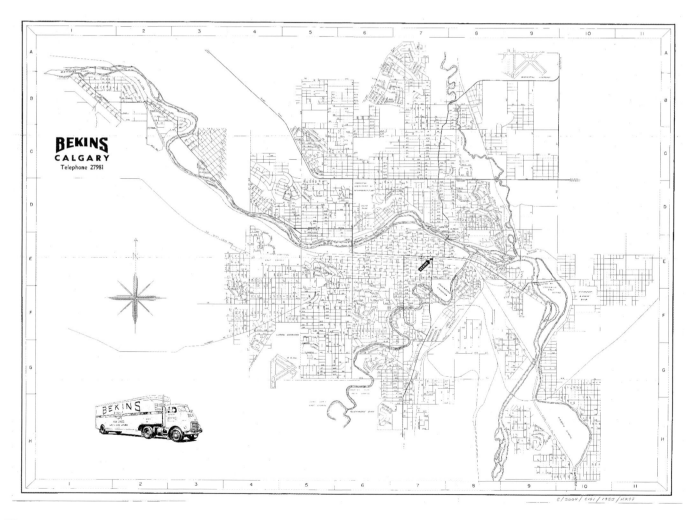

BEKINS
CALGARY
Telephone 27981

5 POST-WORLD WAR II BOOM

5.1   INTRODUCTION

In Calgary, perhaps more so than in other Canadian cities, the post-war years are quite distinct from the interwar years. Within twenty years (1945–65) Calgary grew from a small provincial city to an urban metropolis of national importance, serving as the Canadian headquarters of an international oil industry. Up to the 1950s Winnipeg was the pre-eminent city on the prairies and a major metropolitan centre, while Calgary and Edmonton served as regional centres. Between 1951 and 1971 Alberta emerged as the dominant prairie province, and Calgary started to play a more important role regionally, nationally, and internationally. The city experienced a sustained period of urban growth, related to general national prosperity and also to the growth of the oil business in Alberta.

The 1947 discovery of oil near Leduc came when production from the Turner Valley field was starting to decline. Prairie oil consumption, however, was increasing, with Calgary oil refineries on the verge of arranging imports of crude oil from the United States. The Leduc discovery ushered in a period of much growth and led to the location of numerous oil industry administration offices in Calgary. Alberta again became a supplier, and since Calgary was the location of the refineries and the headquarters of most of the oil companies operating in the west, the city continued as the pre-eminent administrative and financial centre of the Canadian petroleum industry. During this period, oil came to symbolize Alberta and Calgary, similarly to how ranching and the railway had done so before, and it also influenced the city's urban structure and image.

The city's population reached 100,000 in 1948, transforming Calgary from a town to a city, and it now had the population base necessary for development of more expensive amenities and services. Calgary commenced another period of sustained growth following the oil discoveries, this time characterized by the proliferation of suburbs, and the functional relationships of the city's component parts underwent significant changes. The oil boom made for a broadly based rising standard of living, and relatively higher income levels in Calgary permitted the majority of families to purchase single-family dwellings. Suburban expansion took off, as the affordability of housing combined with the ready availability of low-cost automobile transportation.

5.2   IDEAS, PLANS, AND PLANNING

The second general phase of modern urban development in western cities such as Calgary corresponds to modernism, corporate development, and the invention and

63
Bekins Map of Calgary, 1955.
courtesy Glenbow Library

institutionalization of methods for town planning. This coincided with the period of economic growth following World War II and reached its zenith in the 1960s and 1970s. The early paradigm of history was replaced by one of space, where architecture and urbanism attempted to express functional and experiential space. History, tradition, and local and regional identity were thought to be anti-progress and old-fashioned – huge pieces of many Canadian and American towns, cities, and landscapes were destroyed to make way for progress. The lifestyles that go along with the spatial forms that were produced – the suburbs, housing projects, shopping centres, and strip malls – are now taken for granted, while at the same time they contribute to several contemporary urban problems, including suburban sprawl, decline of the central business district, and a neglect of the traditional public realm – the street and the public square.

Although planning legislation had existed in Alberta since the early part of the century, it had little force, and this era saw the institution of more formalized planning processes, which changed transportation and residential priorities and redirected traditional growth patterns. The Town Planning Commission, established in 1929, was an active proponent of planning, after World War II. A town planning engineer, a land surveyor by training, was appointed in 1946, and a planning consultant was engaged in 1949 to administer planning.

Calgary's Planning Department was officially established in 1950 and was comprised of a permanent staff of three to work on Calgary's first plan. In 1951 city council replaced the advisory Town Planning Commission with a Technical Planning Board composed of the heads of the civic departments responsible for development, and it became the major decision-making body on planning, especially design and development of new areas. In 1963, the City prepared the Calgary General Plan, which was the first municipal plan in western Canada.

By 1965 the Planning and Building Department had a permanent staff of ninety, and planning as a process had become fully institutionalized.

Zoning was one of the planning tools of choice at this time, and it aimed for, and resulted in, a pattern of distinct and separate land uses. In addition to functionally separating incompatible land uses, the Central Business District became distinct from the suburbs, in terms of relative density and intensity. This pattern of development also contributed to the need for transportation systems in order to link the various functions of the city. The 1958 City Zoning Bylaw was far from a benign tool, as it started to put into play the processes that would result in the destructive practices of urban renewal of the 1960s and 1970s.

64
View of 10th Street NW, Louise Bridge and downtown, looking southeast, 1973.
Glenbow Archives NA-2864-23932

65
Mayfair area and Glenmore Reservoir, with Elbow Drive in foreground, looking west, 1958.
Glenbow Archives NA-5093-587

Residential neighbourhood planning was perhaps the most notable aspect of the post-war era. Most subdivisions that existed at the end of World War II were registered during the land boom of 1908–12, and most were still vacant in 1948, although they sometimes included streets, utility lines, and streetcar tracks. Many large tracts of land had seen no permanent economic use in forty years.

At the end of World War II, the edge of Calgary was a patchy zone of sub-urban development. The post-war demand for housing was first addressed by infilling in existing, but not fully built out, subdivisions. The developing edge of the city eventually caught up with the fringe developments, which were typically substandard as they were built outside the jurisdiction of some of the planning and construction regulations. By the early 1950s, the city's serviced land supply was exhausted and infilling of the subdivided land had run its course.

The City of Calgary had control of the land supply and the utility systems (it had acquired much land during the Depression), and it therefore came to have almost absolute control over the forms and patterns of land development. Most of the city up until this point had been laid out in a modified grid, and this pattern prevailed during the first years following World War II. With the exceptions of Mount Royal and Scarboro, the grid was the usual land subdivision pattern for the first seventy-five years of Calgary's evolution. This early period of Calgary's development is often referred to as "unplanned growth"; however, it managed to produce much of the city's high quality inner-city neighbourhoods that are held in esteem now.

Up until the early 1950s, builders normally bought lots one by one. This produced a city that was built not just block by block, but, often, lot by lot, and during the first phases of development when tradition and historical precedent influenced decisions, the resultant urban form was fairly cohesive. With the beginning of the population boom, and influenced by emerging social planning ideas, Canada Mortgage and Housing Corporation (CMHC) started to promote "sound community planning." There was also much discussion about the need for parks and recreation space for families, and the idea of the residential district as a community service unit began to emerge.

In 1951, Calgary had a new planning director, A.G. Martin, who promoted "orderly growth" and the neighbourhood unit concept as the basis for the spatial and functional organization of suburban development. This was closely based on Clarence Perry's 1920s Regional Plan for New York in which the "neighbourhood unit" became the basic planning module. Martin advocated the neighbourhood unit for Calgary, defined as the area served by the average elementary school. It was a form that was intended to produce safe and healthy living environments, un-invaded by major traffic, but with ready access to thoroughfares and transit and good local shopping. Its wholesale implementation was hampered by partially developed land, which absorbed the early post-war demand for housing, and therefore the early years of this new neighbourhood form involved compromise. However, once the land supply was exhausted, the neighbourhood unit was imposed exclusively, and the grid fell out of favour.

Procedurally, the technical planning board was made the subdivision approval authority and was therefore self-contained within the civic administration. The city held a monopoly on the land supply, with phasing and land development carried out by civic utilities departments. While school boards had input to the planning process, there was very little from private industry. This situation changed through the 1950s as municipal land was depleted and attention shifted to privately owned land under the control of development companies.

The city cancelled many of the paper subdivisions and replaced them with newly designed layouts on neighbourhood unit principles, with curvilinear street layouts, unit boundaries defined by major collector streets, and self-contained arrangements of schools, playgrounds, and convenience shopping. This policy continued even after the city-owned land supply was exhausted, and land development reverted completely to the private market.

The suburban developments of this period of expansion are therefore remarkably similar, as Calgary's planning machinery and the neighbourhood unit became well-established. CMHC had a financial interest in the new homes, as it provided loans and mortgage insurance, and therefore had the right to review residential subdivision plans. Perry's principles also seemed to be supported by the provincial government's subdivision regulations of 1953 that covered minimum road width, dedication of land for community reserve (schools, parks), maximum safety and privacy in design of the street system, and convenient relationships of neighbourhood elements.

According to Perry's model, traffic was to be diverted around the neighbourhood, and a system of collector roads emerged. Neighbourhoods developed during this time included the same array of schools, parks, shops (commercial services were now integrated with design of residential areas), churches, and social service outlets. Commercial zoning was commonly granted to all four corners of an intersection on one of the collector roads, and the greatest demand was for service stations, which

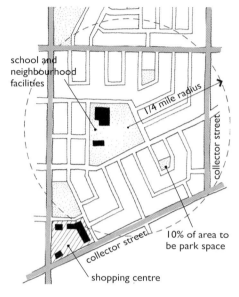

66
Diagram of neighbourhood unit, based on Clarence Perry's 1920 New York plans, that would heavily influence post-war suburb planning.
diagram K. Meehan-Prins and F. Alaniz Uribe based on Clarence Perry 1922

often pre-empted sites intended for local convenience shops. It was not uncommon to see two or three corners of an intersection with automobile service stations.

Although the neighbourhood plans initially included a range of land uses, rezoning often took place to permit even more residential development, and by the early 1960s the trend shifted to fewer but larger commercial sites. The low densities did not support the full extent of commercial development that was initially proposed in the plans; however, there was a huge demand for more single-family housing. The single-family dwelling therefore dominated planned unit developments, and where multi-family housing was included, it was placed on the less desirable edge of the neighbourhood near the major roads. Clusters of other housing forms such as walk-up apartments and terrace houses became increasingly common through the 1960s, but the neighbourhoods developed during this time were predominantly low-density havens for families with children. With the school and park as the social and functional centre, residents, typically families, began to think of themselves as belonging to a neighbourhood first, and the city second, and community associations became well established and took on some of the business of management of facilities such as skating rinks, as well as organization of neighbourhood social events.

5.3   SPATIAL STRUCTURE

By 1965 Calgary was an "oil city," largely dependent on a single industry, and Calgary's hinterland expanded from the regional to the global context. The city was the focal point of the Canadian oil industry, with over 900 oil company head offices and the majority of the oil-related industries headquartered here, and approximately half of the city's population owed their jobs to oil and gas. Expansions in educational services, construction, retailing, and manufacturing all reflected the dynamic growth of the oil industry, and a new era of prosperity took hold.

Calgary's earliest downtown office towers and construction of a new airport at McCall Field helped to solidify the city's emerging modern image. Post-war de-industrialization also changed some of the land use patterns. The airport assumed much more importance following the war, when the city resumed control of the facility. In 1956, a modern air terminal opened at McCall Field in the northeast, and several expansions ushered in the jet age. Development restrictions around the airport affected the evolution of this northeast area of the city. Several military facilities had expanded during the war, and they now occupied large land areas at Lincoln Park, Currie Barracks, and Sarcee Military Camp.

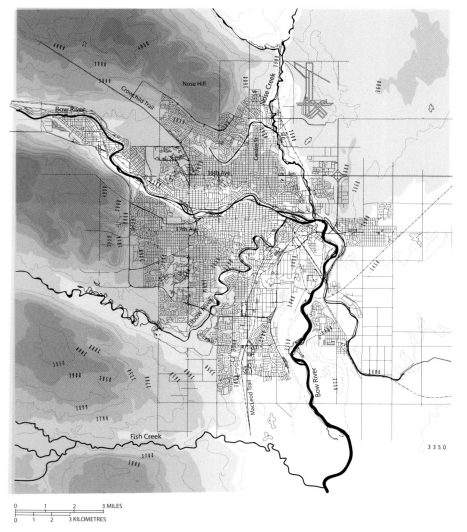

67
Post-war development considerably expanded Calgary's land mass. New suburbs up to 1965 took the form of distinct planned unit developments, although still functionally connected to the city. Most growth was to the north, west, and south and was constrained by Nose Hill at the north, Glenmore Reservoir at the south, and the plateau at the west.
drawing A. Nicolai

68

The automobile age was reflected in the urban structure of Calgary in 1965, and development related to roads rather than streetcar lines. New highways west and east connected Calgary more easily to a broader region, and several auto-oriented commercial strips intensified. An internal freeway system was initiated and included Glenmore, Sarcee, and Barlow trails. The downtown core was still the office and commercial centre, although with the expanding suburbs came Calgary's first shopping malls. North Hill, Chinook, and Westbrook Malls served a regional population base and were located on major roads. Industrial development was still related to the railway, but new industrial areas were located along the highway. It was said during this time that you could drive to anywhere in Calgary in twenty minutes.

drawing F. Alaniz Uribe and B. Sandalack

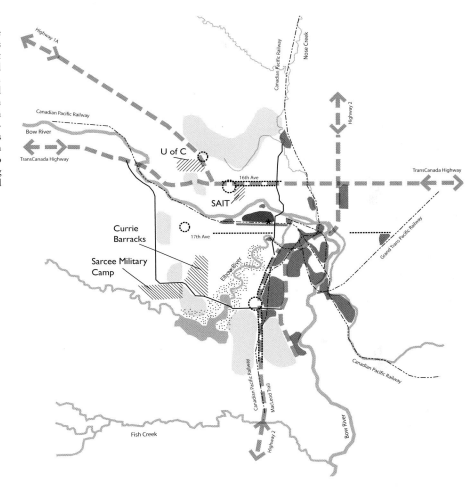

Commercial
Industrial
New Residential
Park
Commercial node
Commercial strip
Major entry corridor
Railway

The suburbs became the residential base for the increasingly single-use downtown, and a high-density commercial district emerged from the old business core. Retailing patterns also changed to include development of several outlying shopping malls and numerous strip malls that were built to serve the newly expanding suburbs.

At the same time, other sectors also grew, including agricultural production, regional distribution, the food and beverage industry, and service industries. This period saw huge growth in the construction industry as the downtown area was transformed and modern subdivisions were created, and locally based housing corporations came to comprise 10 per cent of the city's employment.

Some specialized businesses, including the provision of accommodation and ancillary service for through-travellers and the sale of new and used automobiles, became established during this time, and underwent locational shifts as a result of the rapid increase in highway transportation. Prior to around 1950, both of these businesses were found in the Central Business District (CBD); however, during the 1950s, the demand for new transient accommodation was satisfied by motel concentrations at the highway entrances to the city, and tourist and highway services became strung out on 16th Avenue North, especially around what would develop as "Motel Village," and Macleod Trail. The downtown would remain the prime location for hotels. A new and used auto sales corridor emerged along Macleod Trail, benefiting from the continuous strip development that enables buyers and sellers to make easy comparisons of products and prices.

The University of Calgary also became a force at this time. The new Calgary campus of the University of Alberta was established in the northwest on an open stretch of prairie, remote from the downtown at the time, and it opened in 1960 with two buildings on the campus and McMahon Stadium located just to the south of the campus. In 1966 the University of Calgary was created through the Universities Act. By that time, several other buildings had been added, and the campus had started to develop its distinct landscape character as the prairie had been ambitiously transformed to a park-like setting.

Transportation

The post-war era saw the emergence of the automobile as the dominant mode of transportation, the conversion from streetcars to buses, and the decline in the use of public transportation. In 1946, the Calgary Municipal Railway became the Calgary

69
Science A building in the left background was one of the original buildings at the University of Calgary. *photo F. Alaniz Uribe 2005*

70
Workers tearing up street railway tracks, ca 1947. *Glenbow Archives NA-2891-26*

71
The Hudson's Bay Parkade and the first skywalk, looking east along 7th Avenue SW.
Glenbow Archives NA-5093-328

72
Streetcar, trolley bus and truck on Louise Bridge, 1947 - the end of one era and the beginning of another.
Glenbow Archives NA-2891-28

Transit System, heralding massive changes in public transportation modes and structures. The first phase in the conversion from streetcars to buses took place in June 1947 with the Crescent Heights, Capitol Hill, and Manchester lines. Later in 1947 all streetcar service on Centre Street North to Mount Pleasant and Tuxedo Park was also converted to diesel buses. By the end of 1947 South Calgary and Beltline service changed to trolleys and buses. Streetcar operation in Calgary finally came to an end in 1950, with the last run of the Ogden route, and the conversion from streetcars to trolley cars and buses was complete.

Traffic concerns soon started to dominate downtown planning and development, due to suburban expansion combined with the continued dominance of the downtown as an employment centre and the growing reliance on the private automobile. By 1964 40 per cent of the population worked downtown, but only 2 to 3 per cent of the population lived there. The downtown accommodated the increasing numbers of cars through development of surface parking lots, addition of metered curbside parking, and construction of parking garages.

The Hudson's Bay Parkade was at the time the largest downtown parking structure of its kind in Canada, with a capacity of over a thousand stalls. A "skywalk" connected the parkade with the Hudson's Bay store, a precursor of the extensive Plus 15 system that would emerge in the late 1960s.

In 1954, Elboya and Mewata bridges were built in response to rapid increase in car traffic, and downtown businesses were made more accessible to the developing suburbs. Mewata Bridge's five lanes helped to carry rush hour traffic into and out of the downtown. 6th and 9th Avenues S were established as Calgary's first one-way street couplet, and conversion of other streets to one-way was seen as important in keeping Calgary's downtown vital. This notion of traffic circulation was expressive of modernist ideas of separation of uses and functional efficiency, and the ability of one-way streets to carry increased volumes at higher speeds was praised. Many of the downtown street trees were removed with the one-way conversions.

The post-war era also ushered in a massive expansion of trucking services and several new transportation corridors were developed to address the growing truck and automobile traffic. Blackfoot Trail on the east side and Sarcee Trail on the west were elements of the partial ring-road complex that had started to form. These roads diverted traffic from the high-density areas, and in 1962 work started on Glenmore Trail as a new east-west freeway.

The automobile also influenced leisure and entertainment at the city scale. Several drive-in theatres were built during this time, including Chinook (now the site of Chinook Mall), Sunset (Edmonton Trail and 31st Avenue NE), Cinema Park (Bowness), 17th Avenue (17th Avenue and 45th Street SW), and the Corral (Macleod Trail and Anderson Road). They remained popular up to the end of the twentieth century, when large multi-screen theatre complexes started to dominate the entertainment industry.

Downtown and other commercial areas

Following the discovery of oil at Leduc, numerous oil companies located offices in downtown Calgary, first in buildings that were left over from the 1906–12 boom, and then westward and parallel with the railway tracks, most notably along 9th Avenue, or "Petroleum Row." A building boom soon transformed the city's skyline as demand for office space soared, and several notable modern highrise buildings were constructed, including the Barron Building, one of the first new buildings to respond to the rising demand for office space, and Elveden Centre, Calgary's first "super-block." Downtown building heights had been limited to twelve storeys; however, a 1958 bylaw permitted construction of the twenty-storey Elveden House. The emergent high-density business core was contained by the railway and the river, and the downtown retail functions still clustered in the original core.

Much pre-1914 housing still existed in the downtown core, and it had undergone a process of succession and subdivision for multi-family living. In some areas, such as the Beltline, much of this housing was replaced over time by low-rise apartment buildings. The downtown was commonly described at this time as a modern downtown core isolated in a sea of substandard housing. A "zone of deterioration" (P.J. Smith 1959) was typical of how the heterogeneous land-use patterns were described. These higher-density areas (twelve units per acre) were compared unfavourably with the post-war suburbs that had a density of six-to-seven units per acre. Mixed uses and high relative densities were presented in a negative light and this would help to pave the way for massive urban renewal and social relocation.

The mood of the time reflected the economic boom, and ideas of continued downtown expansion influenced many of the plans and proposals. In the early 1960s, the City attempted to negotiate a re-routing of the railway along the Bow River. It represented an attempt to redirect the historic patterns of commercial development and transcend the physical barriers (the railway and the rivers) to expansion of the downtown footprint. The CPR redevelopment plan of 1963 proposed a $35 million project that would

73
Railway, downtown and Centre Street Bridge, looking north, pre-1961.
Glenbow Archives NA-2399-40

74
Downtown, looking west, with 9th Avenue on left hand side, 1966.
Glenbow Archives NA-2335-1

75
A plan to re-route the railway included a freeway and railway tracks along the south bank of the Bow River, which would have encapsulated the downtown between the two railway lines, and created a barrier along the river.

76
Buildings on 'Petroleum Row,' 9th Avenue SW, 1958.
Glenbow Archives NA-5093-479

have included rerouting the railway along the south bank of the Bow River and construction of a freeway to move huge volumes of traffic through the downtown.

The project included plans for an international-calibre convention centre to be erected on the east side of the Palliser Hotel, a rail relocation that would remove existing subways and free 102 downtown acres (the existing right of way) for commercial development (with the associated increase in tax revenues), a transportation centre adjacent to the convention centre (to include Greyhound Bus Lines, Calgary Transit, and several airlines), and relocation of the CPR and CNR to the banks of the Bow where they would share a new union station near the site of old Fort Calgary. An eight-lane parkway, described as the equivalent of a road going through a park, but essentially a freeway, was proposed as a primary traffic mover. The plan was generally welcomed as it promised employment, investment, and the removal of the problematic trackage through the downtown. However, opponents to the plan pointed out that the original railway tracks would not be removed, so the city would then have two sets of tracks, rather than one, bisecting its downtown.

The highly controversial plan to re-route the railway took precedence over the Downtown Plan for some time but was eventually dropped, as escalating costs made it unfeasible. Council then returned to the downtown master plan, and the notion of dedication of a green south bank on the Bow River. At the time, the riverbank was industrial and derelict in character, and difficult to envision as becoming a place of amenity value; however, general opinions about the potential of this area started to change.

In 1950, the city's population was 120,000 and the radius of the built-up area averaged only 2.5 miles. Retailing was concentrated in the CBD, with some ribbon developments along the main access streets (10th Street NW, 14th Street NW and SW, 17th Avenues SW and SE, 4th Street SW, 1st Street SW, and Centre Street N), and some retail clusters at termini of the streetcar tracks. Ultimately, the rapid spread of low-density residential areas caused the city's dimensions to exceed the downtown's ability to act as the sole retail and service centre, and shopping patterns changed.

By 1961, the population had increased to 265,000, the urban radius to an average of five miles, and the number of dispersed shopping areas to sixty, including two regional centres each with a department store and approximately fifty smaller stores, service facilities, and offices. In 1958, North Hill Mall opened as the first of the car-oriented regional shopping centres. In 1960, Chinook Shopping Centre replaced the Chinook Drive-In Theatre in the south. Many minor strip shopping centres developed on local collector streets. The specialized retail character of the central area became differentiated from the dispersed and more localized centres that addressed the day-to-day needs of the population, and by 1961 the business core accounted for only one quarter of the city's retail sales. The use of automobiles meant that commercial functions could be more widespread, and they now related to the street system rather than the street railway system and were located on the main axes from the downtown, accessible by the new suburbs.

Annexation and expansion

A total of six annexations by 1965 expanded the city's land base. Calgary has its entire urban area under a single jurisdiction (the "unicity" concept), distinguishing it from most other Canadian cities. In large part, this arose from the recommendations of the Royal Commission on the Metropolitan Development of Calgary and Edmonton that met in 1955 and reported that the most effective way of controlling fringe development and preventing urban sprawl was to extend the city's boundaries well beyond the built-up area. This met with mixed reactions, as Council was not enthusiastic about annexing the three neighbouring towns of Forest Lawn, Bowness, and Montgomery, with their relatively poorer quality of urban services and commercial and residential buildings.

But ultimately Calgary's boundaries enlarged as several annexations added to the land base, including the additions of Forest Lawn in 1961 and Montgomery and Bowness in 1963 and 1964. The city's corporate area swelled from approximately 100 to 150 square kilometres, establishing annexation as Calgary's primary method of dealing with urban growth.

Suburban development

60,000 new homes were added to Calgary between 1948 and 1965, and most of this construction took place in the rapidly expanding suburbs. Developers acquired land further and further from the city centre, aided by the cooperation of the city in providing necessary services, as extension of utilities was now a prerequisite of new housing construction.

The suburbs developed in a characteristic Calgary pattern, as a concentric ring around the core, modulated by the valleys and escarpments. A tier of neighbourhoods was built in the late 1950s on the west edge of the city and was held up there for several decades by a ridge that made provision of utilities cost-prohibitive. The Sarcee (now Tsuu T'ina)

77
Cambrian Heights area in the north west, 1956.
Glenbow Archives NA-5600-6843i

78
Show homes, Thorncliffe Heights, 1955.
Glenbow Archives NA-5600-6295a

Reserve formed a barrier at the southwest. To the south, the bluffs of the Elbow River and the shores of Glenmore Reservoir were limits to southward expansion. This southwestern corridor with its natural amenities has been the location of much of the more exclusive and expensive housing, although large areas of cheaper housing have been drawn with them as well.

There is a steep gradient between higher- and lower-priced housing to the east where housing abuts Macleod Trail and the industrial sector. A similar pattern emerged east of Nose Creek and around Forest Lawn, where lower-priced housing was developed near the industrial areas. These areas have little amenity but are easily and cheaply serviced, and it was planning policy to encourage house building for the industrial labour force in those areas.

A new district emerged in the northwest in association with the establishment of the University of Calgary in the early 1960s, and a very large area of moderately priced neighbourhoods expanded further to the northwest, influenced by the presence of highways, the deliberate provision of services, and also by the desirable mountain views.

Although the majority of Canadian housing starts were apartments, apartment living in Calgary was never as highly valued. However, in addition to the high numbers of single-family houses, some construction of multiple dwelling residences was also found, especially in the Beltline, which continued to develop as a high-density residential and multiple-land-use area, but also in other neighbourhoods where a lower-price housing alternative was sometimes provided in the form of duplexes, fourplexes, and apartments.

Industrial

The original agricultural and transportation industries expanded following World War II by adding the manufacturing of construction materials and the processing of chemical and petroleum products. Until this time, industry was located in response to the railway as the chief means of distributing materials and goods. With the shift to highway transportation, the location and distribution of industrial land uses changed.

A mixed wholesale-industrial zone had extended westward on the south side of the tracks, building on the established warehouse district, and also contributing to the isolation of the downtown from the adjacent areas. This district was oriented to railway transportation, and as truck transportation increased, it eventually became inefficient. The old multistorey stores and warehouses were not suited to modern techniques of handling goods, and the relatively narrow streets and the lack of loading spaces off the streets hindered the movement of trucks and goods. The growing dispersal of commercial facilities beyond the core meant that a central location for the distribution of wholesale goods was no longer necessary. Many of the warehouse buildings fell into disuse, or changed to office or long-term storage.

Although the principal concentration of industry remained in the Bow valley, the industrial district in the river valley became inefficient primarily because its street pattern was disrupted by railway lines and topographic features and did not lend itself to easy traffic movement. The rise in highway transportation became an important factor in industrial location. In 1955, two planned industrial estates were opened on municipally owned land between the Bow valley and Highway 2. These areas were fully serviced and provided excellent access to both highway and rail facilities. Newly emerging light industrial districts west of the Bow valley and east of Nose Creek were served by railways and were also well connected to Alberta's major north-south highway.

Parks, public spaces, and streets

New Parks Superintendent Alex Munro took over a system in 1949 that had badly deteriorated due to lack of finances and labour during the war, and a renewal program was launched. This period saw an emphasis on the provision of parks and open spaces for the booming post-war population and on a renewed interest in street tree planting.

Work on boulevard tree planting was resumed after the war, as many of the older districts were still without street trees. A planting pattern of alternating a tree (typically birch, ash, elm) and a shrub (dogwood, honeysuckle, Nanking cherry, lilac, cotoneaster) became common for a short time. Provincial and municipal government subdivision regulations came to dictate a minimum road width, and several changes from the earlier Calgary street typology resulted. Treed boulevards were excluded in favour of increased roadway width, and sidewalks with rolled curbs (easier on car wheels than the older square curbs) became common. By the end of 1955, public tree planting was included in the local improvement bylaw system in Calgary and community associations were asked to submit petitions for tree planting, specifying the variety of tree and shrub they would prefer on each block, with residents paying a nominal amount. The developer planted one (or sometimes two) trees per lot, and the tree canopy was now situated some distance from the sidewalk on private property. The absence of the treed boulevard, the new sidewalk forms, and the wider driving surface created a much different street (see Perry [2005] for a discussion of the evolution of street tree planting in residential areas).

79
British American Oil Refinery in southeast Calgary, 1950.
Glenbow Archives PA-3637-24a

80
Outdoor rink at Glendale Meadows.
photo B. Sandalack 2006

The Arbour Day tree planting program started in 1958 largely due to the efforts of Alderman Grant MacEwan. Spruce seedlings from the Provincial tree nursery were distributed to Grade 3 students. This was continued up to the late 1970s, adding countless spruce trees to the urban forest, and instilling at least a short-term interest in trees in suburban children (and their parents) who nurtured these seedlings in their yards.

Important work was also carried out in Calgary's large parks. In 1947 Prince's Island was purchased by the city, and efforts to clear it of underbrush and locate picnic tables began. During the early 1950s work at Prince's Island included building dikes and clearing twenty-three acres of "underbrush" to provide space for sports and play-ground areas. Bowness Park was popular for several decades, but declined somewhat in the late 1950s, including closure of the swimming pool, and in 1961 the park was turned over to the city following the annexation of Bowness (it had been admin-istered and maintained by Calgary Transit). The urge to clean up and clear out the old combined with some new development opportunities to destroy a number of important sites, including William Pearce's property and house (Pearce Estate and Bow Bend Shack).

Outdoor public swimming pools were constructed during this time at South Calgary, Mount Pleasant, and Millican, although the pool at Mewata was demolished to make way for the extension of 6th Avenue SW. Renfrew Athletic Park was constructed to replace the loss of ball diamonds at Mewata. A football stadium remained operational for the Calgary Stampeders Football Club, who used it until construction of McMahon Stadium in 1960, and Mewata was re-dedicated to high school and junior football, and other athletic functions.

Other parks developed at this time included Riverview Park, from land donated to the City by Eric Harvie; Senator Patrick Burns Memorial Rock Garden on the west side of 10th Street, incorporating sandstone from Burns' house, which had been demolished; Sandy Beach, from land that had been set aside as a park in 1946 as a result of the efforts of J.C. Leslie (elected as Calgary's mayor in 1965); and a new civic nursery in Glenmore, south of Eagle Ridge on the site of the Sam Livingston homestead.

Development regulations were adopted during this period for new residential subdivisions whereby a minimum of 10 per cent of the land within a planned development was be dedicated as public reserve for school, park, and playground use. Many new parks were constructed, primarily for recreation, although some floral parks were also included, in neighbourhoods throughout Calgary.

In 1960, Alex Munro retired and Harry Boothman was appointed Parks Superintendent. The Parks Department entered a new period of growth and expansion, reflecting the importance of leisure as the baby boom population reached the teen years. Boothman's agenda was centred on the idea that "parks are for people," signifying a radical shift from beautification and decorative parks and playgrounds to family and athletic parks, and to the provision of more public golf courses. In 1960 the City purchased the Edworthy land to complete a right-of-way for Sarcee Trail, leaving the remainder for park usage and what would ultimately become part of the river path system. Stanley Park and Heritage Park were other river parks developed during this time.

Glenmore Park, an area of 1,500 acres of land plus the reservoir, was established as a strictly public park. Land for Glenmore Park had been set aside in 1955 and development began in 1960 with the building of a connecting road between 37th Street to 24th Street SW through the park, and location of picnic facilities at the Lakeview end of the project. The Weaselhead was a result of some land being transferred to the City by the Sarcee Band. This land consists of floodplain and the last meander of the Elbow before it enters the reservoir. It resulted in a somewhat isolated natural area, largely due to the land ownership patterns in the area.

Infrastructure and urban form

Water

In 1952, a new water reservoir was constructed at 42nd Avenue and 14th Street NW. Additional pumping stations were also added at North Hill and Calgary South to serve the expanding suburbs, which by 1956 extended to Glenmore Reservoir.

Sewer

Sewage treatment needs also increased during this time of suburban growth, and in 1956 the Bonnybrook plant was expanded, and the Fish Creek disposal plant was added. In 1960, the Ogden Plant was constructed, which represented the end of raw sewage outfall into the Bow River.

Power

The Calgary Power Company had constructed the Lake Minnewanka Power Plant to supply power to the Alberta Nitrogen Plant in Calgary, an important wartime in-

81
Part of the infrastructure of the city includes the structures required for the efficient distirbution of electrical power, in this case at the Highfield substation.
photo D. Lee 2003

dustry, and had therefore avoided a serious power shortage during the late war years. With the post-war suburban growth in Calgary, and the start of a period of prosperity, energy needs also increased, as did the need for additional distribution facilities.

As well, as the City converted its streetcar system to electric trolley buses, additional demands were placed on the utility, and new infrastructure was required. The demand for electrical power increased from 38,000 kilowatts in 1948 to 140,000 kilowatts in 1960. By 1953, the old 12,000-volt ring main which had been built around the perimeter of the city in 1911–12 had reached its capacity, and the existing distribution system had become outdated. A new ring main was constructed around the expanded city, and plans developed for a number of substations to reduce the voltage at appropriate locations.

The Bearspaw hydro plant west of Bowness was constructed during the late 1950s, although its primary function was ice control to alleviate flooding of the Bow River. The Bearspaw plant became the western terminus of the new 66,000-volt ring. The line ran from Bearspaw along the southern edge of Nose Hill to Barlow Trail, and then south to terminate at Calgary Power's East Calgary Substation at Highfield. By 1955, the 66,000-volt ring was extended around the southern half of the city to serve the new developments. Along with the expansion of infrastructure came an increase in office and service staff, and a need for new facilities. In 1957, the City of Calgary's electric system was consolidated in a new complex in Manchester on Spiller Road.

During this time, the old Calgary Water Power Company power plant on 1st Avenue SW was dismantled, with some of the machinery relocated to the Victoria Park Power Plant. It operated until the development of the Spray Lakes hydro project in the early 1950s, which was to be the last major hydro development on the Bow River.

Several aesthetic improvements were seen during this time, including the levelling and seeding of the Calgary Power line easement adjacent to 50 Avenue SW between Elbow Drive and Macleod Trail. This was in keeping with the general trend towards the development of "green space" during this era and attention to aesthetic issues.

Telephone

The physical infrastructure related to telephone services changed somewhat during this era of modernization. By the 1960s, Alberta Government Telephones pole lines had become outdated, as they were replaced by microwave and buried cables.

5.5 URBAN FORM AND URBAN TYPES

Downtown

The concentrated high-rise downtown was now clearly identifiable, and it sloped down to warehouse buildings and then low-rise residential development.

Commercial form

Shopping patterns, and the form of shopping centres, changed dramatically during this era. With the expansion of the suburbs and the growing reliance on private automobiles, neighbourhood shopping centres were constructed.

The shopping strip at Britannia took the form of a street, situated perpendicular to Elbow Drive, a major collector road. A parking aisle between the two frontages provided good access, and it included tree plantings therefore functioning like a boulevard and providing amenity and human scale. However this was a type that had limited applications, and a more generic shopping centre model soon dominated.

Planning of neighbourhood units included provision of a shopping mall on one of the collector roads. Its typical form was a large parking lot in front with a strip of shops and large grocery store edging one or two sides. A service station was usually included.

The sector shopping model was also introduced, where a larger conglomeration of stores and services served a cluster of neighbourhoods. These were automobile-oriented and included vast parking lots edged with strip malls and interior-oriented malls, with one or more grocery stores. Brentwood Village Mall, constructed in 1960, typifies the sector shopping model.

The first regional shopping mall was constructed at North Hill in 1958, followed by Chinook Mall in 1960, and Southridge Shopping Centre in 1963. These were anchored by major tenants, normally two department stores, and a limited array of retail outlets and professional services. They took the form of inward-focused buildings in the middle of a large expanse of parking.

82
By 1965 the commercial district had expanded further north, and some lands on the downtown fringe had been cleared and awaited redevelopment. Industrial development was still present along the Bow River, and the warehouse district was a functional band to the south of the railway tracks. Residential neighbourhoods lay to the north and to the south where some slightly higher density development had occurred.
drawings J. Zhang, F. Alaniz Uribe, K. Meehan-Prins, A. Nicolai, B. Sandalack

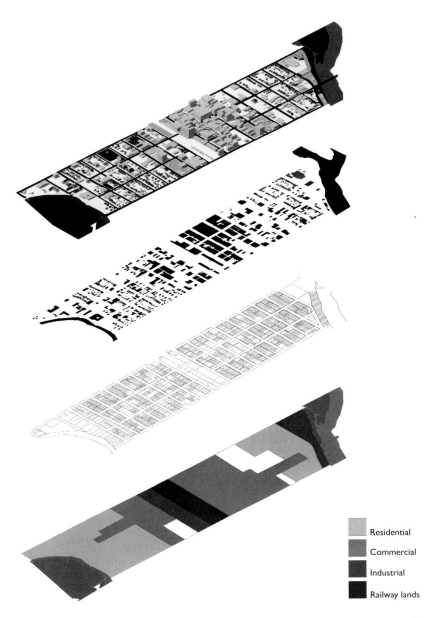

Residential

Commercial

Industrial

Railway lands

Neighbourhood form

Residential expansion during this phase of Calgary's development was almost exclusively suburban and followed what had now become the established pattern of suburban growth, based on residential lots with fifty-foot frontages.

Much of Calgary's growth took place during this period and contributed to a broad band of similar developments ringing the early gridded core. The old grid network of permeable public streets was abandoned for curvilinear streets enclosing semi-private clusters of houses. Concurrently, town planning lost its interest in physical form; its practice became more concerned with orderly growth, social process, and the idea of space, and less with morphology, shape, and structure. Planning became a technical exercise carried out in the service of a municipal government that was pro-development and pro-growth, and street design migrated into the domain of the traffic engineer.

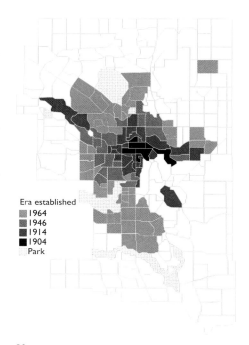

Era established
- 1964
- 1946
- 1914
- 1904
- Park

83
Post-war neighbourhood development took the form of planned neighbourhood units to the north, west, and south of the downtown, and to a limited degree to the east.
drawings J. Zhang, J. Marce Santa, F. Alaniz Uribe

Glamorgan

Glamorgan was on the developing edge of the city during the 1950s through the 1960s, a distance of approximately six miles from the city centre, and it is typical of the broad ring of neighbourhoods developed in the post-war boom.

From pre- and post-development air photos it is possible to identify landscape features and to discuss the degree of correspondence between original landscape and built form. The pre-development landscape consisted of an early trail at the north edge, which was later developed as Richmond Road, a major east-west thoroughfare, grid roads resulting from the Dominion Lands Survey (37th Street at the east, 50th Avenue at the south, which defined the city limits from 1910 to 1954, and what was to become Sarcee Trail at the west), farmsteads and rectangular agricultural fields, and irregular occurrences of aspen bluffs and sloughs and seasonal wetlands. With development of the new suburb, the aspen bluffs were destroyed, and the sloughs and seasonal ponds were filled in and graded over, and there is no remaining evidence of any of the natural features.

Glamorgan was structured according to the neighbourhood unit. Phase 1 of the development (see Figure 77) was organized around a centrally located school and park area. Clustered in this central area were public and Catholic elementary schools, a community centre, and large recreation fields. This constituted the only public space in the neighbourhood, with the exceptions of a piece of land at the northeast too steep for construction, which was developed as "green space" or undifferentiated open space with no apparent functional purpose, and another "green space" developed adjacent to the multifamily node. Phase 2 (to the west of Phase 1) was clustered around another large school reserve. It has not been built on to date and recreation fields occupy the land. A minimum of 10 per cent of the land within a planned development was required as public reserve for school, park, and playground use, and it was typically set aside as one large parcel of land.

Arterial roads formed the edges of the neighbourhood. Richmond Road and the grid roads came to define the edges of the neighbourhood, and secondary grid roads (45th Street and 46th Avenue) became internal collectors. The street system is hierarchical, with few through internal streets, and curved streets and cul de sacs were intended to break what was considered to be the "monotony" of the grid.

Located at the northeast corner, Glamorgan's shopping centre originally consisted of a grocery store and strip mall containing an array of services and amenities (drug store, bank, professional offices, hairdresser, restaurants, bowling alley, drycleaners, shoe repair), with a large parking lot in front. There was a presumption that residents would have cars, and this is clearly the favoured mode of circulation; it is easier to navigate this neighbourhood by car than on foot, although the neighbourhood is internally fairly walkable. The northeast corner intersection contains three gas stations; the fourth corner is occupied by a Junior High School serving a larger regional sector. A small strip mall with a parking lot in front is on the east edge of the neighbourhood.

Phase 1 consisted almost exclusively of single detached dwellings, although a limited amount of multifamily housing was provided on the edges.

Glamorgan streets conform to post-war specifications, and sidewalks are directly adjacent to the roadway since treed boulevards have been generally eliminated. Street trees are located some distance back from the public sidewalk, resulting in much less of a sense of enclosure on the street.

The housing types included primarily bungalows and split levels, and all included large picture windows in front. 50 x 120 foot lots were the norm, and the only deviation in lot size occurred at the inner and outer corners of the crescents and cul de sacs.

Neighbourhood planning of this era reinforced the post-World War II emphasis on family life, with an idealization of home life finding expression in the development of back yards as family area. The front yards were primarily for display, and had a higher level of maintenance, but little use. The differentiation between public and private space was now less clear, as the front yards were publicly visible, but not public, and yet not private.

Although several builders were involved in the development, there was little variation in house type and price. However, there was some variation in quality from builder to builder. The neighbourhood form is visually homogeneous, and Glamorgan is indistinguishable from other neighbourhoods of its type developed at the same time, whether they are in Calgary or elsewhere in Canada.

84
In 1924, the land that would be developed as Glamorgan consisted of agricultural fields and aspen woodlands, with a wetland to the northwest. Richmond Road (an early trail) defined the north edge, and roads deriving from the survey grid formed the other edges. Glamorgan was a typical neighbourhood unit, with single-family houses arranged around centrally-located schools, community centre, and recreation fields. A shopping centre was located at the northeast corner.
drawings J. Marce Santa

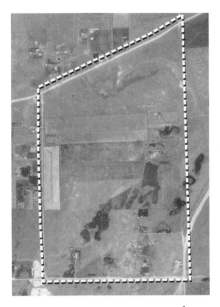

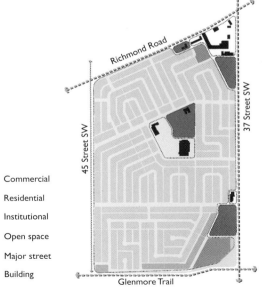

Commercial
Residential
Institutional
Open space
Major street
Building

Richmond Road

45 Street SW

37 Street SW

Glenmore Trail

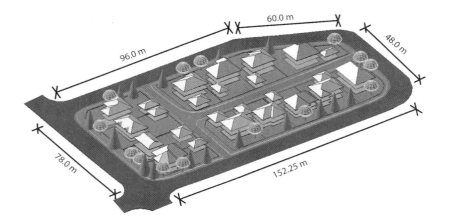

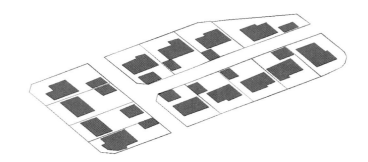

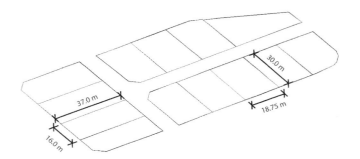

85
Block size still provides a relatively walkable neighbourhood, however treed boulevards are now no longer included. Street trees are provided on private front yards. Front and rear garages are more common.
drawings J. Marce Santa, streetscape drawing C. Chen

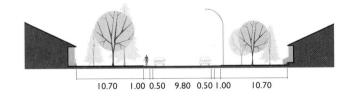

10.70   1.00 0.50   9.80   0.50 1.00   10.70

5.5   SUMMARY

The modern city that emerged during this era was still compact, however, the rapidly expanding population and spatial dimensions of the city led to a more complex city and a more dispersed land base. Skyscrapers, subdivisions, and regional shopping centres started to visually dominate the urban landscape, and the character of the city was also transformed. A new era in urban expansion and development started to take the form of lower densities and a preponderance of single-family houses. An important shift in city building from the public to the private domain took place, and while there were variations in housing quality, the overall form was single-family low-density residential suburbs, interrupted with scattered apartment and shopping centre developments. Transportation had shifted from the streetcar to the private vehicle.

The central business and wholesaling district was still dominant, as was the valley industrial zone; however, market forces led to several other distinguishing features, including shopping centres or strips along the highway thoroughfares, and new industrial areas in the southeast and northeast, resulting in several nuclei by the end of this period. The major public land uses were the airport in the northeast, the new university in the northwest, and the military bases in the southwest. They formed strong edges, and acted as potential stimuli for housing and specialized commercial and industrial functions. Sarcee Reserve in the southwest was the other barrier to development.

As Alberta's economy changed after World War II, Calgary developed an identity and interests very different from the rural hinterland that it had been linked to for several decades. However, Calgary's oil industry, like its ranching industry, kept it tied firmly to the West, and as such it supported Calgary's character and distinctiveness.

The city underwent enormous annexations in 1956 and 1961, and Calgary was the Canadian city with the largest area in 1965 (which had also been true in 1911). The city limits remained until the third boom in the mid-1970s which brought further annexations. It is not surprising that Calgary also had the most cars per capita at this time.

Calgary had also started its habit of perennial newness. The city's rapid expansion took place at the height of the modernist movement, giving Calgary much of its visual character. There was little of the past that was evident by 1965. Old buildings were not considered to have much value, and Fort Calgary lay under weeds, tracks, and warehouses. This was contrasted by the Heritage Park movement of the 1960s, sponsored in part by the City of Calgary, which foreshadowed the need for some

86
The Jubilee Auditorium has a magnificent site on the North Hill overlooking the city.
Glenbow Archives NA-5093-625

physical links with the past. This led to some glorification of heritage resources and the creation of a museum, but did little to impede the destruction of much more, and Calgary's modernity was its dominant characteristic at the close of this era (see Nickle Arts Museum [2000] *Calgary Modern 1947–1967* for a broader discussion).

This period saw the rise of the powerful development industry. It also saw the intensification of the American influence that had first emerged in the days of the open range and its easy north-south mobility. The oil industry had an even more significant impact, and in 1965 over 30,000 Americans lived in Calgary. Since those involved in the oil industry were usually in the higher income brackets, this community figured prominently in Calgary's social and economic life. Calgary became, especially during this time, more white-collar and affluent than other Canadian metropolitan centres.

The city was predominantly Anglo-Saxon, especially in the more affluent southwest and northwest. The northeast quadrant was the most ethnically hetereogeneous. A viable Chinatown had existed unchanged since the 1910 move to Centre Street. Calgary also had a sizeable immigrant population, which joined a small nucleus of Calgary-born residents. Most came from other provinces, mainly Saskatchewan and Manitoba, although throughout the city's history, immigrants from other countries also figured in the population growth.

The city of the 1960s was very different from the city of the 1940s. It was a young, new city, providing all the amenities of city life, but little of the crime or social problems that often went along with larger places. A general prosperity was evident, and the city amenities included community services such as schools, parks, and swimming pools. However, and strangely for a centre of its size, there was still not much in the way of cultural resources, and the university had made little impact on the cultural life of the city. A plebiscite on a new public library was defeated twice in the 1950s, even though the old one was inadequate. The magnificently sited Jubilee Auditorium was the only large multi-purpose hall, there was no public art gallery, and the nucleus of a museum and archives had only been recently established through the benevolence of oil millionaire Eric Harvie.

However, the western flavour and identification, and cowboy culture, were consciously cultivated, and the Calgary Stampede was a major local event and tourist draw. The mayors of the era encouraged and participated in this culture. Mayor Don Mackay advertised the white Stetson hat as Calgary's emblem, Mayor Harry Hays instituted and served the Hays Stampede breakfast, and Mayor Grant MacEwan authored books on frontier life and Calgary history.

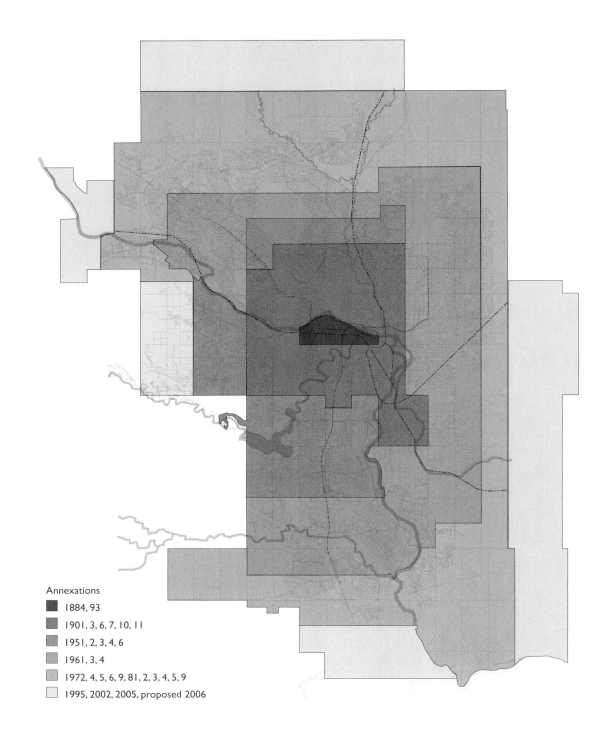

Annexations

■ 1884, 93
■ 1901, 3, 6, 7, 10, 11
■ 1951, 2, 3, 4, 6
■ 1961, 3, 4
□ 1972, 4, 5, 6, 9, 81, 2, 3, 4, 5, 9
□ 1995, 2002, 2005, proposed 2006

6 URBAN RENEWAL AND SUBURBAN EXPANSION: BOOM AND BUST

6.1 INTRODUCTION

Calgary came of age as a modern city during the late 1960s, 70s, and 80s; a still-new urban landscape with a young and predominantly white-collar population that more than doubled in the twenty years between 1961 and 1981. The city's population grew from over 250,000 in 1961, to 400,000 in 1971, to almost 600,000 in 1981, filling out a land mass that was third largest for any city in Canada, with annexations bringing the total area to almost 500 square miles. Although Calgarians voted overwhelmingly in the 1974 municipal election against a proposed annexation that would have doubled the city's size, annexation was to proceed on a project-by-project and development-friendly basis (Reasons [1984] discusses this period of Calgary's development and political history), and the city's footprint continued to grow. The working population increased as people from across Canada were attracted to Alberta's buoyant economy.

Much of Calgary's distinguishing growth took place during this period and came to characterize it as a modern city. While, for example, Halifax was established as a city during the 1800s, and has a downtown fabric that still expresses that period, and Winnipeg has an extensive and rich fabric of warehouse buildings from the early 1900s, much of what distinguishes Calgary was built during the 1960s to 1980s. This was a period during which the International Style dominated architecture, the main planning tools were zoning and urban renewal, the emphasis was on the single-family house, and the impact of the car was seen in the construction of freeways and suburban malls. The downtown would ultimately be almost completely rebuilt during this phase, including redevelopment of several of the important landmark areas.

Mayor Ralph Klein (1980–89) compared Calgary's downtown to a factory, fuelled by the needs of commerce. The city's skyline was transformed by office towers that sprang up to form a dense and concentrated business core, and much of the historic urban fabric of commercial and residential buildings was removed in a vast urban renewal program (buildings were destroyed at the rate of 600 per year at the peak of the boom) (Reasons 1984: 70) and replaced by institutional blocks including a new municipal centre and some major cultural facilities. The construction crane was referred to as Calgary's official bird during this time; for five consecutive years (1978 to 1982) the city set a Canadian record for construction permit applications, and millions of square feet of office space were constructed.

However this boom was followed by a catastrophic bust, set off by the effects of the National Energy Program (NEP) that imposed federal authority over energy resources

87
Calgary's land mass has grown through several major periods of annexation.
drawing F. Alaniz Uribe and N. Zoldak, based on City of Calgary History of Annexation 1995 and proposals

and established new price and revenue sharing schemes, without western consent, and by the subsequent collapse of the Athabasca Tar Sands project. The disastrous effects of these events were somewhat offset by the award of the 1988 Winter Olympics to the city, which initiated another wave of development and optimism.

6.2   IDEAS, PLANS, AND PLANNING

A number of important city planning documents were produced during this time, and they reflected the prevailing paradigm. In 1965, the City, the Province, and the CMHC entered into a cost-sharing agreement to prepare an urban renewal scheme for the thirty-one blocks of Churchill Park (today's East Village). Urban Renewal Scheme No. 1A was prepared and approved to deal with the area between 1st Street E to 3rd Street E and roughly between 8th and 4th Avenues. Only the Federal Public building (8th Avenue and 1st Street SW), the Anglican Cathedral and the Roman Catholic Church (1st Street East at 7th and 6th Avenues S) were thought to be worth preserving and the rest was slated for "complete redevelopment."

Urban renewal was one of the planning strategies of the age, and it managed to destroy huge pieces of the downtown. It was an approach taken by many cities to try to get rid of actual and perceived blight and to encourage revitalization. This situation was not unique to Calgary. Halifax (see Sandalack and Nicolai 1998) and Montreal (see Lortie 2004) are among the Canadian cities that underwent similar processes and changes. In Calgary the period of urban renewal was responsible for the destruction of much of the early fabric, and it set in motion several processes that are still influencing urban quality and function.

The 1966 Downtown Master Plan was another highly influential document. It recognized the continuing central role of the downtown, and set out strategies to improve its accessibility and simplify its structure. Its policy thrusts were to reinforce the linear east-west axis, to introduce a pedestrian mall and a north-south walkway, and to consolidate the office core. It proposed plans to address "blight" in the east end, and it accepted that the desire of every person to drive and store his/her automobile in the downtown must be accommodated. An emphasis, therefore, was high capacity roads and interchanges.

The 1966 Plan was a product of the values of the time that emphasized modernity and newness along with functional efficiency, and brought on much demolition and rebuilding. Since Calgary was such a young city this redevelopment had a devastating effect on any sense of historic continuity.

88
A conceptual drawing from the 1966 downtown plan shows an auto-oriented core surrounded by ring road. The plan was attempting to double the number of cars that could enter the downtown.
1966 Downtown Master Plan, City of Calgary, Plate 1, p. 3, Glenbow Archives G3504-C151-1966, courtesy of City of Calgary

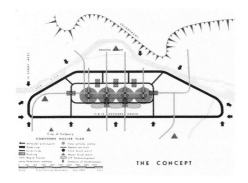

89
Downtown prior to urban renewal (1966) showing low-rise downtown, continuous urban fabric, and intact residential neighbourhoods in Eau Claire and Churchill Park (today's East Village).
Range Aerial Survey Ltd. and University of Calgary

90
Downtown after urban renewal projects (1978) with institutional blocks north of City Hall composed of more massive single structures, higher rise commercial core, and many empty lots and surface parking lots in East Village and Eau Claire awaiting redevelopment.
National Air Photo Library and University of Calgary

In contrast to Thomas Mawson's three-dimensional drawings and his emphasis on the public realm, the 1966 plan lacked this vision and detail and seemed to reduce the downtown and its functions to two-dimensional diagrams. Transportation was the emphasis, and the plan's number one objective was to double the number of cars that could enter the downtown. Two concentric ring roads were intended to increase the downtown's vehicle-handling capacity, and a network of one-way couplets would feed several parking structures. The outer ring would include a major east-west freeway, realignment and widening of 10th Street NW, and upgrading of Memorial Drive with grade-separated intersections at 10th and 14th Streets NW, Centre Street N and 4th Street NE.

Pedestrian circulation was similarly rationalized and organized in a hierarchical and diagrammatic way. A proposal for the 8th Avenue pedestrian mall emerged in this plan, along with other north-south pedestrian connectors.

Public transit was also emphasized and the downtown core was to be confined to an area within 500 feet (approximately 150 metres) of the main transit spine situated on 7th Avenue, which would consolidate the office and retail core. Drawings of an underground LRT system were included; however, the cost was considered too prohibitive. Despite the inclusion of these plans, the emphasis was private automobiles, and not public transportation, and the plan states "We cannot force people into any action they don't deeply desire. If they don't wish to use public mass transportation they just won't do it" (City of Calgary Planning Advisory Committee, 1966: 2).

The plan attempted to spatially segregate different land uses, and various historical accounts of this time talk about the "negative heterogeneous land uses" that had been allowed to develop and that needed to be addressed. This contrasts with today's approach of encouraging mixed uses as a quality necessary to vibrancy.

The plan identified six "comprehensive renewal areas," which were found to have varying degrees of "substandardness," defined in terms of "overcrowded homes, the inadequate nature of schools, parks and playgrounds, worn-out buildings, inadequate water and sewer services, traffic congestion, a poor visual environment, and use of land that is unreasonable within the overall framework of the neighbourhood or of Downtown." The plan also identified the need to restore the residential component of the downtown, and redevelopment was proposed for the West End, Eau Claire, and Churchill Park (East Village), which had traditionally been residential but had started to deteriorate. The plan hastened the demise of these neighbourhoods over the next decades, and lost were many of the amenities and services required to support residential development, including grocery stores, corner stores, and small retail businesses, and the planned higher residential densities haven't yet materialized.

Churchill Park, described as "skid row," was a particular target. The plan paved the way for its clearance, and it was to sit vacant and to become even more derelict after the interventions began. Eau Claire was composed of the negatively viewed mix of uses and was occupied by old housing stock and poor families. The Bow River was identified as a potential site for public enjoyment, and Eau Claire was described as a "dormant" area, and suitable for redevelopment. The West End of downtown was assessed as an aging community, chopped up by major thoroughfares, and therefore eligible for redevelopment. Centre Street south of Chinatown was a smaller area targeted for redevelopment.

Two other areas identified in the plan were located south of the tracks. The Beltline was described as being composed of pleasant tree-lined streets, although a shortage of parks and open spaces, and "spoiled by heavy traffic and excessive street parking," particularly the eastern section. However, the plan was proposing even more traffic. Victoria Park was identified as being populated by low-income families of long tenancy, and "aged" because it had undergone very little change, which was seen as a negative quality. The area was described as an intact neighbourhood but with a high proportion of social problems and a preponderance of "certain ethnic groups." The scene was carefully set for redevelopment.

Several major projects were completed in the downtown, with scores of buildings razed to make way, and an institutional district was created to include the Glenbow Museum, Convention Centre, Education Board buildings, Library, Performing Arts Centre, Municipal Building, and Federal Government Building. Most of these were massive concrete structures, with little regard for the creation of the public realm of streets and squares that could have helped to define this district as a more urban and pedestrian-friendly precinct. Combined with the one-way streets and the prohibition of on-street parking, the resulting pedestrian quality was very poor, and the district ultimately became a functional and visual barrier between the river and the downtown, and between the west and east parts of the core.

A system of development bonusing was proposed which would permit higher densities in return for provision of amenities such as plazas, arcades, and parking. The intentions were to achieve higher standards of urban form and create a better pedestrian environment by rewarding developers with the opportunity to maximize the potential of their property. This was ultimately adopted and resulted in much higher densities in the downtown core than would ordinarily have been permitted and created numerous semi-public outdoor spaces of variable quality at the bases of the towers.

91
Several blocks were converted to more massive institutional buildings (shown here the Board of Education Building, with the Public Library in the left background, on Macleod Trail and 5th Avenue SW) that do not positively contribute to the public realm.
photo F. Shaw 2005

The rivers were identified as boundaries to the study area and were treated as borders along which roads and industrial lands could be stacked. No direct links to the rivers were shown in the drawings, and they seemed to have been viewed as an inconvenience to outward development of the downtown and an impediment to road construction.

In 1963, the City had considered the CPR downtown development proposal involving the relocation of the downtown railway lands to the south side of the Bow River, and in 1967, there were plans for a six-lane throughway along the south side of the Bow. This was a critical time for Calgary, and the proposals galvanized interest and passionate debate about the alternative futures for this land and the entire downtown, and many notable Calgarians, including architect Jack Long, became politically active in opposing the plans. Many groups and individuals charged that the river, which should be Calgary's most important natural amenity, was being allowed to be further degraded for irrelevant transportation purposes (Styliaras 1964). The plan to relocate the CPR to the riverbank was ultimately abandoned due to a combination of economic and political reasons, and the 1966 plan acknowledged that the slow rate of acquisition of the banks of the Bow River was a subject of complaint by the citizens, and helped create the context within which notions of a river path system could develop.

It was also within this period that one of Calgary's most distinctive and controversial features was introduced. The Plus 15 system refers to a grade-separated pedestrian circulation system, approximately fifteen feet above the street. It emerged from a 1960s proposal by the City Planning Department to bridge the streets of the Churchill Park Urban Renewal Project. In 1967 the Montreal firm Desbarats, Dimakopoulos, Lebensold, Sise (now Arcop) worked with Harold Hanen, Mike Rogers, and Stu Round of the Planning Department to refine the pedestrian network of the urban renewal scheme. The consultants had also collaborated on the urban renewal plan and the projects were ideologically linked. The plan was rationalized along climatic lines, with the intent to provide a pedestrian circulation system that was sheltered from the elements and safe from traffic, and was promoted as a parallel and livelier street system that would allow Calgarians to escape the weather, while facilitating commerce as office workers could quickly and easily move from one office building to another.

It was enthusiastically and emphatically promoted on the strength of a vision of down-town efficiency and vibrancy. The Plus 15 was soon formally incorporated into City of Calgary planning policy, and developers were granted density bonuses for including Plus 15 connections, and by the mid-1970s, Plus 15 connections were required in all new projects. As this coincided with the 1970s oil boom and its construction frenzy, Calgary

92
Calgary's Plus 15 system (shown in white) now connects many of the downtown buildings.
drawing K. Meehan-Prins, based on City of Calgary +15 Walkway System map

soon had the most extensive elevated pedestrian system in North America. Although the system, which also now includes Plus 30 and Plus 45 levels, was originally conceived as a completely public system, open twenty-four hours a day, and completely accessible, it eventually evolved into a quasi-public, limited hours, security patrolled system, and has been criticized for drawing pedestrians off of the street and into the interior commercial spaces. By the 1980s, as new development subsidized construction of the missing links, the system was virtually continuous – an analogous city (Boddy 1992).

Calgary does not yet have the downtown population to make both pedestrian systems (streets and Plus 15) commercially viable, and businesses along the street have struggled. The planners of the system envisioned a much more complex, livelier, and denser city, which has not materialized. The bridges have also made the street-level environment much less comfortable, blocking the sun, creating wind turbulence, and interrupting views, and creating dark half-block outdoor spaces on what were the continuous grid streets.

93
Mid-block Plus 15 overpasses shadow the street and break up the blocks, and compete with the true public realm of the street.
9th Avenue SW photo B. Sandalack 2003

The Planning Department went through much change during this period. In 1968, Director Martin died in an auto accident, and Deputy Director M. H. Rogers took over the helm, replaced by George Steber Jr. in 1972. By 1970, the Planning Department had a permanent staff of 113, and this was to increase to 270 by 1979, indicating both the greater workload that the department had to cope with, as well as increasing bureaucratization of the planning process.

The 1970 Calgary Plan was the successor to the 1963 General Plan, and it reflected changes to the city's economy. It supported the 1966 Downtown Plan, and it also emphasized transportation as being critical to the health of the downtown. Public transit improvements were proposed, including development of transit corridors to the northwest, south, and southwest, and designation of 7th Avenue as a transit corridor. In order to increase vehicle capacity of streets, on-street parking was to be reduced or eliminated, and the Plan recommended that the City retain its interest in downtown parking. There was a strong emphasis on mobility but not necessarily on urban design quality.

This Plan also focused on public open space needs. It widely quoted the Mawson Plan and identified the opportunities to develop a continuous city-wide park and open space system in which the rivers, Glenmore Reservoir, Nose Creek, Fish Creek, and the escarpments would figure prominently. It identified several issues that needed to be addressed, including deficiencies in the amount of recreational land, a lack of continuity of existing open space systems, encroachment of industrial and residential uses into the river valleys at the expense of recreation potential, and under-utilization of river valleys for recreation purposes.

94
Many downtown streets (5th Avenue and Macleod Trail SE shown here) became bleak one-way freeways in the quest for more efficient traffic circulation.
photo G. Carra 2001

95
7th Avenue was dedicated as a transit corridor. The first version resulted in a street devoid of pedestrian interest and many businesses declined or failed.
photo G. Carra 2001

Recognizing that many public spaces (including Riley Park, Shouldice Park, Woods Park, and River Park) had come from private donations of land, it identified public acquisition as the tool for the provision of open space and outlined the methods and processes of acquisition. The plan recommended development of the river valleys as an open space system to include continuous public access to all river banks at all times and public footpaths throughout the city. The plan also included a section on flood management. It recognized the river system as a dynamic system and the risks associated with such an active river. Flood plain maps, based on engineering studies, were included.

The Calgary Plan (1977) included a section on balanced growth, and the Growth Strategy was accepted by Council in 1977. It emphasized increasing the residential population, density, and mix in the inner city and at transit nodes, decentralizing new employment along the corridor, and advocated filling in vacant or under-used land.

A special team dealing with downtown and inner city planning next developed the proposed 1978 Downtown Plan, noting that the downtown was becoming a single-function area, and warning against the negative effects on the area's stability and image. The goals included development of a high quality pedestrian environment, and an integrated series of public spaces and at-grade pedestrian system; ensuring a high standard of new development, especially where private development shapes the public realm; increasing housing throughout the downtown; increasing accessibility by transit and for pedestrians; making better use of existing roads, emphasizing the functional and physical relationship between the downtown and the inner city; and ensuring conservation of heritage sites and buildings. As redevelopment had still not taken place in the Churchill Park area following the urban renewal clearances, it also addressed east end issues, by proposing a broad range of residential development, services, and social housing throughout the downtown.

The plan reiterated Mawson's emphasis on the development of a complete park system, the development of riverside promenades and the need for a very visible, majestic civic centre to serve as a focus for public activity. It advocated development of a large major open space in the downtown, development of a series of smaller parks to serve as local gathering places, and development of the riverbank for public use. The plan was approved in 1979, with amendments, and Council directed the Planning Department to prepare a detailed Area Redevelopment Plan for six sub-areas of the downtown: Commercial Core, East End, Chinatown, Eau Claire, Core Transition Area, and the Riverbank.

The Downtown Area Redevelopment Plan (1981) was then prepared by the downtown and inner city planning group, and it consisted of a document plus seven posters showing the image, objectives, and specific initiatives for each area. This plan was a radical departure from the two-dimensional plans of the past decades that had focused on transportation issues and zoning. It richly illustrated a comprehensive concept of an integrated system of public streets and spaces, recognizing the need for urban as well as natural spaces in the city, and it provided both an overall framework for development, as well as detailed plans for several character areas. The plan was more visionary than anything that had emerged since the Mawson Plan and might have had the power to inspire a downtown renaissance, had it been passed. It criticized the existing public environment and proposed that very specific improvements to publicly owned land (streets, parks, etc.) be addressed before suggesting guidelines or controls for private development. It then followed with environmental objectives for the protection and enhancement of the public environment, performance criteria and bonuses for private development, and public action plans to implement public improvements.

The plan continued to question the idea of separation of vehicular and pedestrian circulation as originally envisioned in the Plus 15 system, and it proposed height restrictions in order to allow sunlight penetration into downtown streets and public spaces. These recommendations attempted to provide a mediating influence on development in the interest of creating a downtown of quality and character worthy of Calgary's prosperity. However, the plan was believed to be interfering with developers' rights and with the function of the downtown as an economic engine. What followed was the elimination of almost eighty planning positions and the resignation of the director. The message was clear that planning should be carried out in the service of development. The Downtown Area Redevelopment Plan was rejected, although the Downtown Handbook of Public Improvements, a background document and manual detailing the character and cost of priority public improvements, was passed, and development proceeded largely according to free market forces (Reasons 1984).

The Core Area Policy Brief, adopted in 1982, was derived from the Downtown Plan; however, it was non-statutory and was a much weakened and diluted document. And, as the city was readying for the 1988 Winter Olympic Games, some development processes had also started to take precedence over plans and policies, so what could have been construed as a scandalous series of moves was overlooked as the city started to prepare for a major international event.

Towards the end of this period the City eventually had in place policies for special areas such as the Downtown, LRT Corridors, the Inner City and the River Valleys. It had also adopted more detailed policy documents for specific communities in the form of

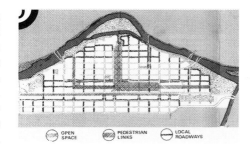

96
Four drawings from the proposed Downtown Plan emphasize the pedestrian-oriented public realm that was advocated in this plan, and illustrate a higher intensity and mixed-use downtown.
Proposed Downtown Area Redevelopment Plan (1981), Glenbow Archives, courtesy City of Calgary

Design Briefs, Area Structure Plans, and Area Redevelopment Plans, and the focus also shifted to suburban growth and development.

In 1986, the City approved the Long Term Growth Management Strategy. It was based on forecasts of moderate but sustained economic growth and continued population growth and housing. The strategy expected a continued demand for new single-family housing, and therefore, continued expansion along the city's edges, a process that could be influenced by the City through Area Structure Plans and by the City's willingness to finance services. Density and housing mix were identified as the two key determinants in the amount of land that would be required for growth, and the Strategy appeared to favour a mix of housing types.

The policy directions of the Strategy reinforced the practice of the City to have a supply of developable lands. An Urban Fringe was identified that would provide land for future urban expansion for at least a thirty-to-sixty-year planning horizon, and to act as a buffer from incompatible rural uses. Further annexation of at least 35 – 45 square miles of land was therefore seen as desirable. It was expected that the downtown would continue to be the primary employment and retail centre and that suburban office space and suburban regional shopping malls would not significantly alter the transportation patterns.

6.3   SPATIAL STRUCTURE

Two major processes of intense development transformed the downtown – the massive $21 million urban renewal scheme proposed in the late 1960s and the construction of an expanded office core as Calgary's head office status increased in the 1970s with the corresponding construction of dozens of signature towers for banks, oil companies, and other institutions.

Calgary's role as a management centre for the oil and gas industry was strongly reflected in the CBD. This was concentrated at the west part of the core, where it had replaced a zone of older single-family residences. The retail and entertainment sector was strung along 8th Avenue, and although it underwent some expansion, it received a decreasing share of Calgary's retail business as more shopping malls were constructed to serve the expanding suburbs. In the west end, small office buildings, a few high-rise apartment blocks and surface parking lots had replaced much of the earlier residential fabric. Construction of the Planetarium as Calgary's Centennial project defined the west end of the downtown and provided a landmark building.

The east end consisted of deteriorating buildings, lower-end businesses, and significant social problems. The area had always been somewhat lower in value and status, and with the urban renewal processes, it became more functionally isolated with more pronounced differences in physical and social characteristics.

North of the core and south of the Bow River was a mixed hotel, parking lot, and light industrial area. Although the area had been zoned for high-density residential development since the 1950s, it was not redeveloped for some time as investors saw it as a seedy backwater. Eventually some high quality condominium developments were constructed in Eau Claire in the latter part of the boom of the 1970s; however, with the bust in the early 1980s, the area did not fill out as expected.

The railway station on 9th Avenue was one of the most notable casualties of urban renewal, as the CPR and gardens were replaced by Palliser Square, a complex of indoor commercial and shopping facilities, an office tower, and an apartment building, over which rose a 191 metre (626 foot) communications and observation tower with a revolving restaurant. The Husky (now Calgary) Tower was an early symbol of this era of construction and modernization, although it was soon dwarfed by several of the downtown skyscrapers. The new buildings created a broad barrier between the downtown and the areas to the south, and the symbolism of the station and garden were lost along with the public nature of the building.

A version of the railway station was constructed in the windowless basement of the structure and passenger service declined; however, freight service still thrived, bringing in goods, and agricultural and petroleum industry products, and other goods, and keeping the wholesaling and warehousing functions south of the rail lines viable. There was some relocation to suburban business parks, but this industrial area remained intact.

In the 1960s, the Stampede considered relocating to sites such as Lincoln Park (now the site of Mount Royal College) and Happy Valley (now the neighbourhood of Valley Ridge), which would permit its expansion and allow construction of new facilities. But in 1968 the City approved expansion of the Stampede on its present site so that its northerly boundary would move from 17th Avenue to 14th Avenue. This decision led to great uncertainty in Victoria Park, and was a catalyst for disinvestment from the neighbourhood.

The Beltline and Lower Mount Royal continued to develop during this time as the city's highest density residential area, and the tree-lined streets were mostly still intact, lending it an established character. Several highrise condominium and apartment buildings were constructed, raising residential densities. However, despite the advantageous proximity to the downtown and 17th Avenue, it would be some time before inner-city living would become fashionable. The population as a whole actually declined during this time, caused in large part by the clearance of housing in the old neighbourhoods of Eau Claire, Churchill Park, and Victoria Park.

In 1965, Calgary was still a fairly compact form; however, the beginnings of massive suburban expansion had begun, and Calgary's growing population took up residence in these new neighbourhoods. Access to public transportation was no longer a variable in determining desirability of location, as the private car and its circulation and storage had been accommodated in City plans, the streetcar with its permanent lines had been phased out, and only the early legs of the LRT system had been constructed.

The neighbourhood unit concept was expanded, and larger sectors of land were now planned and developed. A deep band of low- to medium-density residential development, shopping malls, and business parks developed around the established city, and several institutions and amenities were built to serve them, including schools, hospitals (the Foothills and Rockyview were built in 1966), sports and leisure facilities, and newly decentralized services such as libraries and police services.

Nose Hill in the north, and the Military Base, Sarcee Reserve, and the plateau to the west had constrained development, and the east was largely occupied by industrial land uses. Construction of a trunk sewer and high-level reservoir permitted development around the lower flanks of Nose Hill, breaking a long-standing development barrier, and by the end of this period, suburbs almost encircled it. Similarly, topography had limited development west of Sarcee Trail, but in the 1970s and 80s new suburbs covered the hill, stimulating further country residential development at the city limits.

Suburban development also extended the city southward to Fish Creek Park, although the absence of a ring road meant that the southwest suburbs were not as accessible. A large sector of housing was developed in the northeast on the eastern side of the airport, but development east of Forest Lawn was still constrained by the CNR line.

The new residential sectors effectively rejected the downtown since they were physically removed from it with poor connections and were self-sufficient in many ways, and major shopping centres provided most services. These sectors were connected to the city, and yet also separated from it, by freeways, which at this time included Crowchild, Deerfoot, and Sarcee trails, and many new grade-separated intersections.

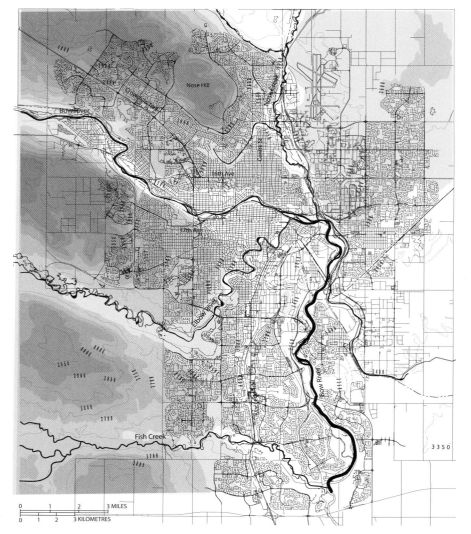

97

Calgary's land mass is much expanded by 1988, and several new residential sectors have extended in all four directions, including significant development to the east for the first time. Suburban growth has almost encircled Nose Hill Park in the north and has also extended south of Fish Creek Park. The former physical limits of the plateaus to the west and north have been transcended, allowing new subdivisions. *drawing A. Nicolai*

98

Calgary is highway- and freeway-oriented by 1988, and the railway is much less important. Most of Calgary's new growth took the form of residential sectors, now separated by major roads, many of which form barriers between parts of the city. New industrial development was along the highways and expanded in the band southeast of the downtown. Numerous suburban regional malls are situated along major roads. The LRT was introduced, but only serviced part of the city form. Several major parks were evident as city-scale elements.

drawing F. Alaniz Uribe and B. Sandalack

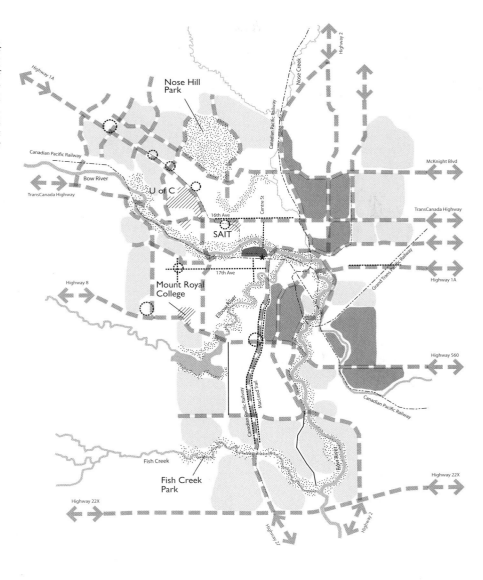

Commercial
Industrial
New residential
Park
Commercial node
Commercial strip
LRT
Railway
Major entry corridor

There was much construction of shopping centres and strip malls to serve the suburbs, and they related completely to automobile traffic. Market Mall, South Centre, Trans Canada, Marlborough, Lake Bonavista, and Northland Village were developed during the 1970s, and Chinook Mall ultimately engulfed Southridge to its north to make it the largest shopping centre in western Canada at that time. Macleod Trail epitomized the automobile-focused street, and it continued its rapid spread, taking on the decided appearance of an American strip, with concentrations of motels, automobile dealers, and restaurants, many of them exhibiting symbolically rich pop architecture (see Boddy 1987: 85–88). Versions of this form developed along other major thoroughfares including 32nd Street NE, 16th Avenue NW, Bow Trail SW, and 17th Avenue SE.

Calgary's post-secondary institutions also influenced new development in the regions surrounding them. The University of Calgary had been established on the edge of the city in the early 1960s; however, through this period, newer suburbs and shopping malls had overtaken it, and construction of several new buildings plus the beginnings of a research park lent it a more substantial presence. Within its vicinity were the Foothills Hospital, McMahon Stadium and Foothills Athletic Park, several retail complexes ranging in size from the regional scale Market Mall, to Brentwood Mall, to several local strip malls. An array of residential areas developed around the university, including two professional-class neighbourhoods and significant amounts of rental housing.

A much-expanded Mount Royal College was relocated to new buildings on the former Lincoln Park military site in the southwest, stimulating housing development around it. SAIT expanded on its northwest location and added several new buildings, including a separate building for the Alberta College of Art and Design.

1988 Winter Olympic Games

In 1981, just as the recession began to affect the city, Calgary was awarded the right to host the 1988 Winter Olympics. This brought the promise of construction of world-class facilities, and it provided a rallying point for government, private industry, and citizens. The Calgary Olympic Development Association (CODA) organized the efforts that gave a new boost to the economy and civic spirits, and another construction boom began.

Several major projects were part of the 1988 Olympic Game preparations, including Canada Olympic Park, a large complex consisting of ski jumps, luge, and bobsled tracks, visitors' centre and Hall of Fame; the Olympic Oval for skating events located at

99
The 1988 Winter Olympics left a legacy of sports facilities (including the speed skating oval in the photo middle ground), residences, and public art at the University of Calgary.
Glenbow Archives NA-5654-238a

100
Olympic Plaza was the site of the medal presentations and is now Calgary's most high-profile public space. *photo B. Sandalack 2005*

the University of Calgary; many other improvements at the university; the Saddledome, constructed on the Stampede Grounds; media villages at Broadcast Hill and Lincoln Park; an expansion of McMahon Stadium; improvements to the Max Bell arena; conversion of the Big Four Building to become the International Broadcast Centre; Olympic Plaza and other improvements downtown; and numerous other small projects in the city and western region.

The Olympics were a significant event and helped to give Calgary a different self-image and international profile. It also reacquainted Calgarians with their city. The construction during the oil boom had for the most part focused on office and commercial development, and on the establishment of the Plus 15 system, with less attention on the public realm. With the Olympics, and particularly the medal ceremonies at Olympic Plaza – which was only the second time in history that the Olympic medals were awarded away from the competition site – suburbanites had a reason to come downtown, and a place to come to. Otherwise, their leisure time had been associated with their neighbourhoods and with the suburban shopping and recreation facilities.

Redevelopment for the Olympic Games also resulted in some expedited urban clearance in Victoria Park, Eau Claire, and East Village, and the removal of the Greyhound Bus Depot from its downtown location to west of 14th Street SW, taking it out of the range of easy walking from downtown, the railway station, and the LRT stations, and eliminating what had become a gathering place for the homeless and other marginalized people.

Industrial

The central industrial area southeast of the downtown (Inglewood, Alyth, Bonnybrook, and Ogden) was still the site of established activities such as meatpacking and stockyards (Calgary's meat processing industry was ranked as third largest in Canada), breweries and distilleries, steel works, refineries, and the CPR shop.

By 1971, upgrading of the Alyth yards had transformed the facility into the modernized Alyth Diesel Shop. Highfield and Manchester, located between Macleod Trail and the railway, had developed to predominantly warehousing, and some agricultural and heavy industrial areas were located to the south and east at Shepard, Forest Lawn, and Hubalta. Construction and concrete-related industries were located in the Burnsland area in the Bow River valley adjacent to Barlow Trail.

Calgary's industrial land uses and heavy transportation corridors were now aggregated along the Bow River and Nose Creek valleys, paralleling the transportation routes. As well, extractive operations took advantage of the sand and gravel deposits in the valleys and provided material for construction.

More modern industrial estates were developed near the Deerfoot/Memorial Drive intersection at Mayland Heights and Meridian Road, focusing on light industrial and warehousing. Small-scale light industrial corridors developed along Macleod Trail South, Edmonton Trail, and near the airport. In the west side of the city, some small scattered warehouse and light industrial activities were located along the railway tracks in the downtown area, along Crowchild Trail near Glenmore Trail, and in Bowness at the intersection of the Trans Canada Highway and Sarcee Trail.

Downtown, the Robin Hood Mills, a landmark on 9th Avenue, were torn down in 1973 to make way for Gulf Canada Square. Although a railway spur line running through the lane between 10th and 11th Avenues S remained into the 1970s to serve the warehouse district, the railway lands lost much of their industrial function and gradually were given over to surface parking lots.

Transportation

Transportation to and from the city, and circulation within it, emerged as more important issues. In 1976 Phase One of the new Calgary International Airport opened, giving the city a much-improved gateway, and heralding its increasingly international position. Air and highway travel had clearly taken the place of passenger train, and the experience of entering the city was now from the outside in, usually on a high-speed freeway. Inter-city highway travel still carried traffic through the city along several routes, including 16th Avenue N and Macleod Trail S.

New freeways were built as Calgary's population spread out further and further from the core, although the downtown was still the major employment centre. Deerfoot, Barlow, and Bow Bottom trails created a high-speed north-south corridor, as well as a broad barrier between the west and east sides of the city.

Work on the much-anticipated Light Rail Transit system began in the late 1970s, a bold move that ran counter to the belief that the city was not big enough to support it. The low density of the expanding city did not make train routes seem viable at this time, even though a high percentage of people continued to work downtown. The LRT

101
Deerfoot Trail continues as an important north-south route.
photo F. Alaniz Uribe 2005

102
Pedestrian bridge connecting Prince's Island and downtown, 1970.
Glenbow Archives NA-2864-5317b

103
Boothman pedestrian bridge over Bow River to Edworthy Park, 1979.
Glenbow Archives NA-2399-138

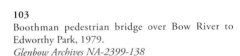

routing attempted to connect the southern extremity of the city with the downtown, the university and northern suburbs, and to provide the newly developed northeast with easy access. However, the opportunity to develop an airport connection was missed, and the LRT stations weren't well integrated with the surrounding communities.

Parks, public spaces, and streets

The concept of a downtown pedestrian mall on 8th Avenue was first proposed in the 1966 Downtown Master Plan, and the first in a series of renditions was developed as an exclusively pedestrian domain. Over time, businesses along the mall declined, as they were deprived of the activity that some vehicular traffic brought and as the eastern section of the mall became taken over by hippies, the homeless, and transients, especially after business hours. Stephen Avenue Mall has undergone several renovations since then, and different combinations of pedestrian and vehicular traffic. With the construction of the Municipal Building and Olympic Plaza in the 1980s, it gained an eastern terminus point together with the increased business day traffic of the thousands of employees and visitors to city offices.

The combination of the new Plus 15 system with urban renewal and the consequent destruction of much of the east part of the downtown had a significant effect on street life and on peoples' perceptions. Downtown Calgary acquired a grim reputation, and although the Olympics brought people back to the downtown for something other than work, the public realm would require significant additional improvement.

Interest in heritage issues surfaced during this time with two major public developments. In 1962, Council had approved a plan proposed by Parks Director Harry Boothman for the Heritage Park area, to be jointly funded by the City, the Woods Foundation, and Eric Harvie. In addition, a number of private individuals had pledged money towards the project. All features were required to date back to at least 1914, and to have come from the three prairie provinces or from the Yukon or Northwest Territories.

Secondly, Fort Calgary underwent development around the same time as the urban renewal plans were in full swing. By the 1960s the fort had become a dim memory, and had become an industrial area and freight yard. In 1967, when plans for a freeway through the downtown were proposed, it was suggested that the site of the original fort be marked; however, there was confusion as to its location, prompting the beginning of archaeological digs in the area. Eventually the city obtained the site through a land swap with the CNR and began to re-create the fort and landscape. In 1978, the interpretive centre was opened, securing the long-term destiny of this part of the downtown.

Although it would still be some years before Calgary committed to the river path system, redevelopment of Prince's Island resulted from a renewed interest in Bow River beautification and a realization of the need for downtown park space. New buildings were added to the Calgary Zoo, including an Avian Conservatory complex funded by the Woods Foundation, and about a hundred acres (40 hectares) north of the Bow River were developed for hoofed animals.

Parks development serving the baby boom generation focused on family and athletic parks, under the leadership of Harry Boothman. Major athletic complexes were completed at Glenmore, Foothills, Kingsland, and Optimists Parks, and similar additions were made to the Renfrew and Shouldice athletic areas. Whereas in 1960 there had been only four outdoor swimming pools, by 1975 there were twenty pools, ten of them enclosed; where only outdoor hockey rinks were found in 1960, eleven indoor artificial ice rinks had been constructed by 1975; and where Shaganappi Golf Course had been Calgary's only municipally operated golf course since 1915, it was now joined by three others.

Dozens of major community recreation complexes were developed by the mid-1970s as a result of the City's cost-sharing program with community organizations. Major new parks included Confederation Park, one of Calgary's most significant Centennial projects, Richmond Green Park, and St. George's Heights Park, and the expanded facilities at Stanley, Glenmore, Bowness, and Edworthy Parks added to Calgary's wide range of family parks.

Later in this period, McMahon Stadium evolved to a multi-purpose community facility in addition to being the home of the Calgary Stampeders football club. Through a land exchange agreement between the City and the University in 1985, both the stadium and the land became the outright property of the University of Calgary. Lindsay Park Aquatic Centre was constructed in 1983 on former CNR yards in anticipation of the Western Canada Games.

In the 1970s, priorities of future park development shifted to the preservation of large natural areas. Nose Hill and Fish Creek Parks were created during this time, establishing two significant environmental reserves at the north and south edges of the city.

Nose Hill and Fish Creek represent two very different ecosystems. Nose Hill is a prairie reserve overlooking the city. It was created in response to organized public protest over a plan to develop much of the hill. The Calgary Planning Commission had endorsed (although it was opposed by the parks superintendent) a residential

104
Heritage Park consists of relocated buildings dating back to at least 1914.
photo F. Shaw 2005

122

105
Nose Hill Park looking west, with Chinook approaching.
photo F. Alaniz Uribe 2003

subdivision on the western slopes of the hill to be known as Leaside; however, City Council was persuaded by a community group assisted by the Calgary Field Naturalists Society to delay this development pending a comprehensive study. The City eventually endorsed a proposal that 4,100 acres (1,600 hectares) of land should be preserved and went about purchasing the land and developing access points and trails.

The University of Calgary worked with representatives from ten community associations to develop an ecological park concept for Nose Hill. Numerous trails now traverse the park, and it provides one of the most spectacular, although windswept, views of the city and the mountains. One of the early intents of the park was to maintain a wildlife corridor to the lands to the west and north of the city; however, Nose Hill is now completely encircled by suburban development.

Fish Creek Park, developed and owned by the Province of Alberta, is one of the largest urban provincial parks in Canada. In 1973, the Province purchased the main section of the Fish Creek valley east of Macleod Trail and placed an environmental protection order on the remainder of the land, and now three quarters of the total of 3,000 acres (1,200 hectares) remain in a natural state. The main focus of recreational development in the park is an extensive system of bicycle and pedestrian trails, with vehicular access limited to eleven locations, and intensive recreation use accommodated at five major nodes. Sikome Lake was constructed in 1978 as one of the high-use public facilities.

Recommendations were also made by the recreation board for other parks centering on natural areas, including Beaver Dam Flats in Millican and Bow River Park in Barlow.

The idea of starting to link up many of these natural areas emerged again during this time, and the concept of a connected system of river parks gained momentum.

Infrastructure and urban form

Water

Calgary's growing population eventually threatened to exceed the capacity of Glenmore water treatment plant, so in 1971 the first phase of Bearspaw Dam was started to address primarily northern growth in the city. This was the first time since 1933 that the Bow River had been used as a drinking water supply. The plant and facilities illustrated a quite different approach to civic design than that at Glenmore Dam. Whereas the water treatment plant and dam at the Glenmore Reservoir were designed to be part of the public realm, Bearspaw Dam and water treatment centre had a much more industrial aesthetic.

The site planning and building design remove the functional aspects of water treatment from public access and view, and the buildings are contained behind chain-link fences and video-monitored gates. By 1984 Phase 2 was under development.

The former Number 2 water pumping station on the south bank of the Bow River was designated a historic site in 1975 and redeveloped as the Pumphouse Theatre.

Sewer

City expansion and population growth also impacted the capacity of existing sewage treatment. The amount of water taken into a home or business is exceeded by that being returned as sewage, with food and beverages that are brought into the overall city system adding to the volumes and necessitating new and expanded sewage treatment facilities.

In 1979, Calgary constructed its first wet pond for storm runoff at 68th Street and 17th Avenue SE.

Power

The increases in downtown development and the huge suburban growth necessitated expansions along with the continued work to provide new streetlighting in the older sections of the city. The new suburbs were now developed by private land developers and not the city, and the additional costs of providing the underground infrastructure were borne by the developers and then recovered in the selling price of the individual properties.

Underground services were now the norm, and the physical landscape of the suburb included fewer of the visible structures related to servicing, with new substations being the most obvious element.

In the mid-1970s, the Government of Alberta established a Restricted Development Area (RDA) around the city to be used as a Transportation/Utility Corridor. The corridor provides a long-term alignment for future ring roads and major linear utilities, such as power lines, telecommunication lines, and pipelines for water and sewer. It includes Highway 22X and Stoney Trail.

106
Ranchlands electrical substation.
photo D. Lee 2003

107
Burns Industrial Park electrical infrastructure. High-voltage transmission lines feed into a substation to be stepped down for distribution voltages.
photo D. Lee 2003

6.4   URBAN FORM AND BUILDING TYPES

Downtown

Calgary's downtown was not only rebuilt during this period, it also drastically changed form.

Tall buildings with extruded floor plans soon dominated the skyline of the downtown, and the characteristic profile of the city took shape.

A pattern of superblocks also began to replace the existing finer grain. Many of the developments during the boom included the assembly of whole blocks, changing the fabric and character of the downtown, and especially the pedestrian experience. Whereas the original lot subdivision pattern had prevailed up until this point, with many commercial development conforming to the twenty-five-foot frontages and only banks and institutional buildings occupying larger lots, the norm for downtown office buildings soon became whole block developments. While this allowed a corporation or developer more economy and efficiency, and permitted greater building heights, it also affected the quality of the street.

The earlier typology had resulted in a street frontage composed of many buildings, a variety of businesses, numerous entries onto the street, and a mix of building materials and building styles. The new typology often resulted in a bland and relatively featureless street facade, with very few entries onto the street, and with only one owner, one building material, and one building style covering the block.

Through this process, back lanes were frequently eliminated (so that service access was provided at one of the building frontages), and the number of business entries along the street was greatly reduced, greatly changing the nature and amount of street-level activity.

Several interior malls were constructed as part of the office tower blocks, including Scotia Centre and Toronto Dominion Square, which included an interior mall parallel to Stephen Avenue and the Devonian Gardens, a large indoor park.

The Calgary Tower emerged as the symbol of Calgary during the early part of this era – a corporate statement with a building base more scaled to the car than the pedestrian, and replacing the civic functions that had been supplied by the railway station.

108
View of downtown with Prince's Island and Eau Claire in foreground - waiting for more re-development, 1984.
Glenbow Archives NA-5654-90

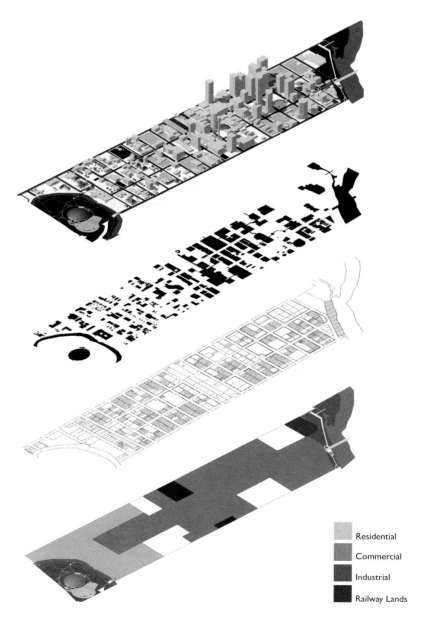

109
By 1988, Calgary's commercial core consisted of high-rise office towers. Redevelopment of the railway station had taken the form of a complex that spanned the tracks. Building footprints were much more massive. The warehouse district underwent redevelopment and included much unoccupied land. Although the residential neighbourhoods south of downtown were still viable, almost all residential use in the north part of downtown had been removed.
drawings J. Zhang, F. Alaniz Uribe, K. Meehan-Prins, A. Nicolai, B. Sandalack

Residential

Commercial

Industrial

Railway Lands

110
Nova Head Office building (currently Nexen).
photo B. Abrams Reid 2006

Other buildings constructed during this era included:

Commercial buildings

1976 Scotia Centre
1977 Toronto Dominion Square
1978 Shell Centre
1979 Mount Royal Village
1980 Cadillac Fairview Office Building
1980 Fifth and Fifth
1980 Atrium One and Two
1980 Gulf Canada Square
1981 Pan Canadian Plaza
1981 Heritage Square 8500 Macleod Trail
1981 Deerfoot Business Centre
1981 AGT Head Office Building
1981 Chevron Plaza
1981 Kensington Place
1981 Delta Bow Valley Hotel
1972–82 Bow Valley Square
1981 Esso Plaza
1982 Nova Head Office Building
1982/3 Bank of Montreal First Canadian Centre
1982 CH2M Hill Building 1110 Centre Street North
1982 Mewata Place
1982 Rockwood Square 1032 – 17th Avenue SW
1983 Crestview Centre 1701 Centre Street North
1983 The Courtyard 320 – 17th Avenue SW
1983 Trimac House
1983 Western Canadian Place
1984 Petro-Canada Centre
1984 Sun Life Plaza
1984 Transalta Utilities Corporation Head Office

Institutional buildings

1972 Mount Royal College Lincoln Park Site
1973 Alberta College of Art

1975 Glenbow Museum, Hotel and Convention Centre
1977 Calgary International Airport
1978 Harry Hays Building (Government of Canada)
1978 Calgary Court and Remand Centre
1978 Main Library,
1978 Board of Education Buildings
1979 Bethany Care Centre
1980 Rocky View General Hospital Expansion
1980 Several new buildings on the University of Calgary campus,
     including the Nickle Arts Museum
1981 SAIT Campus Centre
1981 Tom Baker Cancer Centre
1981 Edgemont Club
1981 Calgary Herald Printing and Publishing Offices
1982 Child Health Centre
1982 Village Square Leisure Centre
1983 Southland Leisure Centre
1983 Calgary Sun
1983 Olympic Saddledome
1983 Lindsay Park Aquatic and Athletic Centre
1985 Calgary Municipal Building
1985 Calgary Centre for the Performing Arts

Residential towers

1983 Estates Condominium Tower and Ranchmen's Tower
1983 Eau Claire Estates
1983 Several 12-plus storey towers in the Beltline,
the west end of downtown, and Eau Claire

Renovation and restoration

1973 Clarence Block
1979 Lancaster Building, Burns Building

(See Guimond and Sinclair [1984] for more detailed information on many of these projects.)

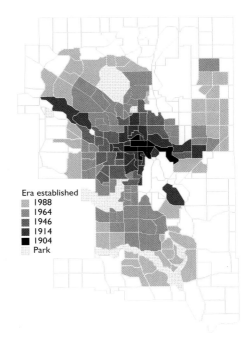

Era established
■ 1988
■ 1964
■ 1946
■ 1914
■ 1904
□ Park

111
New neighbourhoods form a broad band around the city, with expansion constrained only by the airport in the northeast and the Sarcee reserve in the southwest. There is still limited development towards the southeast.
drawings J. Zhang, J. Marce Santa, F. Alaniz Uribe

Residential

The city's supply of developable land was exhausted by 1969, and the building developer began to play a larger role in Calgary's urban evolution. By the mid-1960s, the sector concept of planned growth proposed in a 1962 CMHC publication by Humphrey Carver had replaced the neighbourhood unit. This concept outlined a general plan for overall development within a specified large area, and guidelines were established within which developers were to operate. Sectors were comprised of three or four neighbourhoods with a population to support high schools, shopping centres, places of gathering, recreation and entertainment, and clusters of apartments. It therefore required conceptualization of a more comprehensive system at a larger scale. The Glenmore Sector in the southwest (Bayview, Braeside, Palliser, and Oakridge) and The Properties in the northeast (Pineridge, Rundle, Temple, and Whitehorn) were two of the sectors that were developed during this period. Sectors would typically be bounded by major freeways, and individual neighbourhoods were also defined by perimeter roads, increasing accessibility by car, but decreasing walkability.

One developer could now control the overall image, character and price of a single neighbourhood, and sector development in some cases allowed thematic development to take place on a larger scale, expressed in the names of the subdivisions as well as some of the stylistic elements. In the mid to late 1970s, neighbourhoods like Ranchlands, Marlboro, and Silver Springs were developed. In the 1980s, postmodern developer subdivisions of Strathcona and Prominence Point indicated another stylistic shift (White 1984). However, the general typology was similar, in that each subdivision was comprised of single-family houses arranged in a hierarchical and curvilinear street pattern, and each neighbourhood became a sub-unit of something larger organized around a "sector centre" with a shopping centre, high schools, library, churches, social services, fire and police, and entertainment facilities.

House size by the 1980s was double the size of the average home of the 1940s. During the 1970s, the majority of new housing units were single-family homes; however, by the end of 1978, multifamily starts were more than double the number of single-family, as the construction industry attempted to keep up with the demand. The 1981 record of 15,172 housing starts held as of 2000, and it was up from 7,047 in 1972; however, with the bust, the number of starts declined to 9,600, two thirds of which were multifamily, and 1983 saw a negative net migration from the city, with more people leaving than arriving. The housing bubble had burst, and between 1983 and 1985, there were between 4,500 and 5,500 foreclosures per year, and only 2,700 housing starts in 1986 (see Hope and McCormick [2000] for an overview of the housing industry).

Lake Bonavista

Lake Bonavista is Calgary's first lake-oriented subdivision. The focal point for the community is the man-made lake that was excavated in 1968. A second lake was added to the south a few years later. The street and block pattern is based on a hierarchy of roads. The neighbourhood is bounded by major roads, and two secondary thoroughfares run north-south the length of the neighbhourhood. Smaller roads extend east-west. Local roads are arranged in cul de sacs and crescents, and most of the neighbourhood blocks are laned.

The neighbourhood is a low-density residential area of exclusively single-family houses. A shopping centre with a service station is situated at the centre of the community at the intersection of two major roads. A convenience store and service station are situated at another intersection nearby. Schools and a destination restaurant are the other features. Lake Bonavista backs onto Macleod Trail; however, there is no vehicular access from within the neighbourhood – it is necessary to drive to one of the circumferential roads first.

The lakes and hill that resulted from re-grading the excavated material form the recreation focal point of the neighbourhood. Smaller parks are spaced throughout, and even smaller green spaces are found in the islands of the crescents and cul de sacs. Street trees were a priority in the development and the entry streets and many internal roads are tree-lined. Poplar was the species of choice when the neighbourhood was constructed, and their life span is currently reaching a natural end.

112
Lake Bonavista was constructed on prairie agricultural land with a few wetlands where the lake was situated. The neighbourhood edges were formed by freeways. The street pattern is much less permeable and consists of a hierarchy of curvilinear roads.
drawings J. Marce Santa

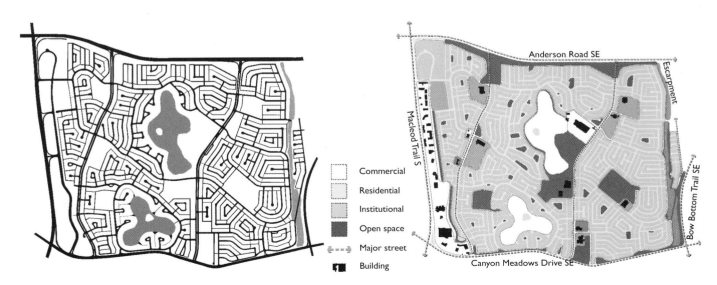

Commercial

Residential

Institutional

Open space

Major street

Building

Anderson Road SE

Macleod Trail S

Escarpment

Bow Bottom Trail SE

Canyon Meadows Drive SE

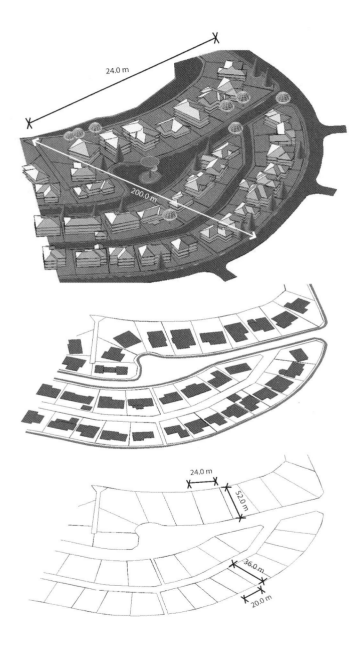

113
Most blocks are laned, and garages open to the front and back of the lot. Most houses are split level or two stories. Some streets include a central treed boulevard, but most street trees are located on private front yards. *drawings J. Marce Santa, streetscape drawing C. Chen*

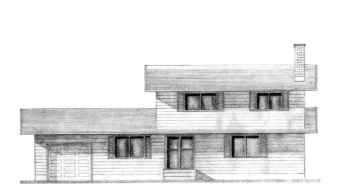

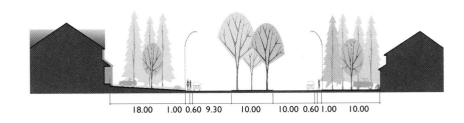

| 18.00 | 1.00 | 0.60 | 9.30 | 10.00 | 10.00 | 0.60 | 1.00 | 10.00 |

Hawkwood

Hawkwood is one of several neighbourhoods constructed in the 1980s as part of a large sector in the northwest. Neighbourhoods were now more typically developed as one coherent concept, with a limited palette of house colours and styles and uniform landscaping creating much of the visual character.

A hierarchical road pattern forms the circulation system, with major roads defining the boundaries, and collectors and local roads providing access to the primarily single-family suburb. A school and small shopping centre with local services is located near the centre. A system of parks and green spaces runs through Hawkwood, and smaller parks and tot lots are found at intervals. A significant portion of the green space in this neighbourhood is found lining the major roads or intersections.

These roads and intersections at the neighbourhood edges form significant barriers to walking to the next neighbourhood; therefore, Hawkwood exists in relative functional isolation, similar to other neighbourhoods of this type. The nearest grocery store or shopping centre is only accessible by vehicle for most.

Both laned and laneless blocks are found. Most houses are large in relation to their lot. Since there is a fairly restricted palette of house style, colour, and material, the neighbourhood conveys a sense of uniformity of taste, economic, and social status.

114
Hawkwood was constructed on prairie landscape, and its edges comprised of major arterial roads.
drawings J. Marce Santa

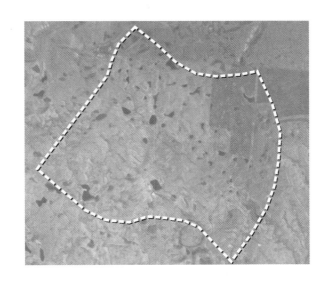

▢	Commercial
▢	Residential
▨	Institutional
■	Open space
◀- - -▶	Major street
▆▊	Building

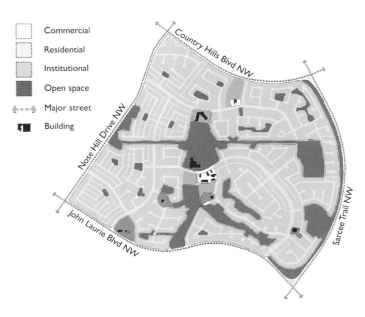

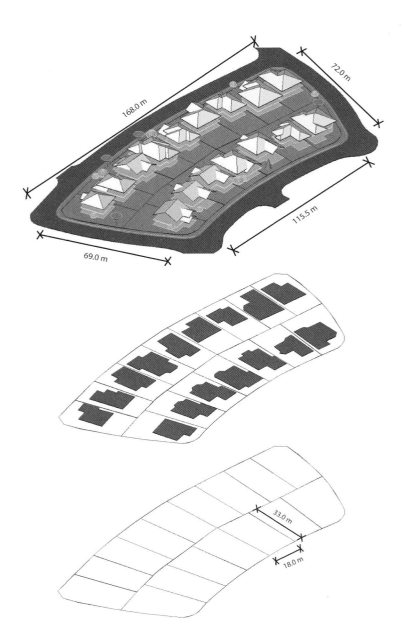

115
Although both laned and laneless blocks are found, most houses have front-facing garages, reducing the area for public street trees.
drawings J. Marce Santa, streetscape drawing C. Chen, photo B. Sandalack

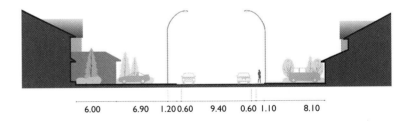

| 6.00 | 6.90 | 1.20 | 0.60 | 9.40 | 0.60 | 1.10 | 8.10 |

6.5   SUMMARY

This era was memorable both for the boom in the 1970s as well as the bust in the early 1980s and is also the period during which the antipathy between the West and the federal government with its perceived Eastern bias became somewhat of a legend. Calgary's economy and prospects were even more tightly tied to the oil industry than before, and the National Energy Policy, along with other federal programs and taxation policies, provoked strong and emotional responses.

During this era, Calgary became the centre of an oil industry that is foreign-dominated, and the American influence on the city was prominent. The movement of capital and personnel back and forth across the border has played an important role in the development of Calgary's character and identity, and Calgary has often been called the most American of Canadian cities.

At the time of the bust, 76 per cent of Canada's oil and gas producers, explorers, and developers were headquartered in Calgary (Reasons 1984:13). The corporate ideology therefore prevailed and was partly responsible for the growing tendency to measure progress in terms of population growth and in house value, rather than in terms of quality of life. At the same time, Calgary continued to be a place where hard work and good ideas could produce success. This appeal to the individual, and the potential for individual reward, was part of the city's attraction, although it was perhaps at the expense of the communal good.

The counterculture of the 1960s never took hold in Calgary, and therefore development generally proceeded unopposed by heritage or social issues (White 1984). It was not until late in the 1970s that the heritage movement arrived in Calgary, too late to have a moderating influence on the urban renewal that was transforming the downtown, but still in time to start to have an effect on the city.

The late 1970s downtown building boom represented billions of dollars of development and could have resulted in a cultural, civic, and social infrastructure along with the business infrastructure. However, much of the development was only average in quality, and little of it led to a high quality public realm. The two physical symbols of the era were the Calgary Tower and Olympic Plaza, both of which signified the increasingly international role that the city was playing, but both of which emphasized style over substance, and image over civic function.

116
PanCanadian Plaza, constructed in 1981, allows views
to the Palliser Hotel.
photo B. Abrams Reid 2006

The 1970s saw a degree of cultural maturation of the city, and development of restaurant and commercial diversity, although with the exception of the gallery row on 17th Avenue, the new Nickle Arts Museum at the University of Calgary, and the Glenbow Museum, there was not the cultural diversity and maturity that might have been expected of a city of Calgary's size and wealth. Calgary continued to distinguish itself more as an active and outdoors city, with Spruce Meadows, Nose Hill, and Fish Creek Park being significant and high quality amenities.

The Olympic Games provided another opportunity for Calgary to invest in its urban form, and to develop an image and character that would take it into the international world. The legacies of that moment would carry into the next era.

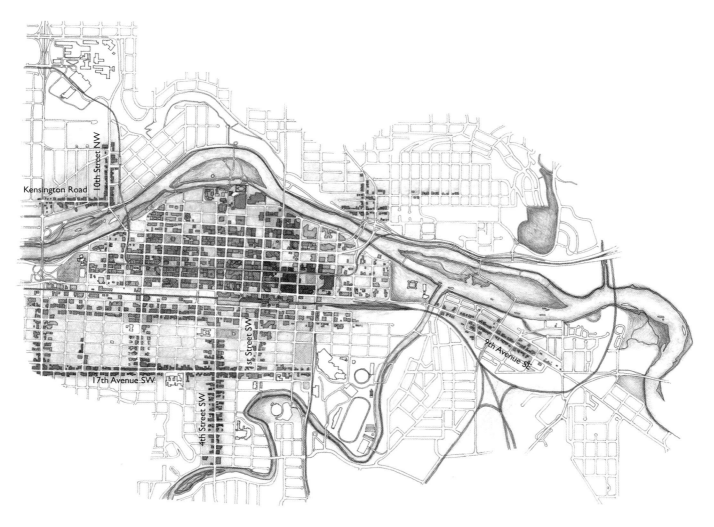

Kensington Road

10th Street NW

17th Avenue SW

4th Street SW

1st Street SW

9th Avenue SE

7 REDEVELOPMENT, EXPANSION, AND MATURITY

7.1   INTRODUCTION

The 1988 Winter Olympics left both a rich physical legacy as well as a sense of pride, and Calgary emerged as a city of international stature. The years following the games were prosperous ones and the city increased its population and land base, while both celebrating this growth and struggling to cope with it.

Calgary has been undergoing the simultaneous processes of continued suburban sprawl and re-intensification of the core. Extensive additions and expansions of the transportation infrastructure have frustrated drivers while at the same time making it possible to live further from the downtown, still the employment core of the city.

Several projects of international note have been completed, including Garrison Woods, on the former Canadian Forces base, and the second phase of The Bridges is currently under development on the old General Hospital site. On the other hand, the East Village still remains undeveloped, and surface parking lots still occupy much of the core.

Extensive exurban development has continued to expand the built-up area beyond the city, especially to the south and west. The City of Airdrie is now a stone's throw from Calgary's northern edge, and towns like Okotoks to the south, Cochrane to the west, and Strathmore to the east function as bedroom communities. The land between Calgary and these settlements is quickly being gobbled up by low-density country residential uses, and land use conflicts occur regularly at this developing edge.

7.2   IDEAS, PLANS, AND PLANNING

Calgary's urban development has both quantitative and qualitative dimensions. Spatially, the city has continually grown outward at a remarkable pace, and Calgary is well known nationally and even internationally for its sprawling form. The outward growth, which has occurred at the expense of the development of a denser and more compact urban form, is, never-the-less, a logical result of the city's development practices and processes. Qualitatively, the city form has gradually become more dispersed, and less imageable. Several notable plans and planning processes have influenced the most recent evolution, and reflect efforts to manage growth and to create a livable city.

It has been City Council policy to maintain at least a thirty-year supply of developable land within its boundaries. The rationale for this policy is that this bank of land allows for the long-term planning necessary to accommodate Calgary's high rate of growth

117
Calgary's core is composed of the downtown plus surrounding established neighbourhoods. This area is strongly anchored by the rivers and railway, with a network of high-quality pedestrian streets and higher density neighbourhoods. It forms an imageable and legible whole.
drawing B. Sandalack, A. Nicolai, J. Zhang, G.C. Carra, (Sandalack and Nicolai 2000)

and to facilitate the planning and budgeting of infrastructure such as power, water supply, sewers, and roads. In order to maintain this long-term land supply, the city must annex land on a periodic basis.

With the demise of the Regional Planning Commissions in Alberta following provincial government cutbacks and restructuring in the early 1990s, the areas adjacent to the city now fall under separate jurisdictions, with the result that there is no longer a comprehensive regional approach to land use and urban development.

Released in 1998, the Calgary Plan's three major policy thrusts are growth management, healthy environments, and healthy communities. The plan's objectives are to:

- increase mobility options for Calgarians;
- protect environmentally significant areas;
- reduce the need for additional river crossings;
- reduce the reliance on the automobile; and
- increase transit use.

The plan proposes several strategies to achieve these objectives, including locating new jobs closer to where people live and providing housing closer to where jobs are; concentrating employment in the downtown and in several employment centres that attract enough people to support transit service; encouraging more people to live in existing neighbourhoods; increasing population densities and the range of housing choices; designing pedestrian-friendly public space systems; and acknowledging the role that urban design plays in fostering a safe and livable city. Despite these broad goals and the comprehensive nature of the Calgary Plan, transportation and road infrastructure issues seem to continue to dominate the agenda.

The concept for an integrated system of public thoroughfares adjacent to the river had its origins in the plan prepared by Thomas Mawson at the beginning of the twentieth century. Heavily influenced by William Pearce, one of the Mawson Plan's aims was to "rigidly preserve the river banks for the use of the public." It would be almost a century before this concept would gain the statutory assistance of an approved plan and, as the city developed, portions of what would ultimately become part of the park and open space system were dedicated as public space. The idea of a system of connected pathways was an obvious one that would recur many times, and the first section of a path system was completed through Confederation Park in the 1970s along with sections along the Bow and Elbow rivers.

118
The Bridges is emerging as a higher density mixed use area on the former General Hospital site.
photo B. Abrams Reid 2006

119
A community centre and large park are at the heart of The Bridges development.
photo B. Abrams Reid 2006

120
The river path system, in this photo south of Prince's Island, includes urban and natural elements and connects most of the city.
photo B. Sandalack 2003

In 1989, the Government of Alberta introduced its Urban Parks Program whereby Calgary was one of several communities that received grants for urban park development. In 1991, the City proceeded with development of an Urban Parks Master Plan for the river valley system, including the Bow and Elbow rivers, Glenmore Reservoir, the Western Irrigation District Canal, Nose Creek, and West Nose Creek. The plan designated 160 potential river valley park sites to entail an estimated cost of $200 million to be shared by the City, the Parks Foundation, and others.

Preparation of the plan involved the City, five landscape architectural firms, several biophysical consultants, and other experts, along with extensive public participation and input. The goal of the program was "the establishment of significant areas of open space to ensure that urban populations have easy access to natural environments and the development of these areas to enable their sustained and unimpaired use for outdoor recreation." The objectives addressed accessibility to urban areas as well as preservation of natural landscape features.

The Calgary Urban Parks Master Plan was completed in 1994, and soon led to the development of the river path system, which extends more than 550 kilometres and is used by thousands of people. Although the plan focused on parks and open space, it also was influential in urban development. Notably, it was opposed to some proposed river crossings, including those being considered for Sarcee Trail at the Weaselhead and the Bow River, Shaganappi Trail at the Bow River, 50th Avenue at the Elbow River, and the South Downtown Bypass. The path system, while extensive, is still incomplete, and there are frequent discussions regarding what the appropriate design strategies and landscape vocabulary might be in the more urbanized parts of the city. The Master Plan has achieved a great deal in dedicating this important system and could now benefit from a better integration with other urban design plans and processes.

The GoPlan, or the City Transportation review, which the City of Calgary released in 1995, also involved significant public consultation. It presented a different point of view regarding river crossings, as its mandate emphasized access and circulation.

The plan was a response to increasing public concern about the damage to the river valleys, loss of arable land, air pollution, and traffic congestion (Jamieson et al. 2000). The GoPlan's extensive participation process attempted to involve all Calgarians in building a vision that would balance economic, political, and environmental issues. The plan attempted to integrate land use with transportation planning "thereby establishing a clear link between car use and urban sprawl."

A Round Table Working Group for the GoPlan was established by the City but was later disbanded, and momentum has not been sustained. However, this planning process was a demonstration in the growth of more direct democracy, and it produced a number of ambitious policy statements. The GoPlan led to other initiatives such as various Growth Area Management Plans and the Sustainable Suburbs Study, which was intended to identify the means of implementing the findings of the GoPlan in suburban development. To date, the Sustainable Suburbs Study does not appear to have had much influence on suburb design (see Sandalack and Nicolai [2001 a,b], Kolody [2003], and Perry [2005]). The Calgary Plan was released in 1998 and outlines in general terms the land uses and transportation priorities.

In 1999, the City completed, in association with numerous volunteers, an ambitious and forward-looking document entitled Evolving Futures. The document outlined several recommendations to achieve a high quality downtown, but few if any of these have been pursued. More recent efforts by the City, with assistance from volunteer committees, to develop a Downtown Urban Structure Plan have attempted to build on the principles outlined in Evolving Futures but thus far the work is still under development. The City is currently engaged in a number of other processes intended to result in visionary and strategic documents for the downtown as a whole.

The failure of the East Village to materialize is perhaps a symptom of the lack of a strong plan for Calgary's downtown. Following the demise of the 1979 Downtown Plan, and the dismissal of scores of city planners, little has been done to set a path for downtown development. Projects are approved on what is essentially an ad hoc basis since, in the absence of a coherent vision for the downtown, each proposal is evaluated in isolation on its own merits. This process does not necessarily lead to a high quality public realm. Council approved a new Area Redevelopment Plan for East Village in 2005 with the hope that this area might finally achieve its promise.

More encouragingly, the City has instituted a process of design review and constituted an Urban Design Review Panel for the downtown. It appears as if there is a new interest and willingness to engage in debate about the quality of the urban form, and to make efforts to improve it, and the requirement of design review may help to raise the expectations of urban form and contribute to the dialogue about the city.

The University of Calgary's recent initiative with other institutions and agencies to develop an urban campus is another project with tremendous potential to help to revitalise the east core and create a pedestrian-scaled neighbourhood.

121
The EVDS Urban Lab has occupied leased space in the former Customs House since 2004 as part of the University of Calgary's initiative to develop a downtown campus.
photo B. Abrams Reid 2006

Calgary Transportation Plan

122
The Calgary Transportation Plan, or GoPlan is one of the most important documents influencing urban development.
City of Calgary 1995a, Glenbow Archives, courtesy City of Calgary

7.3   SPATIAL STRUCTURE

By 2005, Calgary's densely developed downtown core was surrounded by extensive suburbs totalling an area of approximately 720 square kilometres. A broad but discontinuous band of new suburbs forms the outermost ring, and some development has even taken place beyond the Transportation Utility Corridor, established in the 1970s by the Province for ring roads and linear services. New residential development has occurred primarily in the west, northwest, and the south. Additional industrial development has further taken place in the southeast and northeast corridors, with some consolidation and transformation in the central industrial area.

A series of annexations contributed to the land base since the last growth period, and new annexation proposals are under review as of 2006. Exurban development now borders the city on all sides, and land use issues are more frequent as the rural-urban interface comes into focus.

In 2004, the southward development of the city edge abutted Spruce Meadows Equestrian Centre, and the conflict between the established centre and the encroaching suburbs forced the issues of growth and land use into a more public arena. In 1975 Spruce Meadows, then approximately a half-hour drive from the city, was constructed on the site of a cattle feedlot, and it grew to a 120-hectare world class centre for show jumping and other equestrian activities. It now finds itself across the street from the suburban fringe and engaged in a debate over the compatibility of rural and urban land uses.

Urban expansion has still been checked in only a few directions. The Tsuu T'ina Nation southwest of the city has reclaimed land that had been leased to the Department of National Defence, including some former military housing. The reserve has effectively made 37th Street the limit of suburban growth south of Glenmore Trail and has also constrained road development. Neighbourhoods that have developed in the extreme south-west of the city are not easily connected to the downtown, and discussions regarding a connector through the reserve have been underway for several decades, and as of early 2006 there is no clear resolution.

The western and northwestern edges of the city have extended with new suburbs, and Nose Hill Park is completely encircled. A massive 1,400 hectare development at Symons Valley will eventually include retail centres, a business park and suburban housing for over 50,000 people (equivalent to the population of the City of Red Deer) in five neighbourhoods.

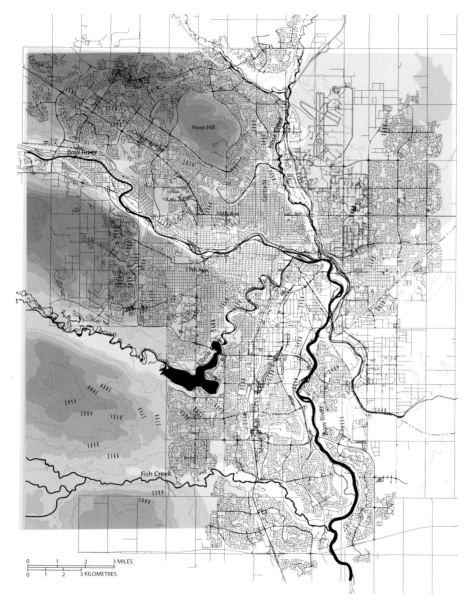

123
A broad band of new suburbs forms the outermost ring of the city by 2003, extending primarily to the west, northwest, and south, and only constrained at the southwest Tsuu T'ina Reserve and the northeast airport. Nose Hill Park is now completely encircled and much new growth is taking place to the north.
drawing A. Nicolai

Nose Hill

Bow River

Coach Hill

Nose Creek

16th Ave

17th Ave

Elbow

Fish Creek

Bow River

0   1   2   3 MILES
0   1   2   3 KILOMETRES

146

124

The downtown is still the commercial and office core and is dwarfed by the large land mass of the city. Several regional-scale "power centres" have developed in the outer suburban rings and are serviced by freeways. Without a perimeter freeway, many roads bisect the city, and many of these act as significant barriers. The west and east sides of the city are separated by a broad band of highway- and railway-oriented industrial lands and by freeways. Newer suburbs are self-contained pods isolated from each other by roads. The LRT lines have extended only slightly.

drawing F. Alaniz Uribe and B. Sandalack

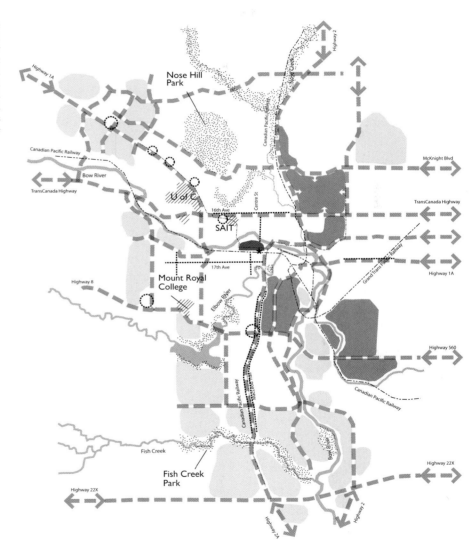

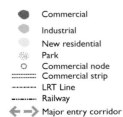

● Commercial
● Industrial
● New residential
⋯ Park
○ Commercial node
⋯⋯ Commercial strip
–·–·– LRT Line
–··–··– Railway
←–‑→ Major entry corridor

The airport has continually constrained suburban development, although new suburbs have developed further east, and the rail line running northeast from Alyth has served as a fairly impermeable border to eastward development with its infrequent crossing points. Combined with the less favourable environmental position downwind and downstream from the rest of the city, the east has experienced less residential development.

The southeast, with the exception of some expansion around Millican and Ogden, has continued to be dominated by industrial uses. The "deep south" has undergone sub-urban development on the east side of the Bow River, and additional suburbs have extended the city's edge almost twenty-five kilometres from the city centre. The industrial lands and freeways have created a broad north-south barrier between east and west Calgary.

125
Main entry to the University of Calgary.
photo F. Shaw 2005

Freeways crisscross the city, and since completion of the south Deerfoot Extension in 2004, it has been possible to bypass the urbanized core when travelling north-south. 16th Avenue N is part of the Trans Canada Highway and carries considerable traffic east-west while attempting to serve as a neighbourhood street. The City is currently widening this thoroughfare, and attempting to create a broad urban boulevard from the unsightly strip it had deteriorated to. Glenmore Trail, Sarcee Trail, Crowchild Trail, Country Hills Boulevard, Stoney Trail, McKnight Boulevard, and John Laurie Boulevard complete a network of high-speed roads.

The existing LRT lines have been extended almost to the city's outer limits, but the future alignments of the LRT have not been set. The Transportation Plan (GoPlan) of 1995 outlines the conceptual expansion of this system and includes general ideas about the need for and location of additional lines.

Other concentrations of employment and nodes of activity include the Calgary International Airport, the University of Calgary, the Southern Alberta Institute of Technology and Alberta College of Art and Design (SAIT-ACAD), and Mount Royal College.

Stampede Park is a seasonal focus of activity and the Greyhound Station, which was relocated from the downtown to west of 14th Street SW, is a secondary node just outside the downtown.

Although Calgary's urban form is largely overwhelmed by its suburbs, there is an important urban renaissance developing in the established inner city.

Downtown and inner city

The downtown is the city's physical and functional epicentre. It continues to be the major employment centre (one quarter of all jobs are found there) and is the focal point for business and entertainment. According to the Calgary Downtown Association 2003 statistics, there were 120,000 people working downtown, 56,000 parking spots, 3,700 businesses, 76 head offices, 124 commercial office buildings, 16 kilometres of Plus 15, 58 Plus 15 bridges (up from 9 kilometres and 42 bridges in 1988, as listed in the *Calgary Urban Explorer*), and 3.25 million square metres of commercial office space.

Office buildings define a concentrated and high-density high-rise core that is interconnected by the Plus 15 system. Rather than expanding along the east-west 7th Avenue transit corridor, this core has migrated to the north. Although plans for freeways through the downtown have been technically abandoned, the street system still favours the car. Several one-way couplets function as freeways, carrying vehicles into and out of the city, providing few opportunities to stop and contributing little to the pedestrian environment.

The LRT system has proven to be a popular form of public transportation, although its above-ground approach through the downtown core has caused a decline in the pedestrian environment along 7th Avenue and contributed to the demise of many businesses. Stations accommodate passengers but don't add value to the trip and are missing the concentration of shops and services one might expect directly around the stops since the stop, street, and shops are separated. In 2005, major upgrades of the LRT stations and the street began to attempt to revitalize 7th Avenue and make the LRT corridor a more vital and vibrant part of the urban form and urban life.

New buildings in the post-Olympics period include Phase Two of Bankers Hall. With its distinctive profile, Bankers Hall is Calgary's second-tallest building at forty-seven stories and is one of the more recognizable landmarks on the city's skyline. Other commercial buildings include the new Trans Canada Pipelines building, the Telus Convention Centre and Hyatt Hotel, Canterra Tower, and a new Eaton's Centre (Holt Renfrew now occupies the old Eaton's building). Projects currently underway include the consolidation of the provincial courthouses and several condominium towers in the West End, Connaught, and Victoria Park.

A YMCA/YWCA, a hotel, and several condominium complexes have been constructed at Eau Claire, but there are still vast expanses of surface parking lots that make the area

126
Stephen Avenue has undergone several renovations and persists as one of Calgary's most popular pedestrian streets. It is a strong retail corridor, and is also the site of several significant office towers, including Bankers Hall, left background.
photo F. Alaniz Uribe 2005

127
New downtown LRT station on 7th Avenue SW.
photo B. Abrams Reid 2006

somewhat vulnerable to street prostitution and criminal activity and less viable as a neighbourhood. Until these gaps are filled, it will be difficult for the downtown to fully benefit from concentrated residential development or to sustain a market at Eau Claire, a feature that was present for only a few years.

Chinatown has been partially redeveloped, and it serves as a character locale and regional shopping centre drawing people from all over the city. Many of the historic Centre Street commercial buildings as well as the texture, scale, and diversity of the area remain. Recent developments include the Chinese Cultural Centre, several residential buildings and public spaces, and some streetscape improvements completed as part of an area redevelopment initiative. However, Chinatown is somewhat functionally isolated by the massive institutional buildings in the east part of the core, surface parking lots to the west, and the uneven pedestrian quality of the downtown streets that inhibit easy circulation between Chinatown and other inner city neighbourhoods.

128
Olympic Plaza summer noon concert.
photo B. Sandalack 2000

Downtown commercial and cultural activity has generally suffered as a result of modernist planning and suburban development. Calgary's downtown is presently composed of discrete functional zones as a result of previous development processes and planning initiatives. A more integrated city should be emphasized in which neighbourhoods are linked, access is easier, and fewer empty lots interrupt the urban fabric. This will require undoing some of the damage that was caused by the urban renewal initiatives and by the imposition of functional zoning and the Plus 15 system.

A viable cultural district is one of the hallmarks of a vibrant and people-centred city. Calgary's emerging Olympic Plaza Cultural District focuses on the blocks surrounding Olympic Plaza and consists of a concentration of civic buildings, public institutions, cultural facilities, and public spaces. The district also includes the cornerstones of urban life: city hall and the municipal building as the place of governance, the library as the place of learning and knowledge, the performing arts centre as the place of high culture and creativity, the museum as the receptacle of the region's material culture and the record of its evolution, the convention centre as the crossroads of commerce, and the cathedral as the place of worship and community service.

Ideally, the urban structure should express the relationships between these key functions and provide the fabric within which all the richness of human life occurs. At present the Cultural District does not meet its potential as a cohesive centre of the city, nor does it function as a neighbourhood to which people are drawn. In 1999, the Calgary Performing Arts Centre initiated a phased process to develop the district's identity

129
Downtown West, Calgary Science Centre, Mewata Armouries and Shaw Millennium Park, viewed from the west.
photo F. Shaw 2005

and to strengthen its image and function as a distinct neighbourhood within which the best of Calgary's public life and cultural expression could be found.

Nearby, however, redevelopment of the East Village is still stalled almost fifty years after urban renewal processes decimated the area. To date, only one high-quality condominium development has been constructed, and, with the extensive surface parking lots, the area is a disappointing underutilization of this prime downtown location. New social service facilities, including the Riverside Drop In and Rehab Centre and the Salvation Army Drop In Centre have been constructed. These facilities serve an important social service function and are of relatively high architectural quality, but in the absence of other balancing residential and commercial developments, perceptions have been further entrenched, and this area is broadly considered as a backwater for criminal and marginal activities.

Partial redevelopment of the inner city has offered a counter-measure to suburban spread and the movement outward from the centre. Although East Village has languished for decades, Downtown West, as the western end of the core is now called, has undergone much high-density residential development, albeit with unsuccessful results in terms of the urban quality (see Alaniz Uribe [2004]).

Although the residential population has increased, primarily through construction of high-rise condominium towers, there has been little attention paid to creation of a high-quality public realm, and developing a true neighbourhood will be difficult. The area is bisected in many places by high-volume one-way traffic corridors, and the connections to the river and to the Science Centre and Millennium Park area are weak and pedestrian-unfriendly. The high-rise towers have few active uses at their bases, and street life is almost non-existent.

130
The Orange Lofts are the only significant recent development in the East Village.
photo B. Abrams Reid 2006

Given the ideal location and the increased population density, there remains much promise for development of a high-quality urbanized environment, but this will only be achieved through much concerted effort.

The process of redeveloping Eau Claire, traditionally a mixed residential and industrial area, to a higher-end residential enclave, is progressing, with more condominium projects adding numbers and increasing density. There are still several blocks of surface parking occupying valuable land in this area, and the Eau Claire Festival Market struggled and eventually failed as the resident population proved insufficient to support the food markets and other retail activities.

The importance of the downtown as an employment, entertainment, and retail core, and the promise of its development as a cultural centre, has made inner-city living much more desirable than in previous periods. There are currently 60,000 residences within a three-kilometre radius of the downtown core and 125,000 residences within a five-kilometre radius. Current development plans for several large mixed residential and commercial projects could have a significant effect on urban form and urban life in the inner city.

The downtown, traditionally defined as the triangle bordered by the Bow River on the north and the railway tracks on the south, is a well-defined and highly "imageable" concentration of office towers and apartment buildings (the downtown can be easily visualized as a triangular area surrounded by the river and roads, and this shape makes it easy to orient oneself to most city maps). As the city has matured, a broader conception of the downtown is called for. The greater downtown, or central city, should now be identified as the core plus the urban neighbourhoods adjacent to it. This area includes most of Calgary's high-quality pedestrian streets and the higher-density neighbourhoods.

The railway lands still define a strong southern edge to the downtown and have for the most part confined the spread of office development. In the Beltline, technically not part of the downtown but conceptually contiguous with it, redevelopment has taken mixed forms. The area between the downtown office core and the residential Beltline district is largely occupied by the railway lands, surface parking lots, and light industrial uses (Marce Santa 2003).

The former warehouse strip has been undergoing a gradual transformation into a themed Warehouse District, and several of the older buildings have been converted to loft condominium and office use, but there has also been some demolition of these versatile structures. The Beltline is currently a construction and development hub; a new Co-op grocery store has been completed, and several signature residential towers were under construction in early 2006.

Particularly in the western portion of the Beltline, a consolidation of the existing high-density residential neighbourhood is taking place, and conversion of many of the apartment buildings from the 1970s and 80s to condominiums is providing much economic and social stability. Several pedestrian-friendly streets are thriving, including most of 17th Avenue SW, 4th Street SW, and a portion of 11th Street SW. If this momentum can be sustained, the Beltline will achieve its ambitions of becoming a high-quality urbanized and pedestrian-scaled city neighbourhood.

131
The Pilkington Building was renovated and now houses Critical Mass, an eMarketing firm.
photo B. Abrams Reid 2006

132
The railway corridor still serves as a strong southern edge to the downtown.
photo F. Shaw 2004

133
The Beltline is undergoing much new condominium development and the community has aspirations of evolving into a high-density urban neighbourhood.
photo B. Sandalack 2005

134
Much of Victoria Park sits vacant in 2005, in advance of Stampede expansion.
photo F. Shaw

Stampede Park continues to be a powerful influence in the east part of the Beltline. The site has been continually upgraded and added to and has become more of an urban fair and tourist attraction, although the western theme is still strong. The events during Stampede animate the entire city, and during the ten days of the fair, over one million people visit Stampede Park. The Stampede Board's ambitions are to become a year-round entertainment centre, and this requires significant expansion (see Hiller and Moylan [1999] for a discussion of the processes and impacts).

In 1994, Calgary was Canada's candidate for the World Expo 2005 bid, and Victoria Park was selected as the site. The bid was not successful, but as long as it was a possibility, investment in the area was at a standstill. In 1998, the announcement was made that the Stampede would expand northward to 12th Avenue, and a comprehensive master plan includes a new agricultural building, expansion to the Roundup Centre, and a more explicitly public face presented through a multi-use green space of rest areas and parkland near the Elbow River. Its location in the centre of the city, picturesque location on the Elbow River, and proximity to emerging high-density residential neighbourhoods gives Stampede Park a higher profile than ever.

East Victoria Park has experienced much deterioration over the past decades, including the loss of the Co-op on 12th Avenue SE, one of the last inner city grocery stores, an incident that was both a cause and an indicator of a declining residential population. Currently the area is dominated by empty lots and surface parking, along with isolated office and residential uses and significant foot traffic generated around the 11th Avenue Mustard Seed homeless shelter and centre for progressive programming, however several new projects are underway.

The area has been renamed Victoria Crossing by the business community to promote its commercial potential as a mixed-use tourism/entertainment destination, a strategy that relies on imagery other than the area's primarily residential and warehouse heritage (Hiller and Moylan 1999). There is growing indication of an urban renaissance in the area, and several high-quality office and residential developments have recently been constructed, signs that the area will undergo significant transformation.

Other neighbourhoods adjacent to the downtown core have experienced varying degrees of redevelopment. Northeast of the downtown and across the Bow River, The Bridges, site of the former Calgary General Hospital/Bow Valley Centre, is taking shape as a high-quality mixed-use area with a variety of housing types, retail strips, parks, and a community centre, a short seven years after the hospital's demolition. Northwest of the downtown, Hillhurst Sunnyside continues to thrive as a residential neighbourhood with pedestrian-friendly streets and a bustling retail area and is well connected to the downtown with a convenient LRT station and a pedestrian bridge across the Bow River.

Cliff Bungalow-Mission and Inglewood are other established communities near the downtown with pedestrian-quality commercial streets that have transformed into destination spots and popular neighbourhoods.

Erlton, to the east of the Elbow River and south of Lindsay Park, was almost completely rebuilt in the last decade and is now an enclave of higher-density low-rise condominiums where single-family housing had previously stood.

Garrison Woods is perhaps the city's most significant recent redevelopment. It involved a successful mixed use urbanization of the former Canadian Forces base and will be followed by development of Garrison Green as a similar residential area over the next years. Garrison Woods is notable for its variety of streets and housing types and for its innovations that include re-use of military housing, conservation of mature landscape, walkable street networks, and commercial frontages provided where surface parking more typically would dominate in front of the grocery store. The increase in property values around Garrison Woods is another indication of the potential in Calgary for development of neighbourhoods with a mix of uses and amenities.

Despite this re-urbanization of the core, where population density and property values continue to increase, the inner city continues to lose services and amenities such as schools, libraries, and swimming pools to closures, through decentralization of services and an increasing focus on suburban growth.

For example, three hospitals in the established city were closed after a century of use. Bow Valley Centre (the Calgary General Hospital) was demolished in 1999; the Holy Cross Hospital was converted to medical offices and a Mount Royal College campus; and the Colonel Belcher Veterans Hospital has relocated to a new centre west of Parkdale. The loss of services and amenities in the inner city has become a source of tension and debate.

Other commercial and retail areas

Commercial and retail land uses are concentrated downtown and along such major roads as Macleod Trail as far south as Shawnessy, 16th Avenue N, 36th Street NE, Bow Trail SW, and 17th Avenue SE. Shopping centres with ever-larger footprints

135
Garrison Woods contains a range of house types, a mix of uses, and higher densities.
photo B. Sandalack 2005

136
Garrison Woods commercial main street includes retail uses at grade and residential or office above.
photo B. Sandalack 2005

137
Chinook Mall underwent extensive renovations, although with an incongruous Egyptian theme.
photo M. Stonehocker 2005

138
Deerfoot Meadows with Bow River in background.
photo M. Stonehocker 2005

now offer a wide array of retail, entertainment, medical and social services, and food services under one roof. Open seven days a week, these centres function as significant magnets.

The recent renovation of Chinook Mall, one of the most extensive and expensive in North American history, was a three-year, $310 million undertaking that yielded 1.2 million square feet (111,000 square metres) of retail space, a sixteen-screen 4,000-seat multiplex cinema, Imax theatre and state-of-the-art customer amenities, all of which further increase the mall's attraction on Macleod Trail.

Major renovations to North Hill Mall (including construction of two residential towers) and Market Mall will likely also rejuvenate these nodes in the northwest.

New shopping complexes, so-called "power centres," include Deerfoot Meadows, West Hills Town Centre, and Signal Hill Shopping Centre. Constructed in 1992, Westhills/Signal Hill involved the development of Battalion Park, an area originally created by First World War soldiers who had trained in the area and returned to commemorate their battalion numbers with over 10,000 rocks arranged on the hill. Development of this huge area involved filling in the gravel pit south of Richmond Road with excavated material from the shopping centre construction, re-grading the slope, replacing the rocks, constructing stairs, and developing the top of the hill to single-family residential.

Other major shopping and employment centres include Shawnessy Centre, Country Hills, and Crowfoot Centre, and a number of shopping centres strung along 36th Street NE.

The new Peter Lougheed Hospital, constructed to replace the old General Hospital, is located on that corridor as well. Some of these shopping centres are nominally connected to the LRT, but the automobile is the favoured mode of access and each of these centres includes extensive surface and structure parking and is well connected by major roads and freeways, but not necessarily to the surrounding neighbourhoods.

An automobile dealership mall at the intersection of Glenmore and Deerfoot trails has created another variation of the shopping centre model.

Brittania Plaza
1950s

4th Street SW Safeway
1960s

Glamorgan Shopping Centre
1950s

Chinook Mall
1960/3, merged 1970s, expanded ca. 2000

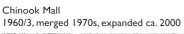

20 40 80 120m

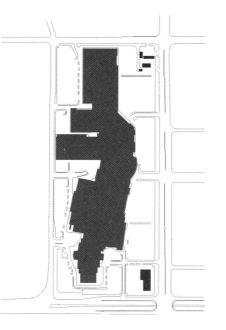

139
Calgary's commercial form has evolved from small corner stores, to small strip malls, to neighbourhood shopping centres, to regional malls, and now to newer and more massive forms. All drawings here are the same scale to allow comparison.

Britannia Plaza illustrates an uncommon form combining parking and two commercial frontages to create a human-scaled environment.

Most grocery stores still follow the model shown in the 4th Street Safeway drawing and photo. A large parking lot is located to be easily seen and accessed.

Glamorgan Shopping Centre is typical of the strip malls constructed with many of the post-war suburbs. When first built, it consisted of an anchor grocery store and a strip of local services, with a large parking lot and gas station oriented towards the street intersection and not the neighbourhood.

Chinook Mall occupies several city blocks. It originally consisted of two separate malls, now merged. Parking lots surround the structure.

Signal Hill and West Hill are part of a large "power centre" west of Sarcee Trail at Richmond Road. Several large big box stores, a cinema complex, and other automobile-oriented services are clustered around parking lots. Walking is not an option here.
drawings J. Zhang

Westhills / Signal Hill Power Centre
1992

20 40 80 120m

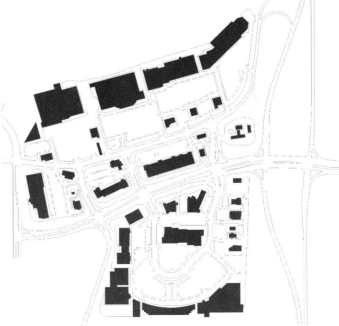

140
Big box stores and an automobile sales mall are two of the newer retail forms. A large intersection and wide buffer occupy much land in this automobile-oriented complex.
drawings J. Zhang

Deerfoot Trail and
Glenmore Trail SE
ca. 2000

20 40 80 120m

Industrial

The early decision to align the railway close, but not directly adjacent to, the Bow River determined the first location of industrial development, and with the construction of the highways, new industrial parks were constructed within easy access of major intersections. This pattern is now entrenched, and industrial land is concentrated today in broad bands northeast and southeast of the downtown and has extended east and south of Ogden.

By 1997, manufacturing revenues surpassed those from oil and gas for the first time in the city's history. Major changes in meatpacking have had an effect on the structures and locations associated with that industry. New meatpacking plants at out of town locations such as Alderside, near High River, and Brooks to the east, have opened up Calgary's former stockyards area for redevelopment for light industrial uses. A new industrial park has replaced the corrals and slaughterhouses, and the Crossroads Farmers Market and Artspace Gallery are the new tenants of the remaining building.

The railway is still an important industry. The Ogden Shops house the CPR's only heavy repair and rebuilding shop, covering sixty-four hectares of land and providing employment for a thousand. The Alyth Diesel and Car Shops remain as the CPR's main marshalling yard in Western Canada, and the seventy-hectare Alyth Yard functions as the CPR's operational hub for Western Canada, with a maximum throughput of 3,000 cars per day.

Public realm

The river path system is Calgary's premiere public open space. It has redefined both circulation and recreation patterns and has quickly become one of the defining features of this twenty-first-century city. It consists of an interconnected series of pedestrian and cycle paths that extend along the rivers and weave throughout the city.

Calgary is located at the interface of the prairies and the foothills, and natural landscapes that are represented in city parks include grasslands, aspen forest, riverine forest, Douglas fir forest, and various aquatic habitats. Numerous golf courses have been developed over the course of Calgary's history, and they comprise public and private amenities within the city limits. Other recreation nodes include Spruce Meadows, a world-class equestrian centre, Eau Claire Market, at the hub of the river path system

141
Part of the river path system along the Elbow River.
photo B. Sandalack 2005

and Prince's Island, and sports and leisure centres such as the Talisman Centre (formerly Lindsay Park) Southland Leisure Centre, and Village Square.

Regional destinations include the major open spaces of Nose Hill Park, Fish Creek Park, Glenmore Park, and the Weaselhead. Many other significant parks and open spaces are strung along the rivers, encompassing a range of landscape types and levels of maintenance. Canada Olympic Park, likely one of the few ski facilities located within a city's limits, provides skiing and snowboarding only a few minutes' drive from many neighbourhoods.

In addition to the squares and plazas developed in earlier periods, downtown Calgary has acquired spaces devoted more to spectacle than to the traditional functions of urban public space. Shaw Millennium Skate Park has emerged as a powerful draw in the west end of the core, bringing young people into the centre of the city. Millennium Park was created on land that had historically been used as recreational space. At various times, the site has been home to an outdoor swimming pool, a football stadium for professional and high school teams, and now a world-class skateboard facility and commemorative park. It also highlights the role that philanthropy and volunteerism have continued to play in making many of the city's public facilities possible.

Construction of Barclay Mall, a limited vehicular traffic road and pedestrian connector to the Bow River, was underway in 1988. This mall attempts to link the downtown core with Prince's Island and Eau Claire, but it lacks the vibrancy that Stephen Avenue Walk enjoys since few of the buildings on 3rd Street face onto the mall or have public uses at sidewalk level. The street, it might be said, is a corridor, but not yet a place.

Eau Claire Festival Market attempted to revitalize the northern core, but so far has done so with limited success. The market is ideally situated near Prince's Island, one of the best known and most heavily used urban parks, and is at the confluence of the river path system and Barclay Mall. However, until the residential population in the area reaches a critical number and density, the area will likely continue to struggle. Plans to renovate the Eau Claire Market block and to fully capitalize on its site were underway in 2006, and with redevelopment of adjacent properties, this central area of the city might eventually become a stronger hub.

Other major public realm renovations underway include Central Memorial Park, and Memorial Drive.

142
The double row of elm trees in front of the Municipal Building provides a comfortable scale and creates a pleasing space.
photo B. Sandalack 2006

Good streets

While Calgary is increasingly well known for its suburban sprawl, a collection of succesful streets reflect a growing interest in more urban and pedestrian places. These streets are where the heart of public life seems to beat at its fullest – where we find "streets full of life" and "places full of time" (Sennett 1990). These are places where something of Calgary's brief history is still evident, and where the pulse of modern city life is also strong.

4th Street SW, 17th Avenue SW, Kensington, Stephen Avenue, 11th Street SW, 9th Avenue in Inglewood, and Centre Street in Chinatown have become destination spots, not just for their picturesque qualities, but for the experience of urbanity they promise. However, these streets represent a relatively small sample in a rapidly growing city, where roads – structures for moving traffic, in contrast to multi-purpose urban streets – tend to dominate.

Good streets in Calgary and in cities worldwide have several things in common. Narrow lot subdivision ensures that there are a variety of businesses (rather than just one large box), and that the shops open onto the street, creating lots of opportunities for people and products to go in and out. This is the quality of permeability that gives a higher degree of choice for the pedestrian and leads to a livelier and more interesting street.

While all of these good streets have many of the same characteristics, they have enough variety in the materials, architecture, and businesses that the result is a unique and individual streetscape.

On streets such as these, smaller lots mean that local businesses also have more opportunity to buy or lease a property, thereby enhancing the character of the street and providing an economic link to the community. On the other hand, a single use, a single design, and fewer street entrances are development characteristics that exclude variety and liveliness and that typify large corporations or franchises with little link to the locale.

The character of the street is also a result of the construction of its edges. The outside of a building can equally be understood as the inside of the street, and from that perspective, buildings are important for the spaces that they create by their arrangement and placement on their lots. An active and continuous street of common building edges fronting onto an amply-proportioned and detailed sidewalk provides the setting for a pedestrian

143
The Bay arcade provides shelter from the elements and a good public / private transition.
photo M. Stonehocker 2005

culture – and people always attract more people. Street trees, well-placed benches in sunny spots protected from the wind, and lack of clutter do wonders for creating a comfortable human scale.

Even in winter, Calgarians flock to places where these simple amenities are provided. The cafes that have provided year-round outdoor seating on the south side of 17th Avenue SW and the east side of 4th Street SW are some of the successful businesses that have benefited from understanding this simple human enjoyment of a sunny place to spend time.

However, even Calgary's high-quality streets are vulnerable to outmoded planning practices. Road widening has an obvious impact on the character and quality both of the streets and of the neighbourhoods around them. Rights of way, or legal easements that the City may appropriate at some time in the future, have been established on several important local streets, including 17th Avenue SW, 19th Street NW, and 10th, 11th, and 12th Avenues SW. The extent of these rights of way is evident in newer developments that are required to be set back from the street, and in some cases in the lack of street tree planting. Although road widening may never actually take place, the setbacks are still required, damaging the street quality.

Context is another variable in the equation that makes for good streets. Good streets require a certain intensity and mix of uses that has been advocated by most urbanists and many city plans, but that seems to be difficult to achieve in practice.

Land use zoning developed as a remedy to Victorian urban problems and was first implemented in Calgary in the 1920s to segregate residential and other land uses that were seen as mutually incompatible. This practice of separating functionally distinct land uses for the sake of efficiency became entrenched during the modernist phase of city planning. Even though it is highly improbably today that an abattoir or tannery would try to locate in the middle of a residential neighbourhood, the continuing dominance of zoning as a planning tool seems to reflect an almost obsessive desire to regulate and oversimplify land use.

It is a curious fact that most of Calgary's good streets would be impossible to create under today's standards and according to today's land use bylaws. The continuous streetwall, buildings framing the sidewalk, narrow frontages, a mix of uses, and an eclectic mix of building design and materials found on these streets are characteristics that are not permitted according to the rules, with the exceptions, for example, of the progressive plans adopted in 2006 for the Beltline communities.

144
The lively neighbourhood commercial node on 11th Street SW would likely be impossible to build under the present land use bylaw.
photo B. Sandalack 2006

145
High-quality pedestrian streets (16th Avenue north of Tomkins Park shown here) usually include broad sidewalks, street trees, and a variety of businesses to attract customers.
photo R. Perry 2004

146
9th Avenue in Inglewood has a mix of uses and small retail units made possible by narrow commercial lots and a building type that allows retail uses on the main floor and office or residential above. The street is also supported by local residential neighbourhoods and has become a destination shopping area.
photo F. Shaw 2005

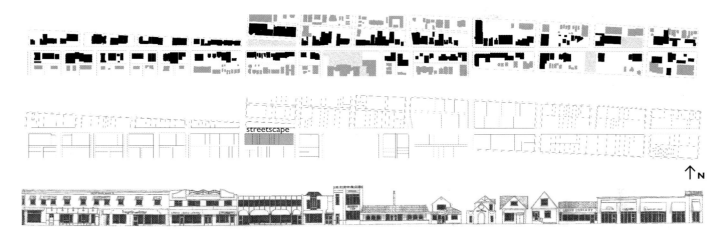

147
17th Avenue SW ca. 2003 (prior to redevelopment of
the Mount Royal Block, currently under construction).
drawings J. Zhang, J. Marce Santa, C. Chen

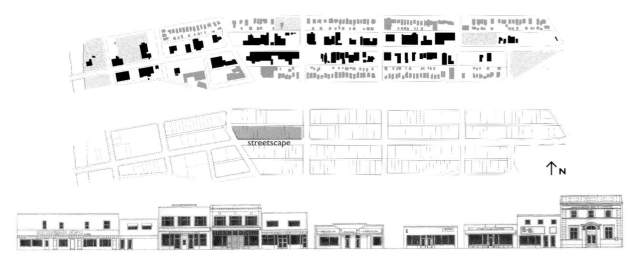

148
9th Avenue SE ca. 2003 (Inglewood).
drawings J. Zhang, J. Marce Santa, C. Chen

149
Centre Street is one of the pedestrian-scaled character streets in Chinatown, and the Chinese Cultural Centre anchors 2nd Avenue.
photo F. Shaw 2003

150
4th Street SW.
photo B. Sandalack 2002

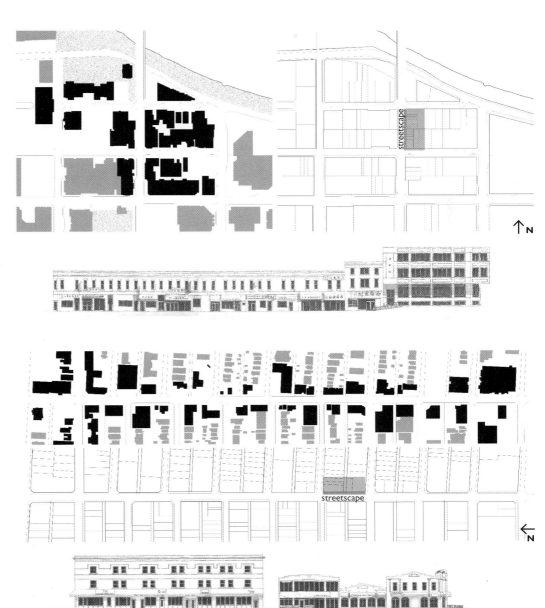

151
Centre Street ca. 2003 (Chinatown).
drawings J. Zhang, J. Marce Santa,
C. Chen

streetscape

N

streetscape

N

152
4th Street SW ca. 2003.
drawings J. Zhang, J. Marce Santa,
C. Chen

Infrastructure and urban form

Water

Calgary now has two water treatment plants that supply safe drinking water to residential, industrial, commercial, and institutional customers in Calgary as well as in Airdrie and Chestermere. The Bow and Elbow River are the two sources of drinking water, and both are surface sources originating west of the city.

The Bearspaw and Glenmore Water Treatment Plants are interconnected, although the Bearspaw Plant primarily supplies water to the north part of the city and the Glenmore plant supplies the south. In addition to the reservoirs, the physical infrastructure includes over thirty pump stations, eighteen treated water reservoirs, and nearly 4,000 kilometres of pipes. With the exception of the dams and treatment plants, much of this infrastructure is hidden below ground.

Sewer

Most of the water drawn from the Bow and Elbow rivers for use within Calgary is returned to the Bow after it is treated. Calgary's two treatment plants, at Bonnybrook and Fish Creek, handle all the wastewater collected by the city's sanitary sewer system and separate the liquid effluent and sludge through a complex filtration process. The effluent is disinfected before being discharged into the Bow River, while the sludge is pumped to the Shepard Sludge Lagoons where it is further treated and eventually discharged or converted into organic fertilizer.

Most of the sewer infrastructure is also hidden underground, with storm and sanitary sewer pipes extending approximately 11,300 kilometres. The technically innovative Pine Creek Wastewater Treatment Plant in the city's southwest will set a new standard.

The storm-drainage system helps prevent flooding by diverting rain and snowmelt into the nearest river or creek by means of a network of underground pipes. The system also includes storm-water retention ponds to hold excess water during heavy rainstorms.

In 1988, the designed capacity for storm drainage systems in new communities was increased to handle one-in-one-hundred-year rainfalls. The former standard was one-in-five-year rainfalls. In some of the older communities, the standard was one-in-two-year rainfalls. In the 1993, The City constructed the first retrofitted dry

153
Water treatment plant discharge into Bow River.
photo F. Alaniz Uribe 2004

154
Downtown ENMAX substation on 4th Avenue and 8th Street SW. At one time it was envisioned that a highrise residential office tower would be built above this substation. The building contains equipment for di-electric non-conductive gas with insulating properties, or SF6, which allows a smaller footprint than conventional substations. ENMAX utilizes this technology for three downtown substations (Numbers 1, 5, and 8).
photo D. Lee 2003

155
Victoria Park electrical structures.
photo D. Lee 2003

pond in Marlborough Park. In 1994, City Council amended the Drainage By-law to establish a Storm Drainage Upgrade Charge, which generates about $3 million a year for storm drainage improvement projects that will reduce flooding from high-intensity rainfalls.

Power

Alberta's electric utilities were restructured in the 1990s to establish a competitive, open-access energy market across the province. In 1998, City Council made the City of Calgary Electric System a wholly owned subsidiary called ENMAX Corporation. ENMAX Energy became an affiliated retailer whose role is to buy and sell electricity and natural gas for domestic consumption. It also owns half of a wind power generation project. ENMAX Power is responsible for transmission and distribution of the electricity.

Most of Alberta's electrical energy is thermally generated from coal or natural gas. The electricity that is generated flows through transmission wires after being boosted to 400,000 volts by a transformer, since higher-voltage current travels long distances more efficiently. The electricity reaches substations where transformers lower the voltage to usable levels. It then leaves the substation on smaller distribution lines. These lines were once entirely overhead, but now, quite often these distribution lines are installed underground. Once the distribution lines reach each neighbourhood, another small transformer, either pole mounted or in a utility box, lowers the voltage again for domestic use.

In the suburbs, ENMAX Power works with developers and others to bring four-party trenching to new areas. This is a relatively new process of bringing all the underground utilities (power, gas, cable, telephone) together using one common shallow trench rather than multiples. This increases the amount of plantable space that might be available for trees and is safer and more economical (Perry 2005).

In the downtown, the City of Calgary has a very significant electrical and fibre optics network that helps to attract and serve major national corporations. ENMAX and Calgary Transit have collaborated to power the LRT on wind power generated by turbines on a wind farm in southern Alberta and distributed by ENMAX's Greenmax system. Calgary's LRT is the first North American public transit system to be operated on wind power. Residential customers also have the option of choosing wind-generated electricity.

7.5   URBAN FORM AND BUILDING TYPES

Commercial

Calgary's downtown has continued to reflect the city's maturation as well as its fortunes and foibles. The office commercial concentration has intensified north of the railway tracks and has moved even further northward. Surface parking lots still dominate the area closest to the river; however, development is starting to renew this area. Office buildings have drifted south across the railway tracks into the Beltline, and many new developments along 1st Street promise to rejuvenate what had been for some years a discontinuous fabric.

The 8th Avenue corridor is also notable for its relationship to Calgary's two rivers. The potential for a more meaningful connection of the rivers through the downtown is still an unrealized opportunity. At present, Barclay Mall (3rd Street) is the only formal connection between the downtown and the Bow River. The other grid streets could make stronger links, but the focus seems to be on east-west circulation and related to traffic efficiency.

Several north-south streets have the potential to form higher quality pedestrian streets and connect the river with the downtown and the residential areas in the Beltline. Since there are limited access points across the railway tracks, these streets could also provide important gateways into and out of the downtown.

156
The Saddledome, Calgary Tower and downtown office buildings create a distinctive profile.
photo F. Shaw 2005

157

As of 2006, downtown office development has spread almost to the Bow River and extends south of the railway tracks. 1st Street is emerging again as a strong commercial street. There is little residential development in the north part of the downtown but increasing residential development in the Beltline. The land along the river is devoted to recreation and amenity uses now. Lot size has increased, and there are several areas awaiting redevelopment.

drawings J. Zhang, F. Alaniz Uribe, K. Meehan-Prins, A. Nicolai, B. Sandalack

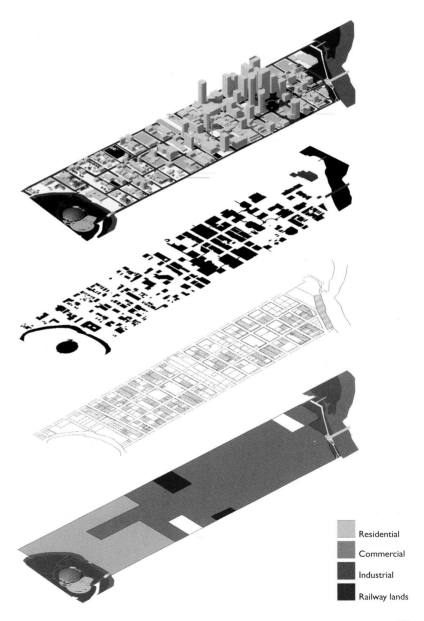

Residential

Commercial

Industrial

Railway lands

Neighbourhood form

Housing starts climbed again in the late 1990s after modest recovery from the 1982 crash, and by 1989 there were 6,200 starts (Hope and McCormick 2000). The housing market was further stimulated by two external influences. In 1992 the minimum down payment requirement was reduced from 10 per cent to 5 per cent, creating a housing boom, and later, CMHC announced its Home Buyers Plan which allowed tax free withdrawals from RRSPs to be used towards house purchases.

By 1996 there were 7,100 starts, the highest since 1982 (CMHC). Single-family housing dominated this market, with multifamily construction comprising only a fraction of this total (City of Calgary 1999). By 1999 multifamily starts experienced a 22 per cent increase over the previous year.

This growth has largely been accommodated in amenity-oriented subdivisions with a strong focus on the private realm. At the same time there have been notable innovations in neighbourhood form in such areas as Garrison Woods and McKenzie Towne.

The wide range of possibilities is expressive of the third phase of contemporary urban development corresponding to postmodernism (Relph 1987), or to a paradigm of ambiguity (Vidler 1996). Time and space are now arbitrary – they are no longer the result of functional requirements or of cultural constraints but are more often determined by the marketplace.

In Calgary, the marketplace has been providing primarily conventional single-family suburbs, although marketing has become a much more significant part of selling, with themes and lifestyles being advertised in addition to houses. Anything is possible, which means that design and planning are really more difficult, not less. The imposition of constraints, such as environmental restrictions, economic limits, cultural norms, social objectives, etc., leads to true creativity. Without these constraints, urban development is subject more to economic aspirations or individual expression.

However, these forces do not necessarily lead to developments that express a sense of place or satisfy the multitude of objectives that cities imply. Issues of local and regional identity have become more important as globalization and corporatization have reduced the distinctiveness of places that used to come from tradition and from the constraints that each place imposed.

158
McKenzie Towne includes a mix of housing types and several public squares, although with an ambiguous character and architectural style.
photo F. Alaniz Uribe 2004

159
Residential streets in McKenzie Towne include front porches and treed boulevards, attempting to create a higher quality public realm.
photo B. Sandalack 2002

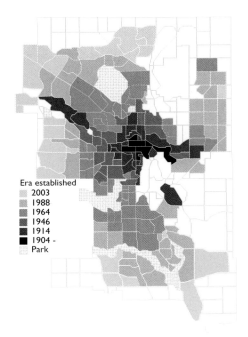

Era established
- 2003
- 1988
- 1964
- 1946
- 1914
- 1904 -
- Park

160
New neighbourhoods have developed in most sectors, although the east is still primarily industrial. Calgary's suburbs have spread beyond Nose Hill Park in the north and Fish Creek Park in the south.
drawings J. Zhang, J. Marce Santa, F. Alaniz Uribe

In Calgary, the possibilities of neighbourhood types range from a version of New Urbanism in McKenzie Towne, to various lake-oriented communities, to enclaves of single-family houses of single price points and styles, to exclusive walled and gated communities, to the mixed use development of Garrison Woods, to country residential lots in East Springbank.

Lake Chapparal

Located in Calgary's southeast, Lake Chapparal was established in 1994 on land annexed by the City in 1981. It is located eleven miles from the city centre, and as of 2006 is no longer at Calgary's edge, following additional annexations.

Suburban development planning in areas such as Lake Chaparral is now carried out in larger geographical units and reflects the sector planning approach introduced earlier. Sector plans determine large residential and service areas and development occurs in phases with major roads typically defining each neighbourhood. Lake Chaparral is marketed for its "lake" – an artificial body of water twelve metres deep filled from the municipal water supply and stocked with rainbow trout.

Air photographs from 1976 and 1999, taken before and after the development, reveal few similarities. One of the main features of the area before urbanization is Macleod Trail, an early trail that later developed into a major north-south highway. Other important features are grid roads at the north and south and a ridge of land sloping down to the Bow River valley at the east, which borders an otherwise fairly flat area. Ephemeral wetlands are present along the western edge of the neighbourhood. Rectangular agricultural fields are lined by a shelterbelt of trees at the south, and small bluffs of aspen are also found.

None of the landscape elements were retained as the land was redeveloped to housing. The lake, a major feature of the area today, corresponds to neither the topographical nor hydrological attributes of the pre-urban landscape.

The edges of Lake Chaparral are highways at the west and north edge, and a very wide buffer of land separates the housing from the northern highway. There are very poor connections with adjacent neighbourhoods, and only one safe road connection, should a resident be inclined to try to walk beyond Lake Chaparral. The slope at the east defines the edge of development, and a grid road is at the south. It will be developed to a major collector road as development to the south takes place.

The internal street pattern is strongly hierarchical, and most internal streets are loops or cul de sacs. It is a highly impermeable street pattern.

Lake Chaparral consists entirely of large single-family houses of a single type (one or one and a half storeys with attached two- or three-car garage at the front), and a limited palette of pastel colours, augmented by artificial stone and brick trim. An enclave of multifamily housing is provided on the east side but is not integrated with the rest of the neighbourhood. There is no school at present, but a partial elementary school (K-4) is scheduled to be built within a few years. There is a small convenience commercial node near the entry at the east, in the form of a strip mall with parking in front.

The lake, with its artificial waterfall, is the area's primary amenity. It is a private amenity and can only be accessed by residents of the neighbourhood. The neighbourhood also includes twelve smaller playgrounds, located within walking distance of each house, and there are over two kilometres of walking paths.

Sidewalks have been eliminated from many of the street designs, and most of the neighbourhood does not include back lanes. Two- and three-car garages dominate the front facades. The combination of large house footprints on the lots plus the loss of plantable area to the driveway has eliminated much of the potential for street tree plantings. There is very little vegetation visible on the street.

The public function of the street is now almost completely corrupted and its main role is that of traffic mover. There is no public face to the street, even though many neighbourhood children use the street for play and three-quarters of the area's homeowners have children under the age of twenty-five.

161
Lake Chaparral was sited on agricultural fields and derives some of its edges from the survey grid. Major roads form three edges, and connections with adjacent neighbourhoods can occur only by car. The street pattern is highly impermeable and forms a very private neighbourhood.
drawings J. Marce Santa

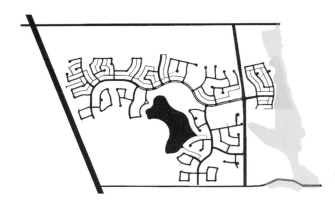

Marquis of Lorne Trail

River Valley Edge

Highway 2/MacLeod Trail

City Limits

Commercial

Residential

Institutional

Open space

Major street

Building

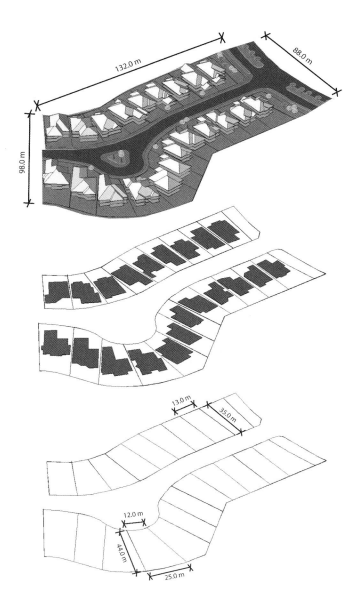

162
Most houses have two and three car garages, and sidewalks are missing from many streets.
drawings J. Marce Santa, streetscape drawing C. Chen

132.0 m

88.0 m

98.0 m

13.0 m

35.0 m

12.0 m

44.0 m

25.0 m

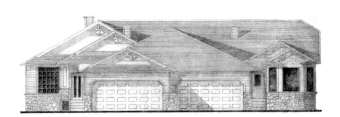

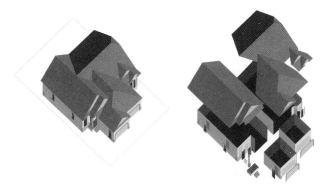

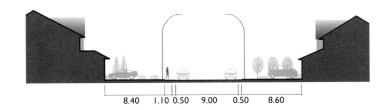

8.40   1.10 0.50   9.00   0.50   8.60

7.5   SUMMARY

Calgary emerged from hosting the 1988 Olympic Games rejuvenated, transformed, and with a place on the international scene. It is known as a bright, young, fresh city in an enviable geographic setting, but one that is also overwhelmed by its suburbs and growth-induced issues that have created political and economic tension. Calgary is also decidedly a white-collar city, with approximately one quarter of almost half a million jobs occurring downtown. It is one of the richest cities, in the richest province, in one of the richest countries, in the world.

While Calgary has been very good at providing a high-quality private realm and in addressing the needs of vehicular circulation, the public realm, culture, and education have not received the same emphasis. Calgary's maturation is evident in projects such as the river path system, in the redevelopment of several of its older inner city neighbourhoods, and in a renewed interest in urban form and quality. However, it is remarkable that this world-class city of a million has only a handful of world-class streets and public spaces.

163
A 3D computer model of the city ca. 2004 illustrates a compact downtown core bounded by the Bow River and the railway corridor.
3D computer model Jinwei Zhang, The Urban Lab

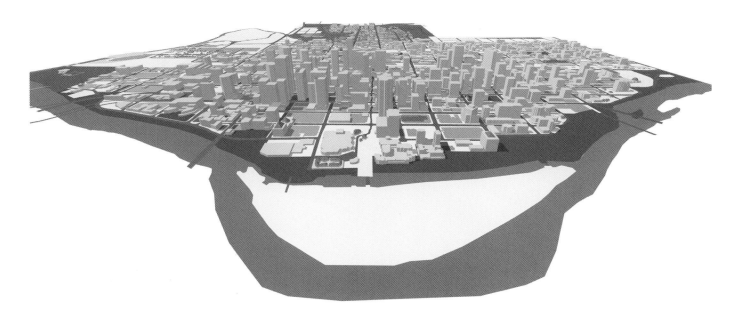

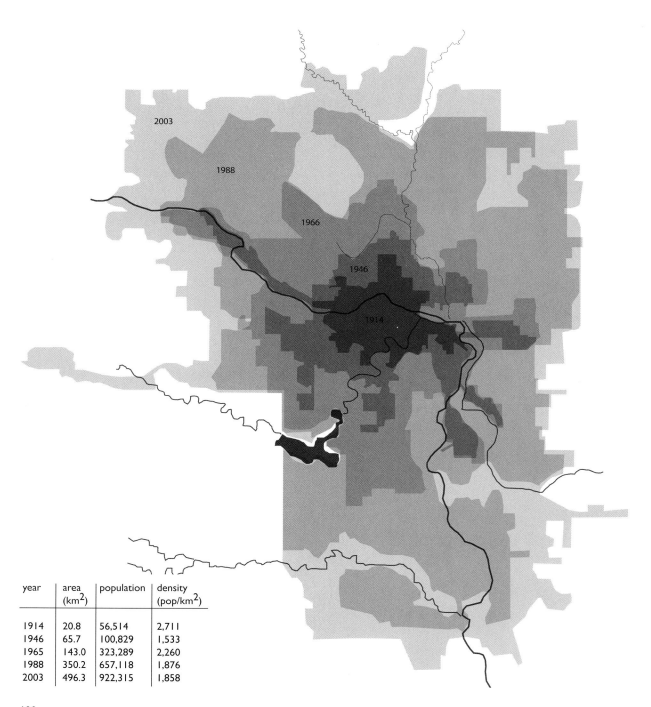

year	area (km^2)	population	density (pop/km^2)
1914	20.8	56,514	2,711
1946	65.7	100,829	1,533
1965	143.0	323,289	2,260
1988	350.2	657,118	1,876
2003	496.3	922,315	1,858

8 WHERE TO NEXT?

8.1 PROCESS AND FORM

Calgary's history so far is one that has many heroes and many stories. The city form that we have inherited is a legacy left by visionaries and entrepreneurs, by ordinary citizens making a home in a new place, and by opportunists attracted by the potential of the West. Its history has been brief but has progressed through all the phases of urban development, from establishment as a frontier town, to consolidation and expansion in the modern world, to emergence in a global setting. Its brief story might have meant that maintaining a sense of historic continuity would have been more vital, but Calgary seems to be afflicted by a short-term memory. The city has always been striking for its perpetual newness and the relative lack of a physical historical record.

Although Calgary still has a relatively compact inner core, it is a city now overwhelmed by its suburbs. There are some recent local examples of developments that attempt to provide a more resilient mix of forms and uses, but they are far too few for this city of a million people.

Calgary has always been a low-density city and has been little constrained by geographic or economic limits. Calgary's urban edge has moved from one mile (1.6 kilometres) from the city centre in 1900, to seven miles (11.3 kilometres) in 1960, to fifteen miles (24.1 kilometres) in 2005. Its developed land mass has grown from a few square miles, to over fifty (130 km^2) by 1965, to over 200 (over 500 km^2) today. The population was approximately 4,000 in 1900, growing to 325,000 in 1965, and is now at a million. This growth, especially since the end of World War II, has been primarily in the form of single-use suburbs. These are low-density developments, by definition, and are unusual in world terms, and particularly unique to western North America.

The combination of sprawling suburban development and the practice of segregating distinct land uses through zoning has contributed to the prevalence of automobile traffic as a dominant and publicly debated issue. Indeed, Calgary's relationship with the car has deep roots: oil has always had positive connotations, the western independent spirit has traditionally favoured the mobility and freedom that a private vehicle can provide, and the city form is closely tied to a development industry that depends on a growing market for the single-family house.

Annexation has been Calgary's method of choice for dealing with growth, but one that has perhaps had the greatest influence on its form and quality. The City has a practice of maintaining a thirty-year land bank and satisfies that by the process of

164
Mapping Calgary's built-up area and population illustrates that the density has decreased since the 1960s, and since the high point of 1914. This has occurred despite calls to increase density and control expansion of the city's footprint.
drawing F. Alaniz Uribe

annexing land for future growth. But this guarantees that the city will continue to spread as low-density suburbs and also ensures that public transportation will become more expensive and that everyone will become more and more preoccupied with the inevitable traffic problems.

Ideas, plans, and planning processes have also had a profound influence on the city's evolution and its quality. Calgary has had some history of rejecting long-term planning, from the failure of Mawson's plan to be accepted, to the outright abandonment of the similarly visionary plan proposed in 1978 for the downtown, both of which might have secured for the city a more humanly scaled urban structure, and both of which might have led to a stronger connection between the river and the system of city streets.

However, other plans were better received, such as the 1966 Downtown Plan that set the stage for a vehicle-centred circulation system and the havoc of urban renewal, and the Plus 15 Plan that completed the process of dissociating street and pedestrian activity. Other smaller plans, of greater or lesser inspiration, have had to contend with the effects of these two major strokes, and it will take great effort to reinstate the pedestrian and the public realm as a focus of city planning and development strategy.

Calgary has also distinguished itself through its ability to weather extreme boom and bust cycles. This resiliency is an asset that enabled the city to take on an event such as the 1988 Winter Olympics and turn it to its advantage. However, with the exception of the Olympics, Calgary has invested little of its considerable wealth in the public realm or a civic culture.

At the middle of 2006, Calgary's skyline is again populated by construction cranes, and many new and very costly traffic structures are being built. Many more buildings are being planned, and there is a sense of optimism and economic well being. New plans for the downtown are in their final stags of preparation, and it seems as if Calgary has yet another opportunity to live up to its promise. Likely this will require a paradigm shift, and a different way of working together.

The shaping of the many components of the public realm needs a high degree of coopera-tion and coordination between the actors involved in its development and management: city planning and engineering departments, the various owners and designers involved in the development of its edges, as well as the community that uses it. Over the past several decades, city planning and the design professions have grown apart. While the various design disciplines have been pre-occupied with staking out their individual

165
Two figures of the Famous Five sculpture on a winter day in Olympic Plaza.
photo B. Sandalack 2006

166
Buildings from all eras can still be found in some sections of the downtown, although most of Calgary appears uniformly new. View southeast from 7th Avenue and 1st Street SW.
photo B. Abrams Reid 2006

167
Construction cranes currently dominate the skyline of
Calgary's Beltline area.
photo F. Shaw 2005

jurisdictions, the public realm has been neglected, and urban form values and principles have fallen into the domain of the private realm and private developers, who have had the strongest influence on the image and quality of the built form. As a result, the public realm has been lost as a comprehensive area of inquiry and concern, and the natural environment has in many places become a themed and regulated private amenity.

It is the public realm, the spaces now created mostly by default, that needs to become an important focus of the design and planning professions, and, first of all, the community. This is achieved through a renewed urban planning process grounded in the belief that the public realm should be crucible for civic life, and the embodiment of local and regional identity and culture. Within this framework, the role of a renewed urban planning process is to support a cultural and environmental memory, as it relates to the public realm. This should include a generous and deliberate provision for the arts and culture, and for education in all its forms. These institutions function best within the city when they are interconnected by the urban structure.

The challenge of the public realm relates directly to more fundamental questions of "what do we aspire to become?" and "what kind of society do we value?" In Calgary's case, there are few practical constraints on urban form, such as severe economic restraints or the geographic limits imposed by a sea or ocean, and therefore a greater need for some idea or vision of what the city should be in order to guide development. We need to define the qualities of urban form and urban life that are desirable, and to make these things part of the public vocabulary and part of public education, and then to publicly debate them.

A vision considers the problems and opportunities that face the city within a comprehensive picture of overall urban form and structure. For example, a relevant and realistic vision would link the pattern of continuing sprawl to the issues of downtown urban quality and would also situate this within the context of regional development. It is a holistic approach that requires an accurate understanding of the situation and how it has been and is currently shaped.

A vision provides direction for the future, and it talks about desirable outcomes, and a desired way of life. To be useful, a vision has to go beyond generalities and deal with the particularities of place and culture. The roles of specialists such as traffic engineers, planners, urban designers, architects, and landscape architects would then be clear as enablers of this vision, and all decisions would be subservient to the greater good – that of the public nature of all development.

But what would the appropriate forms be for this contemporary western city? How can Calgary continue to capitalize on its location, its wealth and its privilege, and mature into an urban community that has a distinct sense of place and retain a high quality of life? What is the appropriate urban design approach to realize such a city?

8.2   URBAN DESIGN AS A METHODOLOGY FOR CITY MAKING

A city is built brick by brick. This does not mean that city building is about individual buildings – it is about fabric, structure, and the city as a whole. It is important to key on the environmental setting that makes this city so wonderful, on the historic patterns and ways of building, and on the civic landmarks and monuments as the important punctuation in the structure. The rest of the buildings - the housing, the offices, and the shopping centres - are important as the everyday urban fabric within which the special places are set.

Urban design can provide the methodology for city-making. It has the public realm as its focus, and emphasizes the inter-relationship of all the aspects of the city form. In this urban design approach, various layers constitute the built landscape, and each has a different degree of permanence, and different strength of connection to other layers:

Layer 1 – the land

The land, and landscape character, is the most permanent aspect of the built environment, with the greatest potential to contribute to a sense of place.

Calgary is situated in the midst of productive agricultural land and some of the most breath-takingly beautiful amenity land in the world. Its sense of place is derived from that landscape. At the scale of the city, sprawl and low-density suburbs are just not sustainable in that context. Urban design can be one of the best ways to express good conservation practices and to create places that have a relationship to the landscape. At the scale of the neighbourhood, careful attention to the topography, the natural features, the view, and the connections can help to create memorable places with a strong foundation in the landscape. Good urbanism is good environmentalism.

There was often a topographic logic underlying early forms of settlement. The location in relation to rivers and trade routes as well as the vantage points provided by the landscape – these were some of the reasons for selection of the city site. The rivers have been the single most important determining factor of Calgary's urban form, and key features

168

It is interesting that a street, Stephen Avenue, is Calgary's premiere civic space, while in many other cultures it is the plaza.

photo F. Alaniz Uribe 2005

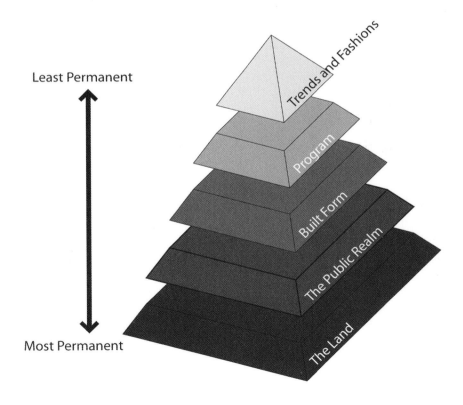

Least Permanent

Most Permanent

Trends and Fashions

Program

Built Form

The Public Realm

The Land

169
The city is made up of several layers of built form with
different degrees of permanence.
concept B. Sandalack, re-drawn F. Alaniz Uribe

in its visual identity. They are also the basis of the most successful and well-loved aspect of the city's public realm – the river path system. However, there are few easy links between the river and the heart of the downtown. Calgary's civic spaces have yet to receive the attention that City policies and growth strategies have given to environmental quality and the provision of recreational amenities.

What is the future of the Bow and Elbow? What effect will further retreat of the Bow Glacier have on Calgary's water supply, and how will the changing river affect the city that it passes through? As Calgary surpasses a population of one million, it may also be heading towards a future in which these basic amenities can no longer be taken for granted.

Layer 2 – the public realm

The public realm is one of the most important components of city infrastructure and is part of its connective tissue, providing space for circulation and gathering and helping to define the city image.

Much of our everyday urban existence occurs within the shared city spaces made up of streets, squares, parks, and plazas. They primarily provide access to buildings – to homes, offices, public buildings and to places of entertainment and culture. They also provide space for the many other functions traditionally associated with urban life, such as markets and public festivals, play, and importantly, the ad-hoc meetings and happenings that make urban life "urban." Within this context, the public realm contains and facilitates urbanity and a type of civility, and it pervades our experience of the city.

The public realm is common ground – it is a place where all citizens can be by right and it is recognition and confirmation that all citizens have something to enjoy in the city, as well as a responsibility to it. This concept of the city is essential to the conception and design of a public realm. This is the main point of urban design and urban planning – not just to protect all our private interests, but to nurture what we have collectively as a community and as neighbourhoods.

The street, most agree, symbolizes public life, and it is mostly from the pedestrian space that we experience the city. How many of us have explored Barcelona, New York, London, Paris, or Quebec City by car? Urban experience is necessarily pedestrian. A city is dependent on sustainable streets to become sustainable itself, and that implies an emphasis on streets that can meet a multitude of demands, rather than function solely as roads or vehicular corridors.

170
As a winter city, Calgary requires appropriate urban design that considers four seasons.
photo B. Sandalack 2006

171
Roxboro was built during the early part of the twentieth century, a time when street trees on boulevards were included in most neighbourhood design.

172
Glamorgan streets, typical of post-World War II suburbs, include sidewalks on both sides. Street trees are part of the private and not public realm.

173
Lake Chaparral is typical of newer suburbs - sidewalks are only present on one side, and there is not sufficient room for street tree plantings.
photos B. Sandalack 1999

In Calgary we have been developing, for the most part, good housing and a high-quality private realm for the rapidly expanding population; but the infrastructure of the public realm – more important than the infrastructure of roads – has been neglected. Streets are usually designed according to traffic flow and road safety rather than according to architectural principles, or according to the dimensions and slower speeds of the pedestrian. The street has therefore become primarily a structure for moving traffic, rather than the multi-purpose instrument that it used to be and still is in the best cities.

There are opportunities at every scale of planning and design of the city – from the street, to the neighbourhood, to the city as a whole – to improve its livability and walkability. Streets as four-season, all-time public spaces need to include sidewalks, street trees, and planted boulevards; otherwise, they become simply devices for moving and storing cars, and hostile environments for people. All neighbourhood streets should be places of quality, and deliberately designed parts of the public realm. Calgary should have more than just a handful of great streets, such as 17th Avenue, 4th Street, and Kensington.

We need to re-learn the vocabulary of the city – street, square, plaza, park are terms that have rich and complex meanings – and develop a higher quality public realm that we collectively inhabit.

Layer 3 – buildings

Buildings are the most visible part of the urban environment and sit within the infrastructure of the public realm. Several generations of built form will come and go within the life cycle of the urban structure; however, if the public realm is intact, the built form has a sense of continuity and meaning over time.

There is a tremendous opportunity for architects to develop a physical response to the landscape, culture, and climate of Calgary – currently only a very small amount of private housing is designed by architects. A new emphasis on everday architecture could lead to the evolution of more place-specific urban form.

But for now, the suburbs are one of the defining features of Calgary, and they are likely here to stay. Most neighbourhoods are too new to have developed a strong sense of community, and one of the defining characteristics of cities like Calgary is the mobility of home owners – "starter homes" and "buying-up" are crass terms for the tendency to view homes and neighbourhoods as commodities first, and places to live second – but this doesn't encourage community building. What would neighbourhoods be like if they provided, as a matter of course, a range of housing types, for a range of incomes and living arrangements, so that one could remain in the same area through all the stages of life?

What would the city look like and function like if the design of new neighbourhoods and housing were done with the intention of producing a high-quality public realm, integrated with the rest of the city form? What would Calgary's housing be like if the design community took on the task of developing unique land subdivision patterns, house types and landscape types that would be recognizably Calgarian?

Layer 4 – activities or program

Each individual building, and each neighbourhood, if it has a resiliency of form, may be used for various activities or programs. The robustness of built form contributes further to the establishment of a sense of place through continuity of form.

174
Too many cars, or too few options of travel?
photo B. Dejun Su 2005

The North American model of suburbia is based largely on segregating activities so we must drive to virtually everything that we do (work, after-school activities, recreation, shopping, entertainment, and so on). The practice of land-use zoning, developed to remedy Victorian urban conflicts, has given way to an oversimplification of land uses and an almost obsessive desire to regulate uses of land. Land uses are crudely characterized as commercial, residential, or industrial, but none of these 'zones' could adequately describe any of the city's really good urban places. They usually consist of a messy but ultimately successful mix of uses and people.

In North America, and in Calgary, the usual way of planning and developing has normalized some very unusual (in world terms) urban forms, such as suburbs and commercial strips, which are proving very difficult to modify to other uses, and made almost impossible the development of a high-quality public realm.

Cities are at their best where there is a mix of uses, housing types, and people, and this essential mix, needed for a healthy and interesting city, is now something that can only come about by design. It will also entail becoming more conscious of the effects that many of our current practices and processes have on urban form and urban life. Urban renewal, zoning, and other processes have discouraged the mix that good places require, and planning policies and development practices therefore need to be changed to achieve a more vibrant and integrated city.

175
New TransAlta building with widened sidewalk and public art in front.
photo B. Abrams Reid 2006

This is also an issue of sustainability: single-use suburbs, single-family homes, and commercial shopping strips, have little versatility as a building type or a land use and cannot easily be adapted for other purposes, as compared to some traditional urban patterns, which can accommodate a changing population and changing needs.

Layer 5 – trends and fashions

The least permanent aspects of the built environment, and of design activity, are the transient and ephemeral trends and fashions. While these frequently add the qualities of delight and contemporariness to the built environment, there is normally a built-in obsolescence to them, and they should be understood as the least permanent, although not necessarily the least important, aspects of urban design.

It is within this layer of environmental design that many aspects of diversity and richness can be expressed, from seasonal changes, to cultural character, to images and emblems. Although this is the least permanent layer of the urban form, it is perhaps the first that is noticed, and it needs the same amount of thought and care as the more permanent aspects. Public art is one way to express contemporary ideas in the city form, and it is more successful if it is connected to the urban structure.

The permanence of the public realm

Good urbanism requires a certain density, intensity, and mix of uses that urbanists everywhere advocate, but which is difficult to put in place, partly due to the persistence of outdated land development and planning practices.

Currently, it seems as if more design intent is applied to individual buildings, to programming, and especially to trends and fashions than to the most permanent elements – the public realm and the landscape. The less permanent elements come and go, but the public infrastructure – the integrated system of public spaces – persists and can give a sense of continuity and quality to a place. What has been neglected has been design at the city scale, and the public realm has too often fallen between the cracks.

8.3   THE FUTURE – A MATTER OF DESIGN

Calgary's development has been defined for the most part by its position as an oil and gas centre, and it has undergone several boom and bust cycles as the industry responded to global forces. The periods of economic growth have resulted in prosperity and urban expansion, but they have not yet led to the establishment of a more multi-dimensional and more mature city.

As Alberta's economy has changed since World War II, Calgary has developed an identity very different from the rural hinterland to which it was linked for decades. Both the ranching and oil industries have established and strengthened Calgary's roots in the western economy and regional character. Ranchers and oil entrepreneurs share a spirit of individualism and a romantic link to the land in a way that farmers, who worked the land without obtaining mineral rights, did not. The proliferation of country estates west and south of Calgary is not a new phenomenon but was established decades ago with the connection between ranching, oil, land, and horses. This is part of the city's identity too.

176
The Calgary Stampede - part of the city image.
photo B. Sandalack 2006

The city, its form, and its qualities, is increasingly a topic of concern to more than the planning and design professions. The 2006 World Urban Forum, held in Vancouver at a time when, for the first time in history, over half of the world's population lives in cities, identified the huge challenges with which twenty-first century cities are faced. Issues of social, environmental, and economic sustainability are likely to continue to dominate urban agendas, and the complex problems and their solutions will require community engagement as well as multidisciplinary approaches and ongoing commitment from all levels of government.

It is now commonly accepted that in order to attract businesses and their employees, cities must be able to offer more than just good jobs, affordable housing, and fast roads. The reasons individuals, families, and major corporations continue to prefer a central location include economic opportunity, person-to-person contact in the business process, desirability and prestige of location, and the presence of a wide network of institutions and services, and these factors have not changed much despite recent technological advances.

However, companies and individuals making the decision to select one city over another now consider other variables; they are increasingly able to choose where they work and live, and they select cities where the quality of life is high, where arts, culture, and education are valued, and where livability, measured in terms of amenity, civility, and urbanity, is evident. If Calgary is to continue to be a desirable location for offices and factories, universities and museums, then it will increasingly depend on its ability to provide a quality of urban life that is competitive with places worldwide.

177
Calgary is now a city overwhelmed by its suburbs.
photo F. Shaw 2005

The Calgary Project examined the city's urban form at various scales, from the scale of the city, to the neighbourhood, to the street; attention to all scales is essential in order to achieve sustainable and high-quality urban form. The length of commuting time, the relationship between places of work, living and recreation, the presence of sidewalks, street trees, parks, and open spaces in a neighbourhood, the location and distribution of schools, libraries, and other services, and the quality of all the urban experiences in those places – these are topics that affect each citizen, and that can be influenced for better or for worse by urban planning and design decisions.

The most recent period of Calgary's urban evolution has exhibited both a tendency towards business as usual, taking the form of land annexations, a focus on road construction, and the prevalence of low-density, single-use suburbs, as well as a waking-up to the need and the possibility of innovative urbanism, evident in the increased interest in public realm issues, the emergence of several break-through neighbourhood developments, and the growing numbers of people moving back to the inner city.

It is also likely that a new convergence of interests will help to further the agenda of urbanism, with health and sustainability considerations bolstering the arguments for a high quality public realm. Recently publicized research in Canada and the United States has started to confirm what logic and common sense have suggested all along – that the way we have been building cities and suburbs is bad for our health, as a result of the decline of neighbourhoods' walkability since the middle of the twentieth century.

While some would say that Calgary is currently distinguished more by its countless Macleod Trail imitations than by its good streets, this might just be a transitional phase – Calgary's adolescent years, so to speak. Cities like Rome have experienced twelve or thirteen generations of rebuilding, whereas Calgary has only had one or two so far. There is time and opportunity. Calgary is a wealthy city in global terms. It is also a teenager in city terms – we need to nudge this teenager, coming from a very privileged background, into responsible maturity as an adult with civic values, environmental ethics, and a respect for education, the arts, and culture.

Calgary's future challenge should not be to build more roads, but to build a sustainable city. Rather than develop simplistic solutions to over-simplified circumstances, such as perceived traffic congestion, we might consider a different question: "How do we build for our desired quality of urban life?" There are no simple solutions, but posing such questions might lead us to develop a vision for the city in which its cultural, social, and architectural aspects are considered together with its functional attributes. Of course, it would need to start with determining what our desired quality of urban life is, along with its spatial and functional implications.

The beginning of the twenty-first century finds Calgary in an enviable position of economic growth and cultural maturing. Foran (1978) referred to the period of 1914 to 1940 as "The Closed Frontier" and that of the period of 1941 to the 1980s as "The New Frontier" (1982). Future historians will no doubt find an appropriate label for the period in which we currently live. With careful development and management, Calgary's evolution has the potential to represent the best urban form and the best urban life that is achievable in the contemporary western Canadian context.

We may be on the verge of an environmental and urban planning revolution in which Calgary lives up to its potential and becomes known for its distinctive places and memorable spaces rather than for its car-oriented strips and suburbs. However, we will need a clear vision that identifies the city's physical and cultural anchors; that is, the aspects of urban development that are non-negotiable, and the qualities that will help to develop a sense of place. But unlike the past, development of this sense of place, to paraphrase Michael Hough (1990), is now a question of choice, rather than of necessity, and is therefore a matter of design.

178
View of Calgary looking east from Bow Trail.
photo F. Shaw 2005

APPENDIX A:
TOWNSCAPE ANALYSIS – APPROACH AND METHODOLOGY

The methodology for the townscape analysis[1] was developed through several previous projects[2] in which techniques and methods from the disciplines of urban morphology, landscape architecture, urban design, and urban planning were synthesized. The methodology, although developed as an approach to pre-design, is employed in *The Calgary Project* as an approach and process through which urban form and its evolution can be illustrated and understood.

The research depends on multiple sources of primary information and considers a number of inter-related aspects of the built landscape, paying particular attention to qualitative aspects of overall city form and in particular the public realm, to historic continuity of process and form, and to the importance of understanding the relationship between the natural/topographic setting and the identity that is derived from that environmental context.

The research consists of documentation and analysis at various scales:

- the city
- the neighbourhood
- the block
- the street
- the building

The form of an object or organism (including the form of the city or a neighbourhood) is a diagram of the forces that have acted upon it.[3] In the case of the built environment, form is the result of the accumulation and interaction of various decisions and acts of design and building. By analyzing the built environment, it is possible to discover the values and choices that shaped it.

The basis for an understanding of urban form is to ask questions about the relationship among the parts, and between the parts and the whole. There are three primary relationships: the relationship between form and nature, the spatial relationships of production, maintenance, transformation, and use of the urban forms, and the relationships involved in the processes of formation and the spatial relationship between built forms. These are outlined in more detail.

a. The relationship between form and nature is expressed in the environmental context, conditions, and features of a place.

There is an inherent logic in the early evolution of any city or town, and this often has something to do with landscape, topography, and hydrography, in addition to social, political, and economic forces. Many towns and cities were originally sited for environmental reasons: the presence of a water body, the prospect afforded by a particular geographic location, the shelter and security provided by topography – these were often important reasons for locating settlements in specific locations and contributed to their unique image and character.

The identity of places also used to be a direct consequence of the constraints imposed by local environmental conditions: extremes of climate, quality of soil, limitation of water supplies, and the availability of certain building materials influenced the form of the settlement as well as the vernacular styles of architecture and gardening. Places tended to be distinctive and unique as a result of individual and community adaptation to local conditions. Now, this relationship is much more a matter of choice than of necessity.

Ian McHarg changed the way that environmental planners and designers gathered and analyzed environmental data, effectively demonstrating that physical planning and the design of sites should be based on a thorough understanding of the ecology of the area together with human values.[4] Through an understanding of environmental conditions and characteristics, more locale-specific and ecologically sound planning and design would be produced and there would be a greater likelihood of producing designs that would be more harmonious with their environmental context and more appropriate to human values and needs.

The field of landscape ecology provides a broad theoretical base to urban ecology and contributes principles upon which urban planning and design decisions can be made.[5]

In order to understand the existing environmental conditions, an inventory of what is there (e.g., topography, hydrology, geology, and vegetation) and their inter-relationships, on a regional and especially a local level, should be acquired. Further, it is necessary to look at the evolution of these conditions over time. Analysis of historic town plans, air photographs, and other archival material from earliest origins and moving forward in time can reveal environmental features or conditions that have been lost or transformed over time, as well as those that have persisted.

As well, the sensed forms of an environment – in particular shade, shelter, sun, and wind – should be understood. This analysis is helpful in providing knowledge of the particularities of the place that can be helpful in making planning and design decisions, and in leading to places that provide more human comfort.

This analysis is of value in understanding places because the relationship between urban development and natural features is an expression of the prevailing values of the time.

The analysis is also useful as a tool in design. Natural features can be important in defining neighbourhood edges, and ecological analysis is essential to development of sustainable places and can also provide design determinants.

b. The spatial relationships of production, maintenance, transformation, and use of the urban forms are expressed through the land uses and functional relationships.

The built environment, particularly the public realm (that is, the collection of spaces of the city, such as the streets, parks, plazas, and squares, in which we live much of our public lives), needs a distinct identity and structure to be legible, successful and enjoyable.[6]

The analysis of a town's or city's spatial structure considers land utilization and the pattern of activities that parts of a town or city generate. It describes the location and distribution of particular uses and the functional relationships between them.

A number of theories of spatial structure have been formulated, with various ways of conceptualizing space. Kevin Lynch saw the city image as a system composed of five basic elements: paths, edges, districts, nodes, and landmarks (or monuments).[7] These urban elements provide physical and psychological orientation and together have significance to the inhabitants forming a mental map. This organizing structure provides a framework by which neighbourhood urban form and its parts and the ways they are related can be analyzed and then used as a basis for design.

Roger Trancik[8] later expanded this framework as he found that the modern urban landscape also included "lost space"; that is, space that does not serve any functional or visual purpose.

In order to be useful as a design tool, spatial structure should be analyzed in terms of its historical evolution so as to discover how functional elements have migrated or been transformed over time, and to show how spatial relationships have changed.

c. The relationships involved in the processes of formation and the spatial relationship between built forms include morphology, typology, and visual relationships.

i. Morphology and the spatial relationships between built forms

Urban morphology is an approach to studying urban form that considers the three-dimensional qualities of lots, blocks, streets, buildings, and open spaces, over time, and their relationship with each other. This approach can encourage a more integrated approach to planning and development and help to avoid the disparate reactions to problems otherwise perceived as unrelated.

There are several schools of thought in morphological studies,[9] which, although rooted in different cultural and linguistic traditions and disciplines, share some common ground and common principles:

- Urban form is defined by three fundamental physical elements: buildings and their related open spaces, plots/lots, and streets.
- These elements can be understood at different levels of resolution. Commonly, four are recognized, corresponding to the building/lot, the street/block, the city, and the region.
- Urban form can only be understood historically because the elements of which it is comprised were formed over time.

The lot is the basic cell of the urban fabric – it links built form to the land and to open spaces. Lots may be subdivided or consolidated over time, a process that influences how properties are developed. Lot consolidation is a powerful determinant of built form. Consideration of land and its subdivision enables the link between the building scale and the city scale and provides a better understanding of the process of city forming and re-forming.

ii. Typology

Typology is the study of elements that cannot be further reduced. Types in built form developed according to both functional requirements and aesthetic considerations. A particular type (of building or public space) is associated both with form as well as with way of life. Types are general (e.g., school, church, town square) but also culture-specific, such as the particular shape and details of a type vary from society to society. Type signifies something more permanent and long-lasting than function. With this understood, the concept of type then becomes the basis of design.[10]

Typology is not neutral – urban spaces should be designed and analyzed in terms of their viability as containers for public life. Typology must also be considered within the morphology of the city. A space or street by itself as a public space is meaningless – it must be conceptualized and designed in relation to its physical and spatial context, in addition to considering the qualities and characteristics of the space and its edge conditions. The typology so defined then informs the layout, the materials, and other design elements.

iii. Visual relationships

It is at the scale of the street and the square that the visual character of the district or city is represented in a condensed form. While the city or the neighbourhood is comprehended as an overall experience, only the single street or space can be held in view by an individual, and this composition is the most important when analyzing visual quality. Space is perceived as a visual relationship between objects. The nature of that space is determined by the building masses and the multitude of relationships between them, primarily their proximity, their continuity as an edge, and the degree to which they create a sense of enclosure.

Currently, the character of building and spatial form is less often determined by considering visual relationships. Land-use planning in our regulated, highly administered cities largely determines function and activities within the public domain, and building forms are determined more often now by program and function (form/content relationship) as well as by building technology, density, and the vehicular – pedestrian circulation system. However, the visual components of built form should be considered together with land-use planning, since they are so profoundly important in contributing to the user's experience.

Urban form analysis, therefore, comprises several ways of documenting, analyzing, and otherwise reading and understanding a place. Of course, what is not considered here are the opinions or perceptions of the residents, or of those who are involved in building the city form. In order for this approach to be practical as a way of providing guidelines for new development or redevelopment, techniques and methods for evaluating the human experiences should also be incorporated.

Notes

1   An expanded discussion of the townscape analysis methodology is included in B.A. Sandalack and A. Nicolai (2006, forthcoming) *"Time, Place and Structure: Typo-Morphological Analysis of Three Calgary Neighbourhoods,"* in The Exurbs: Sprawl and the Ideology of Nature, K.V. Cadieux and L. Taylor (eds.), Boulder: University Press of Colorado.

2   The methodology for this research was first developed in a campus planning project (B.A. Sandalack, *Olds College Campus Plan*, Olds College Board of Governors, 1989) and two small town revitalization studies (A. Nicolai, *Town of Olds Period Restoration and Downtown Revitalization Study*, MScArch thesis, Centre for the Conservation of Historic Towns and Buildings, Katholieke Universiteit Leuven, 1990; and A. Nicolai, *Town of Didsbury Period Restoration and Downtown Revitalization Study*, Master's Degree Project, Faculty of Environmental Design, University of Calgary, 1991) and then refined using a prairie railway town as a case study (B. A. Sandalack, *Continuity of History and Form: the Canadian Prairie Town*, Ph.D. thesis, Oxford Brookes University, 1998) and applied to several more complex projects, including B. A. Sandalack and A. Nicolai, *Urban Structure – Halifax: An Urban Design Approach* (Halifax: TUNS Press, 1998); B.A. Sandalack and A. Nicolai and The Urban Lab, *Calgary Cultural District: A Framework for the Future,* 2001; and B. A. Sandalack and A. Nicolai and The Urban Lab, *Cliff Bungalow – Mission: Townscape and Process*, 2003).

3   Darcy Thompson, in his great work *On Growth and Form* (1917, republished by Cambridge University Press, 1961), studied biological forms from a mathematical perspective. Similarly, the growth of a city can be understood as the product of the forces acting upon it.

4   Ian McHarg, *Design with Nature* (New York: Natural History Press, 1969; reissued 1992).

5   See R.T.T. Forman, *Land Mosaics: The Ecology of Landscapes and Regions* (Cambridge: Cambridge University Press, 1995); and R.T.T. Forman and M. Godron, Landscape Ecology (New York: John Wiley, 1986).

6   Legibility refers to the ease with which a city, or part of it, can be understood. The visual relationships, the way that places connect with each other, and the visual "clues" about what a place is about all give a user a feeling of confidence, and therefore competence, in their surroundings.

7   Kevin Lynch, *The Image of the City* (Cambridge, MA: MIT Press, 1960).

8   Roger Trancik, *Finding Lost Space* (New York: Van Nostrand Reinhold, 1986).

9   See Ann Vernez Moudon, "Urban morphology as an emerging interdisciplinary field," *Urban Morphology* I (1997), for a discussion of the genealogy of urban morphological research and practice. Although urban morphology is an established field of study in the United Kingdom (especially the work of geographers M.R.G. Conzen and J. Whitehand, and the urban design approach of the Joint Centre of Urban Design at Oxford Brookes University), Italy (including typo-morphologisits S. Muratori and G. Caniggia), and France (including the architectural approaches of the Versailles School), in Canada, to date, urban morphological theory has not extensively been integrated into design and planning practice or education in a way that would allow it to inform urban design, and as Moudon points out, relative to the European situation, morphological study of the North American town or city is less related to issues of historicity than to issues of dysfunction. See C. A. Sharpe, "The teaching of urban morphogenesis," *Canadian Geographer* 30:1 (1986), and J. Gilliland and P. Gauthier "The study of urban form in Canada" *Urban Morphology* 10:1 (2006), for a discussion of morphological study in Canada.

10   Aldo Rossi, in *The Architecture of the City* (Cambridge, MA: MIT Press, 1982), based his architectural studies on urban typology. He believed that the memory of the city is embodied in its architecture, whose types can either be "pathological" or "propelling" permanences. Architectural types must preserve their general forms, but also be open to new uses and new interpretations. Typological questions have always entered into the study and practice of architecture – elements of building structure, form, and organization figure into the comfort and appropriateness of any building. They are applied less often, if at all, in the study and practice of urban design, although typology applies to elements of a city as well as to buildings.

APPENDIX B: METHODS FOR GRAPHIC ANALYSIS AND MAPPING

City scale
The topographic base map was overlain with the Calgary street plan, regressed from a 2000 City of Calgary Road Network CAD base map for each time slice.

Population and land area density study
The city's built-up area for each time slice was measured from the street plan. City population was based on the municipal census. Density was calculated by determining the number of people per square kilometre.

Downtown evolution map series
This series was constructed utilizing multiple sources. The current-day series was constructed from the City of Calgary CAD base. Layers were drawn to show land subdivision and building massing (figure ground). A three-dimensional computer model was constructed based on direct observation and photographs. Land uses were inferred from direct observation. Earlier years were then regressed from the 2005 drawings and revised according to information regarding building footprint and lot size. Archival photographs, fire insurance maps, and air photos were used to construct the earlier three-dimensional models. Land uses were inferred from fire insurance maps and from various references in the literature.

Commercial built form evolution
Distinctive commercial types were identified, and a representative example selected from each. These were graphically documented using the City of Calgary Community Maps as a base. Building footprints and lot outlines were mapped, and the buildings were photographed in some cases.

Good streets study
Several of Calgary's "good streets" (i.e., streets popular with pedestrians) were selected and graphically analyzed in several ways. The street facades were photographed, and a collage assembled. The street facades were then redrawn with ink on mylar. Building massing (figure ground) and land subdivision were drawn using the City of Calgary Community Maps as a base.

Neighbourhood evolution map
The dates of the establishment of a community association were considered as the start date of each neighbourhood. The boundaries were taken from the City of Calgary community map. Each era of development was assigned a shade and created as a map layer. Neighbourhood evolution can be read as a composite or as a series of developments.

Neighbhourhood analyses

Neighbourhoods were analyzed according to a methodology designed during this project. Representative neighbourhoods were selected from various development eras.

The 1924 aerial photograph (National Air Photo Library) was used as the base map for showing neighbourhoods prior to development. The 2001 air photo (Foto Flight Surveys Ltd.) was used as base for an overlay analysis and as a base to re-draw a two-dimensional map. Direct observation was supplemented by information from the City of Calgary Communities website. Streets, blocks, major environmental features, and general land uses were drawn. A representative street was selected during a site visit and photographed, then re-drawn by hand with ink on mylar. A cross-section through the street was measured and the elements (sidewalk, boulevard, street tree, right of way, private lot, house, etc.) were drawn. A representative block was selected and analyzed graphically in various ways using the City of Calgary community maps as a base. A three-dimensional model of the block was constructed from photographs and direct observation. A representative house was selected, and photographed, and its lot was measured, and the lot/house combination was drawn in plan and elevation and modeled. In some cases the house was de-constructed into various elements.

REFERENCES AND FURTHER READING

Alaniz Uribe, Francisco G. (2004). *Urban Analytical Comparison: Calgary Downtown West and Vancouver Coal Harbour*. Unpublished report, Faculty of Environmental Design, University of Calgary.

The Albertan. (1963). *This is Alberta in 1963*. Calgary: Albertan Publishers.

Allisson, Rhonda, Marge Lichkowski, Bette Ann Litzenberger, and Margaret O'Reilly. (1975). *Victoria Park: Calgary's Urban Centre Moves West of the Elbow*. Century Calgary Publications.

Anon. (1963). *Calgary: You Won't Recognize the City in Twenty Years*. CPR House Publication.

Baine, Richard P. (1973). *Calgary – An Urban Study*. Toronto and Vancouver: Clarke Irwin.

Barr, Brenton, ed. (1975). *Calgary Metropolitan Structure and Influence*. Western Geographical Series, Vol. 11, Department of Geography, University of Victoria.

Barraclough, Morris. (1975). *From Prairie to Park: Green Spaces in Calgary*. Century Calgary Publications.

Beard, Geoffrey, and Joan Wardman. (1978). *Thomas Mawson: The Life and Work of a Northern Landscape Architect*. University of Lancaster Visual Arts Centre.

Bobrovitz, Jennifer. (1999–2002). 'Cornerstones,' *Calgary Herald*.

Boddy, Trevor. (1981). 'Sky High in Calgary,' *The Canadian Architect*, April: 25–34.

Boddy, Trevor. (1987). *Modern Architecture in Alberta*. Alberta Culture and Multiculturalism, Canadian Plains Research Centre, Regina.

Boddy, Trevor. (1992). 'Underground and Overhead: Building the Analogous City,' in *Variations on a Theme Park: The New American City and the End of Public Space,* edited by M. Sorkin. New York: Hill and Wang.

Breen, David H. (1977). 'Calgary: the City and the Petroleum Industry Since World War II,' *Urban History Review* 2: 55–71.

Calgary Downtown Association and the City of Calgary. (1999). *Calgary Downtown – An Evolving Future*. City of Calgary.

Carver, Humphrey. (1962). *Cities in the Suburbs*. Toronto: University of Toronto Press.

Cashman, Tony. (1972). *Singing Wires: The Telephone in Alberta*. Alberta Government Telephones.

City of Calgary Land Use and Mobility. (2000). *Inner City Transportation System Management Strategy*. City of Calgary.

City of Calgary Planning Advisory Committee. (1966). *The Future of Downtown Calgary*. City of Calgary.

City of Calgary Planning and Building Department. (1993). *Downtown West End Policy Consolidation*. City of Calgary.

City of Calgary Planning and Building Department. (1994). *Short-Term Growth Management Strategy.* City of Calgary.

City of Calgary Planning Department. (1973). *The Calgary Plan.* City of Calgary.

City of Calgary Planning Department. (1981). *Calgary General Municipal Plan.* City of Calgary.

City of Calgary Planning Department. (1995). *The Communities of Calgary.* www.calgary.communities.com. City of Calgary.

City of Calgary. (1963). *General Plan.* City of Calgary.

City of Calgary. (1970). *The Calgary Plan.* City of Calgary.

City of Calgary. (1982). *Core Area Policy Brief.* City of Calgary.

City of Calgary. (1995). *Sustainable Suburbs Study.* City of Calgary.

City of Calgary. (1995). *The Calgary Transportation Plan (GoPlan).* City of Calgary.

City of Calgary. (1998). *Calgary Plan.* City of Calgary.

City of Calgary. (2000). *Growth Area Management Plan.* City of Calgary.

City of Calgary. City and Community Planning Division, Planning and Building Department. (1986). *Long Term Growth Management Strategy.* City of Calgary.

City of Calgary. Special Projects Division. (1981). *Downtown Area Redevelopment Plan.* City of Calgary.

City of Calgary. Special Projects Division. (1981). *Downtown Area Redevelopment Plan Technical Appendix.* City of Calgary.

City of Calgary. Special Projects Division. (1981). *Downtown Plan 1979.* City of Calgary.

City of Calgary. Special Projects Division. (1983). *Downtown Area Redevelopment Plan Handbook of Public Improvements 1982.* City of Calgary.

City of Calgary. Urban Park Master Plan – Citizens Advisory Committee for the City of Calgary. (1994). *Urban Park Master Plan.* City of Calgary.

Conzen, M.R.G. (1960). *Alnwick, Northumberland: A Study in Town-Plan Analysis.* British Geographers Publications No. 27.

Corbet, Elise A., and Lorne G. Simpson. (1994). *Calgary's Mount Royal – A Garden Suburb.* Planning and Building Department and the Heritage Advisory Board, City of Calgary.

Coward, Harold, ed. (1981). *Calgary's Growth: Bane or Boom?* Calgary Institute for the Humanities, University of Calgary.

Czolowski, Ted, and Elaine Johnson. (1975). *Alberta the Emerging Giant.* Vancouver: C & B Publishing.

Dempsey, Hugh. (1994). *Calgary Spirit of the West.* Saskatoon: D.W. Friesen & Sons.

Donaldson, Sue Ann. (1983). 'William Pearce: His Vision of Trees,' *Journal of Garden History* 3(3): 233–44.

Edworthy Park Heritage Society. (1991). *Early Days in Edworthy Park.*

Evenden, L.J. (1997). 'Wartime Housing as Cultural Landscape: National Creation and Personal Creativity,' *Urban History Review* 25(2): 44–52.

Foran, Max. (1975). 'Land Speculation and Urban Development: Calgary 1884–1912,' in *Frontier Calgary: Town, City and Region*, edited by A. W. Rasporich and H.C. Klassen. University of Calgary.

Foran, Max. (1978). *Calgary – An Illustrated History.* James Lorimer and National Museum of Man, National Museums of Canada.

Foran, Max. (1979). 'Four Faces of Calgary,' *Alberta History* 27(1): 1–9.

Foran, Max. (1980). 'The Mawson Report in Historical Perspective,' *Alberta History* 28(3): 31–39.

Foran, Max, and Heather MacEwan Foran. (1982). *Calgary: Canada's Frontier Metropolis.* Windsor Publications.

Forman, R.T.T. (1995). *Land Mosaics: The Ecology of Landscapes and Regions.* Cambridge: Cambridge University Press.

Forman, R.T.T., and Michel Godron. (1986). *Landscape Ecology.* New York: Wiley.

Gilliland, J. and P. Gauthier. (2006) "The study of urban form in Canada" *Urban Morphology* 10:1.

Guimond, Pierre, and Brian Sinclair. (1984). *Calgary Architecture: The Boom Years 1972–1982.* Calgary: Detselig.

Harasyn, D.G., and P.J. Smith. (1974). 'Planning for Retail Services in New Residential Areas since 1944,' in *Calgary Metropolitan Structure and Influence*, edited by Brenton Barr. Western Geographical Series Vol. 11, Department of Geography, University of Victoria.

Hawkins, W.E. (1987). *Electrifying Calgary: A Century of Public and Private Power.* Calgary: University of Calgary Press.

Hiller, Harry H. (1990). 'The Urban Transformation of a Landmark Event: the 1988 Calgary Winter Olympics,' *Urban Affairs Quarterly* 26(1): 118–37.

Hiller, Harry H., and Denise Moylan. (1999). 'Mega-Events and Community Obsolescence: Redevelopment Versus Rehabilitation in Victoria Park East,' *Canadian Journal of Urban Research* 8: 47–81.

Hope, Marty, and Kathy McCormick. (2000). 'The Roofs over our heads: How we've lived,' *The Calgary Herald* HM: 1–16.

Hough, Michael. (1990). *Out of Place: Restoring Identity to the Regional Landscape.* New Haven and London: Yale University Press.

Jamieson, Walter, Adela Cosijn, and Susan Friesen. (2000). 'Contemporary Planning: Issues and Innovations,' in *Canadian Cities in Transition*, edited by T. Bunting and P. Filion, Toronto: Oxford University Press.

Johnston, Emely, Corbet Locke, John Mayer, Tom Moore, Dalwin Stanford, and Lou Zeer. (1975). *Communities Six: Calgary Grows to the Northeast and Southwest.* Century Calgary Publications.

Kalman, Harold. (1984). *A History of Canadian Architecture.* Toronto: Oxford University Press.

Kingwell, Mark. (2000). *The World We Want.* Viking Press.

Kolody, Allison. (2003). *Walkability and Neighbourhood Form: A Comparative Study.* Master's Degree Project, Faculty of Environmental Design, University of Calgary.

Lai, David Chuenyan. (1988). *Chinatowns: Towns within Cities in Canada.* Vancouver: UBC Press.

Lortie, Andre, ed. (2004). *The 60s: Montreal Thinks Big.* Canadian Centre for Architecture.

Lynch, Kevin. (1960). *The Image of the City.* Cambridge, MA: MIT Press.

MacGregor, James G. (1972). *History of Alberta.* Edmonton: Hurtig.

Marce Santa, Julio. (2003). *The Use of Urban Morphology as a Tool for Urban Design Interventions: The Beltline Case Study.* Master's Degree Project, Faculty of Environmental Design, University of Calgary.

Mawson, T.H., & Sons. (1912). *The City of Calgary: Past, Present and Future.* City Planning Commission of Calgary.

McHarg, I. (1969, republished 1992). *Design with Nature.* New York: Natural History Press.

Melnyk, Brian. (1983). 'Residential Buildings in Calgary, 1905–1914,' *Prairie Forum* 8(1): 43–70.

Melnyk, Bryan P. (1985). *Calgary Builds: The Emergence of an Urban Landscape.* Alberta Culture/ Canadian Plains Research Centre.

Morrow, E. Joyce. (1979). *Calgary – Many Years Hence: The Mawson Report in Perspective.* City of Calgary and University of Calgary.

Newinger, S. (1973). 'The Street Cars of Calgary,' *Alberta Historical Review* 22(3): 8–12.

Nickle Arts Museum. (2000). *Calgary Modern 1947–1967.* University of Calgary.

Olds, Kris. (1998). 'Urban Mega-Events, Evictions and Housing Rights: The Canadian Case,' *http://www.breadnotcircuses.org/kris_olds_p3.html.*

Peach, Jack. (1990). *100 Years of Connections: 1890–1990.* The City of Calgary Sewer Division.

Peach, Jack. (1991). *The First Hundred Years – The History of the Calgary Chamber of Commerce.* Chamber of Commerce.

Pearce, William. (1979/1925). 'Reservation of Land at Calgary,' *Alberta History* 27(2): 22–28.

Perks, William T. (1985). 'Idealism, Orchestration and Science in Early Canadian Planning: Calgary and Vancouver Re-Visited, 1914–1928,' *Environments* 17(2): 1–28.

Perry, Clarence A. (1929). 'The Neighbourhood Unit.' *Neighbourhood and Community Planning.* New York: Regional Plan of New York and the Environs Volume 7.

Perry, Ryan. (2005). *The Evolution of the Urban Forest in Calgary's Residential Neighbourhoods.* Master's Degree Project, Faculty of Environmental Design, University of Calgary.

Phillips, Paul. (1981). *The Prairie Urban System, 1911–1961: Specialization and Change.* Canadian Plains Study 10.

Rasporich, A.W., and Henry Klassen. (1975). *Frontier Calgary: Town, City and Region 1875–1914.* University of Calgary.

Reasons, Chuck, ed. (1984). *Stampede City – Power and Politics in the West.* Toronto: Between the Lines.

Rees, Ronald. (1988). *New and Naked Land: Making the Prairies Home.* Western Producer Prairie Books.

Relph, Edward. (1987). *The Modern Urban Landscape.* London: Croom Helm.

Ring, Dan, Guy Vanderhaeghe, and George Melnyk. (1993). *The Urban Prairie.* Mendel Art Gallery, Saskatoon: Fifth House.

Ritchie, T. (1967). *Canada Builds 1867–1967.* National Research Council.

Rossi, Aldo. (1982). *The Architecture of the City.* Cambridge, MA: MIT Press.

Royal Commission on Metropolitan Development of Calgary and Edmonton. (1955). *Brief.* Alberta: Royal Commissions and Commissions of Inquiry.

Saarinen, Thomas F. (1963). *The Changing Office Functions in Calgary's Central Business District 1946–1962.* Master's thesis, Department of Geography, University of Chicago.

Sandalack, Beverly A. (1998). *Continuity of History and Form: The Canadian Prairie Town.* Ph.D. thesis. Oxford, UK: Oxford Brookes University.

Sandalack, Beverly A., and Andrei Nicolai. (1998). *Urban Structure – Halifax: An Urban Design Approach.* Halifax: Tuns Press.

Sandalack, Beverly A., and Andrei Nicolai. (2006). 'Time, Place, and Structure: Typo-Morphological Analysis of Calgary Neighbourhoods,' in *The Exurbs: Sprawl and the Ideology of Nature,* edited by K.V. Cadieux and L. Taylor. Boulder: University Press of Colorado (forthcoming).

Sandalack, Beverly A., Andrei Nicolai, and The Urban Lab. (2001a). *Calgary Cultural District: A Framework for the Future.* Faculty of Environmental Design, University of Calgary, and the Calgary Centre for the Performing Arts.

Sandalack, Beverly A., Andrei Nicolai, and The Urban Lab. (2001b). *Cliff Bungalow – Mission: Townscape and Process.* Faculty of Environmental Design, University of Calgary, and the Cliff Bungalow – Mission Community Association.

Sanders, Harry. (2000). *Watermarks.* City of Calgary Waterworks Division.

Sennett, Richard. (1990). *The Conscience of the Eye: The Design and Social Life of Cities.* New York: W.W. Norton.

Sherrington, Peter, ed. (1975). *Calgary's Natural Areas: A Popular Guide.* Calgary Field Naturalists' Society.

Siefried, N.R. (1982). 'Growth and Change in Prairie Metropolitan Centres after 1951,' *Prairie Forum* 7(1): 49–67.

Smith, Donald B. (2005). *Calgary's Grand Story*. Calgary: University of Calgary Press.

Smith, Donald B., ed. (1994). *Centennial City: Calgary 1894–1994*. Calgary: University of Calgary Press.

Smith, P.J. (1959). *A Preliminary Report on Urban Renewal in the City of Calgary*. City of Calgary.

Smith, P.J. (1962). 'Calgary: A Study in Urban Pattern,' *Economic Geography* 38: 315–29.

Smith, P.J. (1971). 'Change in a Youthful City: The Case of Calgary, Alberta,' *Geography* 56: 1–14.

Soby, Trudy. (1975). *A Walk through Old Calgary*. Century Calgary.

Stead, Robert J. (1948). 'Calgary – City of the Foothills,' *Canadian Geographic Journal* 36.

Stewart, Margaret A. (1999). 'A Newcomer's View of Calgary,' *Alberta History* (Spring): 23–28.

Styliaras, Dimitrios. (1964). 'CPR Redevelopment Proposal,' *RAIC Journal*.

Tanko, Margaret. (n.d.). *Hillhurst – Sunnyside Remembers*.

Thomas, L.G. (1968). 'The Rancher and the City: Calgary and the Cattlemen, 1883–1914,' *Transactions of the Royal Society of Canada* 6(4) June.

Thomas, L.G. (1986). 'The Umbrella and the Mosaic,' in *Ranchers' Legacy*, edited by P.A. Dunae, Western Canadian Reprint Services, University of Alberta Press.

Thompson, Darcy. (1917, repub. 1961). *On Growth and Form*. Cambridge: Cambridge University Press.

Trancik, Roger. (1986). *Finding Lost Space: Theories of Urban Design*. New York: Van Nostrand Reinhold.

Van Rosendaal, Meg, ed. (1999). *Brainstorm: Imagining Calgary's New Downtown Arts District. Calgary*: Calgary Centre for the Performing Arts.

Vernez Moudon, Ann. (1997). 'Urban Morphology as an Emerging Interdisciplinary Field,' *Urban Morphology* 1: 3–10.

Vidler, Anthony. (1978). 'The Third Typology,' in *Rational Architecture Rationelle*. Brussels: Archives of Modern Architecture. 28–32.

Vidler, Anthony. (1996). 'Architecture after history: Nostalgia and Modernity at the End of the Century' *RIBA Annual Discourse,* London.

Von Baeyer, Edwinna. (1984). *Rhetoric and Roses: A History of Canadian Gardening 1900–1930*. Markham: Fitzhenry and Whiteside.

Ward, Tom. (1975). *Cowtown – An Album of Early Calgary*. McClelland Stewart West.

White, Stephanie. (1984). 'Calgary: a new urban morphology,' *Vanguard* 13(5–6) Vancouver Art Gallery.

Whitehand, J.W.R. (1992). *The Making of the Urban Landscape*. Institute of British Geographers. Oxford: Blackwells.

Williams, Vicky. (1978). *Calgary Then and Now*. Vancouver: Bodima Books.

BIOGRAPHICAL NOTES

Dr. Beverly A. Sandalack is Professor and founding coordinator of the Urban Design Program at the University of Calgary. She is Director of The Urban Lab, an award-winning research group in the EVDS downtown centre. Bev is Deputy Chair of Calgary's first Urban Design Review Panel, a Fellow of the Canadian Society of Landscape Architects, and a member of the Canadian Institute of Planners.

Dr. Andrei Nicolai is an architect and planner with a specialization in urban design. He currently teaches urban planning in the United Arab Emirates and is Adjunct Professor in the Faculty of Environmental Design at the University of Calgary.

Francisco Alaniz Uribe is a research associate with The Urban Lab and is completing a Master of Environmental Design (Urban Design) at the University of Calgary and a Master of Projects for Urban Development at the Universidad Iberoamericana in Mexico City. He has practiced architecture and urban design in Mexico.

Julio Marce Santa was the first graduate of the Master of Environmental Design (Urban Design) program at the University of Calgary. He was a graduate research assistant in The Urban Lab from 2002 to 2004 and participated in many aspects of the project. He is currently working as an architect and urban designer in Mexico City.

Jinwei Zhang was a graduate research assistant in The Urban Lab from 2000 to 2004, and was responsible for much of the 3D computer modeling of the project. After graduating from the University of Calgary in 2003 she practiced with consulting firms in Calgary and is now working in the United States.

Other related books

Sense of Place: a catalogue of essays
Eds. Ann Davis and Beverly A. Sandalack
Calgary: The Nickle Arts Museum
2005

Excursions into the cultural landscapes of Alberta
Eds. Beverly A. Sandalack and Ann Davis
Calgary: The Nickle Arts Museum
2005

21st Century City + Urban Design Symposium: papers and positions
Ed. Beverly A. Sandalack
Forthcoming

Other books by the authors

Urban Structure Halifax: an urban design approach
Beverly A. Sandalack and Andrei Nicolai
Halifax: Tuns Press
1998